Immigration and Integration in Canada

Immigration and Integration in Canada

in the Twenty-first Century

Edited by John Biles, Meyer Burstein, and James Frideres

School of Policy Studies, Queen's University
McGill-Queen's University Press
Montreal & Kingston • London • Ithaca

SCHOOL OF
Policy Studies

Publications Unit
Policy Studies Building
138 Union Street
Kingston, ON, Canada
K7L 3N6
www.queensu.ca/sps/

Library and Archives Canada Cataloguing in Publication

Immigration and integration in Canada in the twenty-first century / edited by John Biles, Meyer Burstein and James Frideres.

Includes bibliographical references and index.
ISBN 978-1-55339-217-0 (bound).—ISBN 978-1-55339-216-3 (pbk.)

1. Canada—Emigration and immigration—History—21st century. 2. Canada—Emigration and immigration—Government policy. 3. Canada—Emigration and immigration—Social aspects. 4. Immigrants—Canada—Social conditions—21st century. 5. Social integration—Canada. I. Biles, John, 1971- II. Burstein, Meyer III. Frideres, James S., 1943- IV. Queen's University (Kingston, Ont.). School of Policy Studies

JV7225.2.I55 2008   325.71'090511   C2008-901779-X

In partnership with

Contents

Contents

PART II

Integration Policies in English-Speaking Canada
John Biles 139

6 Integration Policies in Quebec: A Need to
Expand the Structures?
Conseil des relations interculturelles 187

7 Receiving and Giving: How Does the Canadian
Public Feel about Immigration and Integration?
Jack Jedwab 211

8 How are Immigrants Seen—and What do they
Want to See? Contemporary Research on the
Representation of Immigrants in the Canadian
English-Language Media
Minelle Mahtani 231

9 The Discourse of New Individual Responsibility:
The Controversy over Reasonable Accommodation
in Some French-Language Newspapers in Quebec
and Canada
Chedly Belkhodja 253

Conclusion: Canadian Society: Building Inclusive
Communities 269
John Biles, Meyer Burstein, and James Frideres

Index 279

Contributors 283

Acknowledgements

This book began its life nearly four years ago through the combined efforts of the three editors. However, we wish to acknowledge the help of many people. The other two editors owe a debt of gratitude to John Biles, who, from a conceptual stage through to its final publication, personally and through the Metropolis Project, has provided leadership and support. For his part, John Biles wishes to acknowledge the strong influence of Jim Frideres and Meyer Burstein, two of the most senior statesmen in their respective fields, for their invaluable contribution to this volume and to his development as a person. Equally, all three editors are grateful to Arthur Sweetman for encouraging us to pursue this series of volumes.

The manuscript has benefited from comments and suggestions from a number of academics, community leaders, and government officials such as those within Citizenship and Immigration Canada. Through their comments on various versions of the papers, they have contributed to strengthening the manuscript. From the academy, we would like to thank Paul Spoonley, Arthur Sweetman, Dan Hiebert, Lori Wilkinson, David Ley, Marie McAndrew and Peter Li. Community leaders such as Fariborz Birjandian and Carl Nicholson amongst others have provided new perspectives on the issue of integration and forced us to rethink the concept. Erin Tolley, Kamal Dib, and others have provided their support of this project over the years, and Howard Duncan's support of the project needs to be acknowledged. And finally, there are those who straddle the neatly packaged categories identified above: Humera Ibrahim, Ravi Pendakur, and Mary-Lee Mulholland, who have supported this effort over the years and have provided personal, academic, and government perspectives on the issues being discussed.

The manuscript has been professionally handled through the efforts of members of the Publications Unit, School of Policy Studies staff. Mark Howes, Nancy Mucklow, and Valerie Jarus have been able guides who have ensured that the material is complete, well written, and organized to accomplish our goals.

Finally, we would like to thank the nearly 8,000 policy-makers, re-searchers, and practitioners who comprise the Metropolis network in Canada and around the world. Their dedication and commitment to improving the lives of newcomers, minorities, and "host" societies is inspiring. We are grateful for whatever small part we and this volume can play in this worthy pursuit.

Foreword

Metropolis is an international network for comparative research and public policy development on migration, diversity, and immigrant integration in cities in Canada and around the world.

Metropolis has just entered its third five-year funding phase (April 1, 2007 to March 31, 2012). This phase will be marked by an increased focus on knowledge transfer. This volume, and those to follow, represent one of the means by which we intend to pull together research findings completed over the last decade and to examine how they speak to policy and practice. We hope this will make an important contribution to how issues surrounding immigration and diversity are approached, leading to a better Canada.

In large measure, the chapters in this volume are derived from a series of workshops at the 8th National Metropolis Conference held in Vancouver in March 2006. We are grateful for the contributions by participants in those five workshops. It is rewarding to have a volume emerge from the rich discussions provided by one of the largest annual gatherings of experts in the field. We encourage you to participate in both the annual national and international Metropolis conferences. For information on upcoming conferences, visit www.metropolis.net

Part I

Introduction

JOHN BILES, MEYER BURSTEIN, AND JAMES FRIDERES

Zooming in from space on Google Earth, one sees Canada as a huge land mass, bounded by oceans, full of enormous rivers, lakes and plains, and divided by massive mountains. These physical features, along with snow and cold, define Canada and distinguish it from other countries. Imagine, though, a different Google engine, one that observes social and cultural features. Now as we fly over the landmass, the distinguishing elements that come into view are hyper-diversity, prosperity, and a (largely) peaceful co-existence. These features—especially diversity—brand Canada and define the country as much as its physical geography. However, unlike the physical features for which we can take little credit, Canadian diversity is largely the product of human decision-making. Because of this, and because we have been—for the most part—successful in our decisions about building a socially cohesive society, immigration and diversity are a source of pride for Canadians, even though the policy architecture, policy goals, and measures of policy success are frequently contested (Imbert 2004; Winnemore and Biles 2006).

Notwithstanding the focus on policy, this volume is not aimed solely at policy-makers. Its chief goal is to contribute to public debate and public understanding. It does so in two ways: (i) by summarizing some of the main research about immigration and indicating where there are gaps in our knowledge; and (ii) by suggesting a series of indicators we might use to gauge our progress with regard to integration. This goal is more controversial than it might seem, and complexity is only part of the reason. More importantly, immigration has distributional consequences. Some parties gain, while others lose (or perceive that they are losing). The greatest difficulty lies in deciding whose gains and losses to measure, including the gains and losses accruing to present and future generations.

Immigration and Integration in Canada in the Twenty-first Century, eds. J. Biles, M. Burstein, and J. Frideres.
Montreal and Kingston: McGill-Queen's University Press, Queen's Policy Studies Series.
© 2008 The School of Policy Studies, Queen's University at Kingston. All rights reserved.

Any volume purporting to deal with Canadian immigration policy must, at the outset, recognize three foundational points. First, that immigration and the chain of consequences that immigration engenders represent a fundamental choice that Canadians have made and, in one form or another, have adhered to for over a century. Second, all modern societies receive migrants, not only because they have active immigration programs but also because they have made choices in other areas of domestic and foreign policy, including human and social rights. Migration can be thought of as a by-product of these choices. Third, having made choices leading to large-scale immigration, Canada has turned the integration of immigrants into a societal endeavour—an endeavour distinctly defined as a "two-way street," where both immigrants and current citizens are expected to adapt to each other, to ensure positive outcomes for everyone in the social, cultural, economic, and political spheres.

Given these realities, immigration policy tends to be both instrumental and adaptive—all the more so in a country like Canada that already has a large immigrant population and, hence, a large, self-generating, sponsored immigration movement. Partitioning immigration into adaptive and instrumental components may therefore seem artificial. After all, once people arrive in Canada, their rights, entitlements, and benefits have little to do with the factors responsible for their admission, whether adaptive and capitalizing on existing legal (admission) structures or instrumental and responsive to state inducements (recruitment and promotion). Equity and fairness dictate that immigrants be accorded equal treatment, independent of their motives for coming to Canada or those of the receiving society.

The same holds true for social and economic investments in the well-being of immigrants. These investments are guided by anticipated rates of return and have little to do with the original decisions made by individuals to migrate. Indeed, if we were to probe more deeply, even the distinction between immigrants who are sought out for instrumental reasons chosen by the host society (such as filling labour market shortfalls) and immigrants who enter for personal reasons (such as private calculations) would assume a more ambiguous form than that posited by policy-makers. From the vantage point of a majority of immigrants, Canada's immigration laws are a maze to be negotiated, and there is no reason to distinguish between the motives that guided the construction of different parts of the maze (Harvey et al. 1999). Sponsored family immigration and independent economic immigration are simply "routes of convenience" to be chosen on the basis of efficiency and risk management (Hou and Balakrishnan 1996).

However, the vantage point of the host population or, more precisely, the host population that is contemplating opening its doors to immigrants, must also be taken into consideration. From this instrumental perspective, the case for immigration is based on the flow of benefits and costs that would accrue (to the pre-existing population) under conditions of closed or open immigration of various types. Another way to think about this is that instrumental immigration requires a distinction to be made between the interests of immigrants and the interests of their Canadian hosts. This distinction is not, however, symmetrical across all policy domains. In the area of admissions policy, Canada assigns little or no weight to the interests of potential immigrants. Yet in matters of integration and citizenship policy (which become relevant once residency has been established), Canada makes little or no distinction between the interests of migrants and those of their hosts. This asymmetry needs to be kept in mind when considering this book's various contributions.

Depending on one's viewpoint, this volume may be considered either overly ambitious or overly modest. Ambition, as always, is defined by reach: The aim is to take stock of how Canada is doing in its goal of admitting immigrants, integrating them, and forging the connections of citizenship that will pave the way to a prosperous shared future. In approaching this task, the volume does not confine itself to any one discipline or to any one policy topic. Rather, its goal is to provide a comprehensive framework that covers all aspects of immigrant adjustment and associated public endeavour. To this end, contributions were solicited from several academic and non-academic analysts; they were asked to examine the major dimensions of immigrant integration and citizenship behaviour from a policy perspective. The focus was on how Canada is doing and what it could do to improve policy in four critical behavioural spheres: economic, political, social, and cultural. In each article, authors were asked to summarize the main lines of thought and evidence, to consider the principal responsibilities of both newcomers and hosts, and to offer suggestions for how best to measure how well the host society and immigrants are living up to their mutual responsibilities. Rounding out these discussions are several chapters that add texture and context to the policy assessments.

Inevitably, given its ambitious scope, this volume suffers from a certain unevenness in its treatment of different perspectives and in the evidence that is assembled. Furthermore, some arguments are less compelling than others, and some omissions more puzzling. Despite these shortcomings, the volume succeeds in its primary mission. Both the editors and authors of the volume view it as an experiment to determine whether a Canadian index of integration that address both sides of the two-way street can be developed and whether there exists sufficient appetite to improve on this initial experiment, to refine its focus, and to generate the information which will be needed. From this perspective, this volume is sufficiently fleshed out to inform the general reader, while at the same time, it is likely to attract enough interest from the policy and academic communities to determine if the "experiment" is worthy of elaboration in future years.

Certainly on the surface, it is hard to see how such a deeper undertaking could be avoided, given the tumultuous historical period we have entered. Over the past thirty years—a relatively short time span— new tensions have developed that affect both immigration and integration and Canada's capacity to manage either. It is arguable whether policy thinking has kept up. This is not to fault policy-makers: the changes that have occurred are profound and, in many cases, their origins lie outside domestic control. Responding to these changes will require different policy levers pulled by different hands, or, more optimistically, old instruments used in new ways.

The following sections briefly describe some of the tensions that confront policy-makers, prefiguring their appearance in the chapters. The aim of these sections is limited: to note the changes and to signal their policy significance. To ensure that the proposed measures in the chapters remain relevant, these sections will need to contribute to our understanding of these changes as well as our ability to manage them.

Mission Drift

For most of Canada's history, immigration has been associated with nation-building, particularly with producing a more robust economy and developing vast tracts of open territory (Knowles 1997). Despite recurring doubts about the character and compatibility of newcomers, this impetus to develop the country produced sustained support for large-scale immigration throughout much of the twentieth century. Today, many of these original arguments have lost their force and shape (Stoll and Wong 2007). In particular, freer access to overseas markets has reduced the pressure for Canada to develop a larger, domestic consumer base. In turn, demographic arguments that focus on merely increasing the size of Canada's population have been weakened (Simmons 1990). Instead, the focus has shifted to the aging of the Canadian population and the need for immigrant "replacement workers."

But here, the demographic case is less compelling, since immigrant age distributions are similar to those of native-born Canadians.

In a similar vein, arguments focusing on immigrant admissions to address labour market gaps are no longer clear-cut. Labour requirements have grown more complex at the same time as integration has become more problematic and more costly. In addition, other recent economic changes have included outsourcing, new technology, retraining of the domestic workforce, and enhanced internal mobility (Granovetter and Swedberg 2001).

The key question that must be answered is, What are we trying to achieve? This question is important because successful integration requires widespread public and institutional support, extending well beyond the capacity of governments. The drift in mission carries with it a potential loss in essential public support, especially for instrumental immigration policies, such as recruitment, unless the purpose of immigration can be clearly explained. Obviously, the measures proposed in this volume for establishing the success (or failure) of Canada's immigration and integration policies will need to conform to the evolving purpose of the immigration program in order to be persuasive.

Integration Uncertainty

Mounting evidence indicates that the pattern of economic success experienced by immigrants over the last two and a half decades has experienced a profound and lasting deterioration (Picot and Hou 2003; Grant and Sweetman 2004). Until the 1980s, the prevailing picture was one of a rapid increase in immigrant earnings, quickly matching and then exceeding the incomes of similarly endowed, native-born Canadians. Then the picture changed abruptly. New arrivals experienced sharp declines in earnings as well as in other measures of economic success. This decline persisted through the 1990s and is still evident today, though slightly muted. As a result, recent immigrants now appear unlikely to attain native-born earning norms.

The fall in economic outcomes for recent immigrants cuts two ways: from the perspective of the host society, it represents wasted economic potential and declining returns on investments in immigrant selection and integration; from the perspective of immigrants, it represents a deterioration in quality of life and reduced incentives to come and remain in Canada. Either way, correcting the present situation is a matter of utmost importance. The Immigration and Refugee Protection Act (2001) was supposed to accomplish this transformation; but the Act's legislative powers—which must be given effect through regulation—remain underexploited. Furthermore, the immigrants' continuing difficulties getting their foreign skills, education, and credentials recognized suggests that without robust complementary integration strategies and strategies to reduce barriers, the immigration program will continue to struggle.

There are many issues responsible for the slowdown of integration. Among the more important are (i) the depressive effects of globalization on manufacturing jobs, especially in Ontario where the majority of immigrants reside; (ii) overarching structural adjustments that have depressed the earnings of all new labour market entrants, including immigrants; (iii) a fall in the value that markets attach to non-Canadian work experience; (iv) an increase in immigration from countries where Canadian employers discount educational and other credentials; (v) discrimination; and (vi) a pronounced decline in English and French literacy among immigrants. There is a growing consensus that the importance of language has been grossly underestimated and that recent immigrants lack the communication skills demanded by the labour market. Greater uncertainty surrounds the decline in returns to work experience and education, which likely reflects some combination of discrimination, declining returns to age, differences in educational quality, and problems of acculturation (Basaran and Zong 1998; Dreidger 2003; Grant and Sweetman 2004; Pendakur and Pendakur 1998; Li 2000). Ideally, the measures contained in the following chapters will provide insight into immigrant participation and outcomes along various dimensions of integration as well as into the root causes that are responsible for those outcomes.

Social Exclusion

Visible minorities and immigrants from non-English and non-French speaking backgrounds have been hardest hit by the decline in earnings and the capacity to absorb immigrants into the existing social and economic structures. The result has been a significant and sustained increase in immigrant poverty only somewhat attenuated by social assistance. Startlingly high percentages of new immigrants experience persistent low income (Nakhaie 2006; Picot and Hou 2003). Moreover, this poverty seems to be transmitted from one generation to the next (Halli 1999).

The coupling of persistent poverty with visible minority status constitutes a significant threat to the long-term viability of Canada's immigration program (Kazemipur and Halli 2000; Portes and Sensenbrenner 2001). This is especially so if other forms of deprivation accompany income deprivation, creating a state of social exclusion. Social exclusion, as pointed out by Amartya Sen of the Asia Development Bank, needs to be understood in the sense of capability deprivation, which not only impoverishes individuals or groups but also erodes their ability to escape the state (Sen 2000). This spectre of social exclusion requires that we look behind the low incomes and poor employment outcomes of immigrants to the root causes of exclusion that most likely reside in both the individuals concerned and in the society in which they are embedded and with the interaction between individual and institutional factors.

This complexity directs our attention to two shortcomings in the present volume. The first arises from the fact that it treats separately the different aspects of integration—economic, social, cultural, and political. This separation tells us whether economic deprivation is increasing and whether political isolation is deepening; but it does not tell us whether these conditions are converging in the same individual and thus contributing to a more profound isolation than if two different individuals were affected. In part, this treatment results from the analytic choices made by the volume's editors and contributors, but it also reflects the shortcomings of most data sets, which probe only one dimension of behaviour and cannot be integrated with other datasets that probe other behaviours or states. The second difficulty concerns the assessment of institutional behaviour—a key feature of the two-way street. Most research infers institutional behaviours from immigrant outcomes; but this strategy is clearly inadequate, since it is very difficult to distinguish the impact of personal behaviours from the impact of institutional behaviours. The latter are arguably more important over the long-run and, in many cases, more accessible to policy intervention.

Shared Spaces and Changing Flows

Social cohesion and accommodation have emerged as key concerns for immigration policy-makers. Many policy-makers, backed by limited research, believe that integration, particularly the integration of religious minorities (adults and children), is problematic (Hiernymi 2005; Suarez-Orozco et al. 2005). Throughout Europe, public discomfort has manifested itself in high levels of support for language competency tests and courses and for compulsory civics education as a prerequisite for entry and for the right to remain in the country (Association for Canadian Studies 2006). A recent Harris poll shows support levels at 86 percent in Germany, 83 percent in Britain, 61 percent in France and 50 percent in Spain for mandatory citizenship and language tests (Harris Interactive 2007).

Similar, though more polite, discussions are underway in Australia, the United States, and Canada. In Canada, debates over religious accommodation have figured prominently in the recent Ontario and Quebec provincial elections (the first and second largest provincial destinations for immigrants), as well as in federal by-elections. These debates have revealed a deep vein of discomfort with religious minorities and the obligations of the host society to accommodate religious differences. Even more revealing has been the Quebec *Commission de consultation sur les pratiques d'accommodement reliées aux différences culturelles* that has given voice to thousands of Quebecers. Ignoring the pettiness of some of the presentations, three issues have dominated the discussion: gender equality, language, and the (claimed) desire for isolation and separateness. These concerns are not unlike those voiced in Europe; however, while some commentators argue that the similarity is due to common themes of nationalism, it is unlikely that an open discussion in other parts of Canada would reverberate differently.

The most common explanations for the tensions that have surfaced are fears of Islamic militancy and discomfort resulting from the collision between secular and religious values (Freeman 2004). Pluralistic, secular societies emphasize freedoms and rights over obligations and responsibilities, rendering them ill-equipped politically and practically to cope with religious challenges. But other factors also are at play, among them a decline in the attachment by migrants to the nation-state. This detachment is visible in the trend toward multiple citizenships and the growing importance of students, temporary workers, and other forms of temporary and circular migration in the flow of migrants to traditional immigrant-receiving countries (Ferrera 2003). Less esoterically, discrimination—exclusion by the majority as opposed to rejection by the minority—undoubtedly plays an important (perhaps *the* most important) role.

We should be especially concerned with integration because it constitutes both an outcome and a lever. As a lever, successful integration plays a critical role in immigrant recruitment, stimulating investment, and leveraging public support without which integration could not be achieved and social and economic policy goals could not be realized (Burton 2002).

The creation of two new sets of indicators would be helpful for measuring social cohesion and isolation. The first set would focus on the extent to which the values and attitudes of immigrants and the wider society converge, or diverge, over time. The World Values Survey—for which the University of Toronto's Neil Nevitte is the principal Canadian investigator—appears to offer excellent, and generally underutilized, dynamic information concerning the evolution of values in Canada among various sub-populations. The second set would focus on actual behaviour: whether immigrants and members of the wider society live together or in enclaves, where they attend religious services, where they work, and so forth. Ideally this set would examine participation in a range of institutions, including clubs, businesses and not-for-profit organizations. Implicit in this approach is the idea that values are primarily by-products, the result of living and working together on projects in the public domain—the result of such undertakings and not their precursors (Johnston and Soroka 2001).

Indicators providing an insight into cohesion appear in Part I of this volume, and they deal with the many dimensions of integration. Collectively, they should offer a portrait of immigrant behaviour that corresponds to the values and expectations that most Canadians would associate with social responsibility and contributions to national and local well-being. What is missing but would need to be obtained through special survey data is information concerning attitudes and interactions involving members of different communities, including the host community.

New Management

The federal push for greater provincial involvement in immigration, formalized through agreements, extends back over two decades. Signings—federal-provincial agreements now span the country—are seen as *federal* triumphs and are announced with considerable fanfare. Lost in the accompanying hoopla is the fundamental change that has been taking place in the locus of responsibility for managing the core immigration issue—integration. The reasons for this shift have to do with numerous forces, including the decline in federal powers due to globalization, the resulting increase in the importance of provincial inducements, the demographic changes that have boosted competition for skilled migrants, and the compositional shifts that have added urgency to the task of aiding newcomers.

The capacity of the federal government to manage trade relations and to stimulate economic activity has declined as a result of globalization, Canada's binding free trade commitments, and international competition. As a result, efforts to attract corporate investors, new technology, and skilled workers increasingly focus on the provision of physical and intellectual infrastructure—good roads, airports, and universities—and on the availability of social amenities, health care, education, and a peaceful and tolerant society (Boushey and Luedtke 2006). Significantly, many of the levers that govern infrastructure and social amenities are located within provincial, rather than federal, jurisdiction; this means that the success of the immigration program—its ability to contribute to competitiveness and to economic and social development—is, to a large extent, contingent on provincial, rather than federal, actions (Hamilton 2007).

Equally important, if not more so, is the growing role of cities, which also fall under provincial jurisdiction. Cities are important for several reasons. As economic engines, their capacity to compete for and attract investment and skilled workers plays a crucial role in the ability of provinces (and the nation) to compete in the international arena (Castree et al. 2004). The key idea here is that the health of nations depends on the capacity of their major cities to compete for and to attract investment and skilled workers, which means that creating this capacity must become a priority for all levels of government. Interestingly, a number of analysts—best represented by Richard Florida—claim a connection between diversity and competitiveness. The argument is that diversity is a key driver in the creation of *virtuous* circles that begin with an immigration of skilled workers drawn by supportive social conditions. This immigration is followed by corporate investment seeking to capitalize on this talent; more creative workers then follow, attracted by the new jobs; and this, in turn, generates more investment and so forth. The role of public policy, especially provincial policy, is to create and maintain the conditions necessary for diversity to flourish, what Florida (2005) calls "quality of place," a combination of health, education, cultural policies, and investments in local social and physical infrastructure—in other words, the policies that contribute to local integration. To accomplish this goal, provinces and cities need to increase their investments in stakeholder relations, particularly in building partnerships with the private sector—employer groups, chambers of commerce and professional associations—and with municipal and local authorities. This requirement is closely linked to the emerging recognition of the importance of the spatial dimension in immigration.

From the same analytic perspective, but focusing on a different population, some research has gathered increasing evidence (as noted above) that integration is critically dependant on local actions—on the willingness and capacity of local actors (including schools, hospitals, employers, and voluntary sector agencies) to offer support and transform themselves in order to become more welcoming and to reach out to newcomers (Jordan et al. 2003). Without question, these actions are guided by national frameworks and shaped by federal financing; yet fundamentally, they are driven by bottom-up, not top-down, forces.

Because immigration and integration have long been thought of as a federal rather than provincial or municipal responsibility (the shift occurred earliest and most aggressively in Quebec), measures and data sets—including administrative data—have focused on the federal sphere. Far less attention has been paid to measures of local capacity and local activity directed to immigrants. Little is known, for example, about the capacity of the voluntary sector to deliver services to immigrants, even though this capacity is crucial to successful integration. Equally important, and similarly unavailable, are spatial measures that pinpoint personal and institutional interactions. In the chapters that follow, the authors have, by and large, maintained a national or top-down focus in their recommendations. This is understandable, given the paucity of local data; but clearly, this situation will need to change if this project is to continue and to become increasingly relevant to decision-making.

Shifting Power Balance

New opportunities for migration and residency occasioned by global changes in economic organization, technology, demography, and citizenship have altered the balance of power and thus the distribution of benefits and costs associated with migration. There are three protagonists in this "contest" for capturing gains and avoiding costs: receiving states, sending states, and the migrants themselves. Somewhat ironically, the gradual easing of restrictions on migration is producing enormous gains for the world as a whole, but the gains accruing to Canada, an "early adopter" of open migration, may well shrink as sending states and migrants "figure out" how to capture a larger share of the benefits for themselves. Of course, Canada need not remain passive in the face of these transformations; however, policies intended to alter the distribution of migration benefits represent new and uncharted territory for Canada.

The policy contours of the emerging new landscape are shaped by two critical changes. The first change arises from the fact that emigrants are no longer viewed by their countries of origin as surplus labour to be exported and ignored. Instead, they are seen as assets constituting a vital source of development assistance. Countries of emigration have become acutely aware of remittances. As a result, they have evolved policies aimed at inducing migrants to repatriate earnings, diverting a portion of those earnings into government coffers. The existence and form of these policies reinforce the links between emigrants and their countries of origin, promoting both return and circular migration involving the migrants, their immediate families, and the community of co-ethnics and co-religionists.

The second change concerns the "bilateral negotiation" itself—in other words, the balance of power between migrants and states. Until quite recently (settler movements and forced migration aside), Canada and a handful of other countries had the migration market to themselves. Except at the highest echelons of scientific, artistic, sport, and corporate achievement, opportunities for movement were scant. The market was a buyer's market, and Canada was able to enjoy monopolist benefits. This period has come to an end. Competition has materialized—and is expected to grow—from both Europe and Asia. As a result, the skilled migration market is being transformed from a buyer's market into a seller's one. Skilled migrants can now avail themselves of numerous opportunities that allow them to maximize their own well-being and that of their families. Another way to think about this is that globalization has produced a shift in power away from governments and towards migrants. On the losing side (or reduced benefits side) are states such as Canada.

The discussion above suggests that some Canadian policies may be depreciating in value; but which ones and to what extent—a prerequisite for countervailing action—is something we know little about. Similarly, we know little about the opportunities that may result from stronger social and economic networks bridging Canada and countries of origin. What we do know is that the outcomes—both positive and negative—will have something to do with our success in integrating migrants and inculcating a feeling of citizenship and belonging. The following chapters suggest several measures that may prove useful in tracking and possibly explaining shifting allegiances. However, since all of the proposed measures are restricted to Canada and to resident Canadians, several important questions cannot be addressed. Again, this is a task to be considered for future instalments of this project.

Organization of the Volume

The editors have chosen to organize the volume into two parts. Part I partitions integration into four key spheres: economic, political, social, and cultural. Authors of each of these four chapters focus on the fundamental debates, controversies, and assumptions about integration in their sphere. They present both a review of the literature, and measures for evaluating how Canada is faring on both sides of the two-way street of integration in Canada.

Sweetman and Warman provide an up-to-date survey of the empirical evidence regarding relevant economic research and immigrants. In doing so, they look at the issue of immigrant economic integration and the impact of immigration on the Canadian economy. They interpret the evidence and discuss the interrelated responsibilities of the host society and the immigrants.

Anderson and Black identify the rights and responsibilities that define the two-way interaction of political integration. They present a review of the literature concerning three interrelated dimensions of political integration—naturalization, political participation, and representation. They develop a series of indicators that could be used to assess the level of political integration and provide evidence to assess the extent to which both immigrants and native-born Canadians engage in the processes of political integration.

Frideres delves into the issue of social integration. His review of the literature identifies several dimensions in the concept and discusses how the concept has been used over the past two decades. With that in mind, he presents several empirical indicators that might be utilized to measure the extent of social integration of immigrants.

Stone et al. begin their chapter by synthesizing the literature and presenting an operative definition of culture and related concepts, such as "cultural capital." They then discuss responsibilities relating to immigration and integration on the part of both the host society and immigrants. The last part of their chapter discusses the degree to which responsibilities are currently being met and presents several "cultural indicators" as empirically based measures of the social effects of culture.

All of the authors in Part I of the volume perform an "environmental scan" on the use of the concept of "integration" and then tease out potential and existing indicators that might be used to assess the nature and extent of integration within Canadian society.

Part II of the volume offers contextual information for the reader that is intended to provide for a better understanding of integration in Canadian society. These five chapters illustrate that integration is a societal endeavour in Canada. The chapters on media coverage and public opinion polling clearly indicate that there remains considerable room for education regarding immigration. The two chapters on policy suggest that co-ordination, especially avoiding duplication of effort, remains a central challenge for policy and practice in Canada.

Biles's chapter describes integration policy in English-speaking Canada, focusing on the three orders of government and their community partners. He finds that there is no shortage of players seeking to facilitate the integration of newcomers, though, like Rimok and Rouzier in the next chapter, he concludes that a co-ordinated approach appears to be lacking.

The chapter from the Conseil des relations interculturelles discusses several immigration integration initiatives undertaken by the Quebec government. Focusing on three sectors—education, municipalities, and regions—the authors argue that current activity is based on a "siloed" approach that does not lead to integrated policies and programs. They recommend more co-ordinated activities to ensure the integration of minorities in Quebec.

Jedwab, using data from a number of sources, measures public opinion about immigration. He also presents information about immigrant integration and shows that the opinions regarding intake and integration are not independent of each other. However, he notes that the link between the two concepts has not been sufficiently recognized thus impairing policy development.

Mahtani and Belkhodja provide insightful analyses of English and French media and their coverage of immigration and immigrant integration issues. Carrying out a content analysis of major English and French newspapers, they examine how the media portrays immigrants, integration, and the idea of reasonable accommodation. Mahtani surveys the literature on media and immigration over the last decade and finds an ongoing pattern of "misrepresentation" of these issues by English language media outlets. Belkhodja reviews the Quebec media and examines the intrusion of the language of individual responsibility into the debate over reasonable accommodation. He finds that populism has emerged in Quebec, which has both democratic and demagoguery elements that surround the debate.

References

Association for Canadian Studies. 2006. *Canadian Diversity/Diversité canadienne* 5(1). Special Issue on "Integration of Newcomers: International Approaches."

Basaran, G., and L. Zong. 1998. "Devaluation of Foreign Credentials as Perceived by Non-white, Professional Immigrants," *Canadian Ethnic Studies* 30(3): 6–23.

Boushey, G., and A. Luedtke. 2006. "Fiscal Federalism and the Politics of Immigration: Centralized and Decentralized Immigration Policy in Canada and the United States," *Journal of Comparative Policy Analysis* 8(3): 207–24.

Burton, D. 2002. "Incorporating Ethnicity into Marketing Intelligence and Planning," *Marketing Intelligence and Planning* 20(7): 442–51.

Castree, N., N. Coe, K. Ward, and M. Samers. 2004. *Spaces of Work: Global Capitalism and Geographies of Labour*. Thousand Oaks, CA: Sage Publications.

Dreidger, L. 2003. *Race and Ethnicity: Finding Identities and Equalities*, 2nd ed. Toronto: Oxford University.

Ferrera, M. 2003. "European Integration and National Social Citizenship," *Comparative Political Studies* 36(6): 611–52.

Florida, R. 2005. *The Flight of the Creative Class*. New York: Harper-Collins.

Freeman, G. 2004. "Immigrant Incorporation in Western Democracies," *The International Migration Review* 38(3): 945–69.

Granovetter, M., and R. Swedberg. 2001. *The Sociology of Economic Life*. Denver: Westview Press.

Grant, H., and A. Sweetman. 2004. "Introduction to Economic and Urban Issues in Canadian Immigration Policy," *Canadian Journal of Urban Research* 13(1): 1–24.

Halli, S. 1999. "The Changing Colour of Poverty: A Study of Immigrants' Poverty in Canadian Cities," Working Papers series. Edmonton: PCERII.

Hamilton, R. (ed.). 2007. *Routes of Passage*. East Lansing, MI: Michigan State University Press.

Harris Interactive. 2007. *Harris Poll #127*. December 19. Harris Interactive. At www.harrisinteractive.com/harris_poll.htm.

Harvey, E., B. Siu, and K.I. Reil. 1999. "Ethnocultural Groups, Period of Immigration and Socioeconomic Situation," *Canadian Ethnic Studies* 31(3): 95–103.

Hiernymi, O. 2005. "Identity, Integration and Assimilation," *Refugee Survey Quarterly* 24(4): 132–50.

Hou, F., and T.R. Balakrishnan. 1996. "The Integration of Visible Minorities in Contemporary Canadian Society," *Canadian Journal of Sociology* 21(3): 307–26.

Imbert, P. 2004. *Trajectoires Culturelles Transaméricaines*. Ottawa: Les Presses de l'Université d'Ottawa.

Johnston, R., and S. Soroka. 2001. "Social Capital in a Multicultural Society: The Case of Canada," in *Social Capital and Participation in Everyday Life*, ed. P. Dekker and E. Uslaner. London: Routledge, pp. 30–44.

Jordan, B., B. Strath, and A. Triandafyllidou. 2003. "Comparing Cultures of Discretion," *Journal of Ethnic and Migration Studies* 29: 142–54.

Kazemipur, A., and S.S. Halli. 2000. *The New Poverty in Canada: Ethnic Groups and Ghetto Neighbourhoods.* Toronto: Thompson Educational Publishing.

Knowles, V. 1997. *Strangers at Our Gates: Canadian Immigration and Immigration Policy, 1540-1997.* Toronto: Dundurn Press.

Li, P. 2000. "Earning Disparities Between Immigrants and Native-Born Canadians," *Canadian Review of Sociology and Anthropology* 37(3): 289–312.

Nakhaie, R. 2006. "Earnings of Canadian Native-Born and Immigrants, 2001," *Canadian Ethnic Studies* 38(2): 19–45.

Pendakur, K., and R. Pendakur. 1998. "The Colour of Money: Earnings Differentials Among Ethnic Groups in Canada," *Canadian Journal of Economics* 31(3): 518–48.

Picot, G., and F. Hou. 2003. *The Rise in Low-Income Rates Among Immigrants in Canada.* Ottawa: Statistics Canada. Catalogue Number 11F0019MIE No. 198.

Portes, A., and J. Sensenbrenner. 2001. "Embeddedness and Immigration," in *The Sociology of Economic Life*, ed. M. Granovetter and R. Swedberg. Denver: Westview Press, Ch. 5.

Sen, A. 2000. "Social Exclusion: Concept, Application and Scrutiny." *Social Development Papers*, 1. Mandalugong, Philippines: Office of Environment and Social Development, Asia Development Bank.

Simmons, A. 1990. "New Wave Immigrants: Origins and Characteristics," in *Ethnic Demography*, ed. S. Halli, F. Travato, and L. Driedger. Ottawa: Carleton University Press, pp. 141–60.

Stoll, M., and J. Wong. 2007. "Immigration and Civic Participation in a Multiracial and Multiethnic Context," *International Migration Review* 41(4): 880–908.

Suarez-Orozco, M., C. Suarez-Orozco, and D. Qin-Hilliard. 2005. *The New Immigration.* Net Cong, NJ: A1 Books.

Winnemore, L., and J. Biles. 2006. "Canada's Two-Way Street Integration Model: Not Without Its Stains, Strains and Growing Pains," *Canadian Diversity/ Diversité canadienne* 5(1): 23–30.

Chapter 1

Integration, Impact, and Responsibility: An Economic Perspective on Canadian Immigration Policy

ARTHUR SWEETMAN AND CASEY WARMAN

Introduction

Canadian immigration policy has been and currently is primarily about nation-building. Economic evidence and reasoning sometimes enter into the national discussion, and, as in the case of humanitarian flows, economics at times plays the "after the fact" support role of describing and interpreting labour market or other relevant outcomes. On occasion, economic issues drive an aspect of immigration policy. Appropriately, economic evidence is most commonly one of a wide range of inputs into the decision-making process. Regardless of whether economic evidence enters into the decision-making process or not, and regardless of the quality of that evidence, economic outcomes ensue, and they can vary appreciably with alternative policies.

Following this introduction, brief up-to-date surveys of the economic evidence regarding two major areas of immigration-relevant research are provided along with a discussion of the interpretation of that evidence. The first section surveys research on immigrant economic integration, and the second one looks at the economic impact of immigration on the Canadian economy, which is less understood. These two parts form the bulk of the chapter since they provide the foundation on which the later, briefer, sections are built. The subsequent section builds on the extant evidence and theory to discuss the interrelated responsibilities that both Canadian society and newcomers to Canada have towards each other. This is clearly more subjective than the earlier parts and does not build on an established literature, but hopefully it will stimulate

Immigration and Integration in Canada in the Twenty-first Century, eds. J. Biles, M. Burstein, and J. Frideres. Montreal and Kingston: McGill-Queen's University Press, Queen's Policy Studies Series.

discussion. Finally, the last section prior to the conclusion considers how Canada currently measures, and in future might measure, economic issues related to immigration. Although this part is not long because many of the issues about how we measure immigrant-related outcomes are implicit in the survey sections, it is more crucial than some policy-makers might at first believe, since policy commonly responds to what is measured.

Economic Integration of Immigrants

Immigrant labour market outcomes have declined appreciably across successive arrival cohorts over the past few decades, while poverty rates have concurrently increased. Given that the basic descriptive elements of the decline are well known, we will only review it briefly and will focus on some interpretive issues. Recent surveys of the extensive research literature include Picot and Sweetman (2005), Grant and Sweetman (2004), and Reitz (2007); a brief and persuasive economic history of Canadian immigration policy is by Green and Green (2004). An interesting comparison of Canada, the United States, and Australia is by Antecol, Kuhn and Trejo (2006).

Although earlier cohorts of immigrants had lower average earnings than the Canadian-born at the time of entry, their earnings converged to the Canadian-born average relatively quickly. For example, Warman and Worswick (2004) show that male earnings in the 1971–75 landing cohort converged within 6–10 years. The decline in outcomes is, however, not due to a decreased rate of convergence for newer cohorts. On the contrary, the convergence rates have for the most part increased. Instead, the fall in earnings at entry (or landing/arrival) for most recent arrival cohorts has been so very substantial that, even with these cohorts having faster earnings growth, the time to "catch up" has increased appreciably. Looking forward, Frenette and Morissette (2003) suggest that for the most recent immigrant cohorts, average immigrant earnings may never catch up with that of the Canadian-born.

In an apparent effort to improve average immigrant economic outcomes, the federal government has undertaken actions such as increasing the percentage of immigrants in the economic class (especially the skilled worker category), as shown in Figure 1. In part as a result of this policy shift, earnings improved in absolute terms for immigrants entering in the late 1990s. However, conditional on characteristics, there was little, if any, increase (see, e.g., Hou and Picot 2003). Further, recent findings indicate little improvement in the early 2000s (Coulombe, Hou and Picot 2007; Hou and Picot 2007). This confusion raises an issue of interpretation. It is important to take into account that many estimates are statistically (regression) adjusted—that is, they are conditional on a particular set of observed characteristics—while others are unadjusted or adjusted using fewer or different characteristics. The basic declining pattern exists in all cases, but the magnitudes differ systematically and there are some important points of divergence.

Figure 1: Time Series of Total Number of Immigrants by Class

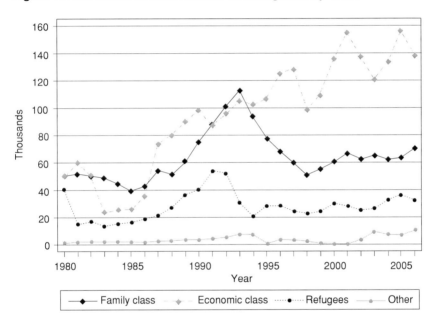

Source: Authors' calculations from Citizenship and Immigration Canada 2007.

Consider again the cohort of the late 1990s. Their labour market outcomes, while still poor compared to those of previous decades, improved somewhat relative to the immediately previous cohorts, when no adjustments are made for characteristics such as education, or when the only controls are for age. However, the improvement is much reduced when statistical controls are added for education and the like. Thus, the outcomes improved because the composition of the cohort changed (largely as a result of government policy changes); but for a person of similar characteristics in both cohorts, there was very little improvement, if any. Once one controls for a range of observable characteristics, immigrant outcomes are found to decline more relative to those of the Canadian-born than without such controls. This is because newer immigrants are, on average, older, more highly educated, more urbanized, etc. and there is an earnings premium associated with each of these characteristics. Once differences in the distributions of characteristics are taken into account and like is compared to like, the gap appears wider.[1] However, neither adjusting nor not adjusting for characteristics is the "better" method; rather, the outcomes of each approach answer different policy questions, and care is needed to ensure an appropriate interpretation and that the "right" approach is employed for answering the question at hand. Estimating multiple specifications and comparing the results can be very informative.[2]

Although there are some mild differences in interpretation across researchers and policy-makers, there appear to be three main proximate sources of the decline in labour market outcomes (most studies focus on earnings) that are, very roughly, of equal importance (see the surveys listed above; for recent direct evidence, see Frenette and Morrisette 2003; Green and Worswick 2004; Warman and Worswick 2004; Pendakur and Pendakur 1998, 2007; Aydemir and Skuterud 2005; and Beach, Green and Worswick 2008).

First, about 30 to 40 percent of the decline—probably on the higher side for males and the lower side for females—is associated with changes in (i) French and English language ability, measured as mother tongue and (self-reported) official language knowledge, (ii) region of origin, which may proxy for several other factors, including ethnicity and a bundle of characteristics that are hard to disentangle, and (iii) labour market and pre-labour market racial and related forms of discrimination.

Second, about one third of the decline follows from a massive reduction in the economic rate of return to (imputed or potential) pre-Canadian labour market experience. Schaafsma and Sweetman (2001) found that recent immigrants receive virtually no return to this measure of their foreign work experience. Aydemir and Skuterud (2005) found that this effect is broadly based, but is somewhat larger for males from "non-traditional" source countries. In contrast, the effect is similar for females from both traditional and non-traditional source countries. Green and Worswick (2004), who studied only males, found a somewhat larger effect for those from non-traditional source countries. An important interpretational issue here is that the datasets employed almost never have direct measures of pre-Canadian (or post-arrival) labour market experience. Rather, potential labour market experience is imputed for immigrants and the Canadian-born alike as: "Age" minus "Years of Schooling" minus 6. This has traditionally worked well for Canadian-born males, but is not as good a proxy for females; and it is unclear how its role as a proxy might have changed across successive immigrant cohorts. A very strict interpretation would say that for earlier immigrant cohorts, earnings increased reasonably strongly as "potential" experience increased, whereas the relationship is now substantially weaker or non-existent. Note that this result has an automatic corollary that can be missed because of the phrasing of the issue. What is being witnessed is a decline in the economic outcomes of older immigrants, since younger immigrants, by definition, have little or no pre-Canadian labour market experience.

The third source of income decline is associated with a general decline in labour market "entry conditions." There are two major issues here. First, immigrants who arrive during recessions appear to have "economic scars" that endure, and the immigration rate increased during the recession of the early 1990s (e.g., Aydemir 2003; Aydemir and Skuterud 2005). Relatedly, Beach, Green and Worswick (2008) found that when the Canadian economy is in a recession, the higher unemployment rate reduces the average (administratively measured) skill level of the entering immigrants. The second and larger part of this third source of decline is that *all* new Canadian labour market entrants have been experiencing declining labour market outcomes. New immigrants, regardless of their age at immigration, and new Canadian-born labour market entrants (e.g., recent graduates) both face the same challenge of declining and stagnant real earnings (see, Picot 1998; Beaudry and Green 2000). This latter phenomenon started in the early 1980s but may have reduced slightly in recent years.

The rate of return to education does not appear to have a primary role in the declining immigrant outcomes. Foreign education has always received a lower rate of return in the Canadian labour market than Canadian education, and this does not appear to have changed enormously. However, changes in the composition of the immigrant stream may be contributing to this effect. Moreover, the economic rate of return for education among immigrants is more complex than it might at first appear. Ferrer and Riddell (2008) show that if credentials and years of schooling are examined separately, then even though immigrants have a lower rate of return for years of schooling than do the Canadian-born, they also have a higher return associated with the completion of a credential. Immigrants who complete their education after arriving in Canada have, on average, substantially higher returns than those who complete their education before landing (McBride and

Sweetman 2003); and those who land as young children have very high rates of return, at least as high as those of the Canadian-born (Schaafsma and Sweetman 2001). There is also important heterogeneity between immigrants and the Canadian-born according to field of study (McBride and Sweetman 2003); and although many do not like to discuss differences in the quality of education, there appear to be important differences both within Canada (e.g., Betts, Ferrall and Finnie forthcoming) as well as outside of the country (e.g., Sweetman 2004) that are reflected in the labour market. In May 2007, the Foreign Credentials Referral Office was established to help foreign-trained workers have their credentials assessed, and this, in conjunction with language training (discussed below), can be very useful to educated immigrants.

That education is not a major cause of the decline in labour market outcomes does not, however, imply that education-related policy might not be an appropriate policy tool to remedy some of the decline. Credential recognition programs may decrease the gap between the rates of return to education between those educated domestically and those educated outside of the country, particularly in countries that are not well known to Canadian employers. However, other education issues are at least as important, as discussed below in the context of educational responsibilities.

One important topic that has received little attention, mainly due to data limitations, is the return migration of immigrants. If a large proportion of immigrants do not stay in Canada, and if the emigration is non-random in terms of such things as skills or labour market success, this can have significant implications for the interpretation of immigrant outcomes. Aydemir and Robinson (2008) use the longitudinal Immigration Database (IMDB) to examine the disappearance of immigrants from the country. They find that a little more than one-third of young working-age male immigrants left Canada within 20 years of landing. Around 60 percent of immigrants who left did so within the first year of arrival. At first glance, the existence of return immigration may suggest that not all immigrants are able to find the type of employment or level of earnings they desire. However, this issue is certainly more complex than a simple response to economic outcomes.

The Economic Impact of Immigration on the Domestic Economy

Although the economic impact of immigration is a topic of popular, government, and academic interest in countries such as Australia, New

Zealand, the United States, and parts of Europe (an eclectic set of references includes Borjas 1995, 1999; Dustmann et al. 2006; Econtech Pty Ltd. 2006; Lowenstein 2006; OECD 2005; Poot and Cochrane 2004; Smith and Edmonston 1997; and Simon 1999), there has not been much recent policy discussion or research in Canada around this topic. The goal is to understand how immigration causally impacts the domestic economy both in terms of aggregate averages and the distribution of outcomes. Of course, causal effects are extremely difficult to estimate, and readers are frequently faced with correlations that may or may not be causally related.[3] Many studies simply trace out trends and do not impose a causal interpretation. Of course, readers may impose their own or reject the authors' (sometimes implicit) causal interpretation.

Two issues need clarification for discussion of this topic. First, alternative populations are relevant in different studies of the economic impacts of immigration and for policy. Three common ones include immigrants themselves, the pre-existing population (comprising non-immigrants and previous, or earlier, cohorts of immigrants), and prospective and/or recent immigrants. Each frame of reference is associated with different policy questions and can have quite different outcomes. It is easy to imagine policies that would benefit the pre-existing population but that would not be beneficial to new immigrants. The reverse is similarly easy to imagine.

A second and related distinction is between types of measures and the policy issues for which each is relevant. There appears to be substantial confusion between these issues in the media and in some research studies. Certain variables measure total quantity, such as GDP or total employment, while others measure GDP *per capita* or the employment *rate*. A further distinction is between an average (or median), such as the employment rate or average annual earnings, and the distribution of that outcome across the population. A concrete example where the distinction between the national average and its distribution matters is seen in the work of Hou and Picot (2003): they found, without any causal interpretation, that between 1990 and 2000, the low-income rate for the non-immigrant population decreased, whereas the low-income rate for the (much smaller) immigrant population increased sufficiently that it raised the aggregate national "poverty" rate. Also, if immigration raises total GDP, this does not imply that it raises GDP per capita. When GDP is used in discussion of a policy issue where GDP per capita is clearly the more appropriate measure, the ensuing confusion is not helpful to good policy-making.

Previous Conclusions on the Economic Impact of Immigration and Economies of Scale

Canadian research on the economic impact of immigration has resulted in mixed conclusions regarding whether the impact is positive or negative; but all the research agrees that any impact is small. The research report for the Royal Commission on the Economic Union and Development Prospects for Canada (the MacDonald Commission) concluded after surveying the research to date:

> The broad consensus is that high levels of immigration will increase aggregate variables such as labour force, investment and real gross expenditure, but cause ... real income per capita and real wages to decline (Marr and Percy 1985, 77).

A later report by the federal government's Economic Council of Canada looked more deeply at the impact of economies of scale and argued that:

> In contrast to previous investigators in Canada and Australia, we do find that immigration enhances economic efficiency within the host community. The effect flows almost exclusively from the greater size of the population that immigration brings. Scale economies result, and these benefit everyone—hosts and immigrants alike. No other efficiency effects of immigration appear to be important.
>
> ...
>
> Our view is that ... the gross efficiency gains are positive but very small (Swan et al. 1991, 36).

However, the Economic Council's report was published a year before the North American Free Trade Agreement was signed; since then, many other changes in technology and globalization have affected the nature of the Canadian economy. By 1999, following on work such as that by Trefler (1998), Green and Green (1999) argued that Canada's economy is best thought of as constant returns to scale, which contrasts with the increasing returns that the Economic Council report saw as the main source of economic benefit.[4]

In brief, in this context the idea behind "economies of scale"—which can be increasing, constant, or decreasing—is that in holding the structure of the economy constant, a pure change in the population can have an effect on productivity (output per person or per hour). For example, some types of production might be most efficient with a certain size domestic market. Increasing returns to scale implies that immigration has a benefit by virtue of increasing the size of the population, assuming that everything else is proportionately unchanged. Constant returns to scale imply that the efficiency of the economy is unaffected by the population's size—it neither helps nor hurts. In general, most economists believe that developed economies appear to operate near constant returns to scale, although we personally wonder if Canada might not exhibit some modest increasing returns to scale, given its low population density (even considering only arable land). Of course, constant returns to scale imply no change in the geographic distribution of the population. While useful, the concept of economies of scale addresses only some of the relevant issues.

Altering the Structure of the Economy including Demographics

Supplementing the concept of returns to scale is the impact of immigration altering the composition, or structure, of some aspect of the economy so as to affect productivity. Commonly discussed beneficial changes include (i) smoothing Canada's demographic "baby boom" hump, (ii) meeting unmet skill needs, (iii) attracting immigrants who can increase access to export markets, and (iv) gaining access to financial capital or entrepreneurial resources.

Looking first at demographics, Canada currently has a historically low fertility rate and a large "baby boom" cohort who will start to retire in less than a decade. As a result, immigration could be considered a means of modifying the age structure of society to reduce the (old-age) dependency rate. Unfortunately, as currently managed, immigration is much less effective at reducing the rate of population aging than at increasing the population's size (e.g., Beaujot 2003). Denton, Feaver and Spencer (2001) show that an immigration rate of 225,000 per year (which is about the current level, but is high for a sustained rate by historical standards) for 50 years will produce a median age of 46.5 years in 2051. A rate 50 percent higher would reduce the median to only 45.1 years, and the implausibly large act of doubling the rate only brings it to 44.2 years. Thus, even over long periods, sustained extremely high rates have only a minor impact on the age distribution for the population and the labour force.

Figure 2 shows the age distribution of non-immigrants, new immigrants, and total immigrants in 2001. These densities are plotted so that the area beneath each curve is the same, whereas the number of new

Figure 2: Age Densities for Permanent Residents, 2001

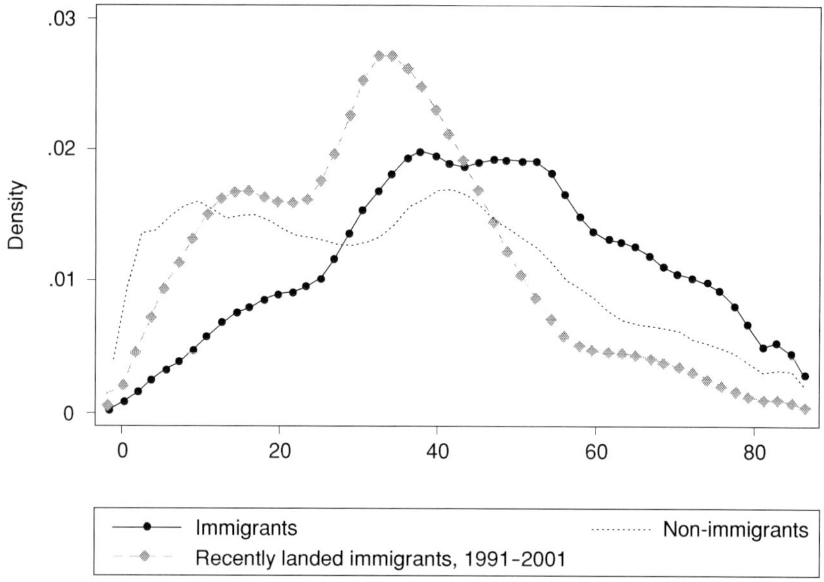

Source: Authors' calculation from the 2001 Canadian Census Public Use Microdata File (PUMF).

immigrants is only a small percentage of the Canadian-born population; it would be difficult to visually observe the details of the new immigrant curve if it were plotted to scale on this graph since it would be quite small. A few characteristics of the plot are worth mentioning. First, it is clear that the entire immigrant population's distribution is to the right of that for the Canadian-born (older, not younger). Second, while new immigrants are younger, they are not so much younger that it makes a great deal of difference to the overall age distribution. Also, the new immigrant distribution has an appreciable fraction of its population that is older than the peak of the Canadian-born baby boom. Further, Beaujot (2003) found that immigrants' average age at entry has been rising. Overall, there may be an economic benefit from the changing age distribution, but its magnitude is extremely modest.

Another commonly discussed issue is "filling skills gaps" in the Canadian workforce. This idea is both complicated and controversial, and we will address only two issues here. First, government policy on this issue (or at least practice, since it is not clear that a coherent policy has been articulated) has shifted considerably over the past few decades. The immigration legislation introduced in 1993 discontinued the practice of using the points system for skilled workers in the economic class to target occupations that were deemed to be in short supply. This was done partly because the initial prediction of a shortage and the arrival of the relevant immigrants could easily be, for example, one and a half years apart, by which time the occupation was frequently no longer in such high demand. (The list of occupations deemed in short supply was updated quarterly, which reflects shifts in demand at far too high a frequency for the way Canada's immigration process is administered.) In addition, the volatility of predicted demand raised questions about what "needs" really were, and there were often geographic mismatches between the location of occupations deemed in short supply and the locations preferred by new immigrants.[5] Although an idea with some merit (but see the discussion of displacement below), occupational targeting could not be administratively executed so as to produce a significant economic benefit within the context of the Canadian system. However, it should be noted that Australia appears to be able to administer its system so as to realize a benefit from this approach.

More recently, the federal government appears to have reintroduced the idea of using immigration to fill short-term labour market needs in particular areas, using the temporary foreign worker program and similar pilot projects, and introducing procedural/regulatory "bridges" to permanent immigrant status. However, the results of this workaround have been mixed, since the government's ability to gauge the labour market's needs and to reduce the flow of specialists after a "need" has been met has not been ideal. The number of engineers admitted as immigrants as part of this effort, which substantially exceeded the aggregate number of graduates from all Canadian engineering schools, is a case in point. Hou and Picot (2003, 2007) point to the poor labour market outcomes that ensued after the "tech bubble" burst and to the more general decline, though from an initially high level, in the relative earnings of highly skilled immigrants.

A second issue closely related to the "skills filling" idea is the potential "positive externalities" and/or (much less positive) "displacement effects" of new immigration for the existing workforce. There is substantial debate whether, and to what degree, new immigration helps increase, or conversely bids down, the earnings of the pre-existing workforce. Lowenstein's (2006) *New York Times Magazine* article is a popular presentation of two of the alternative points of view in the American context. For example, if new immigration reduces bottlenecks in Canada's production process by providing skills or other resources that are in short supply, and/or if new immigrants are complements in production to the existing workforce, then there will be economic "spillovers" to the pre-existing population. If, however, immigrants are substitutes in production, then they may compete for jobs with the existing domestic population and bid down wages. Recent and somewhat controversial work by Aydemir and Borjas (2006) compares the impact of migration on labour market outcomes in Canada, the United States, and Mexico. The same basic economic forces show evidence of displacement occurring in all three, although different national choices have led to very different outcomes. In Canada, a 10 percent increase in the supply of workers reduces wages by between 3 and 4 percent, with the actual impact varying across skill groups. Aydemir and Borjas estimate that the policy focus on high-skill workers has caused wages in this bracket to decrease by 7 percent between 1980 and 2000. The Canadian case is complicated by an early 1990s move away from a policy of adjusting immigration levels in response to the business cycle— increasing immigration in booms and decreasing it in recessions (see Grant and Sweetman 2004).

Overall, many economically-oriented Canadian policy-makers and researchers appear to believe that the impact of immigration on GDP per capita is probably positive but quite small. As most clearly articulated by Green and Green (1999) and Beaujot (2003), some argue that it is not practical to promote immigration as a policy for driving economic growth or demographic structure, unless Canadian society is willing to make some very focused policy decisions. Rather, immigration is better envisioned as a primarily social, cultural, and humanitarian policy that may have very substantial economic implications. Some policy-makers might be concerned about negative consequences of immigration, such as those in some European countries (see e.g., Dustmann et al. 2006 for an analysis of the UK context), but there is no substantive evidence that immigration has negative net economic impacts on the economy. For a slightly more extended discussion of economic impact issues, and references related to fiscal, taxation, trade, capital stock and other topics, see Sweetman (2005).

Responsibilities of Immigrants and the Host Society

Discussing economic responsibilities in the context of immigration's "two-way street" is difficult and potentially controversial. Canada is more accustomed to discussing rights and freedoms than responsibilities. However, the bedrock of our modern society's massively beneficial economic productivity, which allows us to have unprecedented standards of living, is economies of scale and specialization that require individuals to work co-operatively and to exchange the outputs of their specialized production. Modern economies are thus highly integrated and require a form of mutual respect based neither only on the very costly enforcement of the rule of law nor only on a sense of our own rights, but also on an understanding of the rights of others. And, of course, concern for the rights of others is central to the idea of social responsibility and economics as discussed since at least Adam Smith's (1759) *Theory of Moral Sentiments*. We believe that this idea is much more profound than it may at first appear: responsibility is in large part based on a concern for the rights and freedoms of others and is central to the operation of modern economies. Maximizing the economic benefits of immigration requires the expression of this concern by both new arrivals and the existing population.

It is also useful to recognize that although individuals are the fundamental actors, an individual's actions and attitudes are significantly affected by society's institutions. To be sustainable, responsible practices must be embedded in the nation's institutions and frequently must be enacted through them.

At a very high level of abstraction, therefore, for both sides of this "two-way street," there is a need to uphold the rule of law and to respect that central Canadian institution—our form of "responsible" government that both responds to and reflects the population. This includes concepts such as "reasonable accommodation," which have important implications for both immigrants and the Canadian-born in, for example, the labour force. There is similarly a need for both to recognize that society's choice, enacted through its government, with respect to immigration implies that we are part of an evolving multicultural society. Canada also puts an emphasis on, among other issues, maximizing the social and economic benefits of immigration and the importance of official (French and English) language knowledge, as set out in the *Immigration and Refugee Protection Act*.

Next, making a large leap, we turn to a set of concrete examples within the Canadian context. This is not a comprehensive discussion, but it does point out areas that we think of as priorities. Centrally, the receiving society must provide opportunities for immigrants and their children to integrate and succeed economically, while immigrants should seek to be self-sufficient and pursue that same economic success. However, many determinants of economic success occur outside of the Canadian labour market and/or are pre-labour market, so the focus needs to start there.

Information

At the very earliest stage of the migration process, well before landing, potential new immigrants need to receive high-quality information about the nature of the Canadian labour market and what will be required of them. This information needs to go beyond a minimalist process guide and must be accessible to new immigrants.

Incorporating more extensive formal information exchanges for both sides into the application process would be worthwhile. Some immigrant education credentials might not be equivalent to Canadian norms, and not all immigrants might have an accurate assessment of their French and/or English language skills. Obtaining formal assessments of both of these issues as part of the immigration process, not only for skilled worker principal applicants, would be very useful for both sides and represents a useful information exchange about abilities, expectations, and labour market requirements.

Education and Canadian Official Language Skills

Some crucial implications of specialization and co-operation in economic production are that the integration of immigrant children into the education system and the provision of opportunities for language acquisition and occupational/educational upgrading for adults are crucial for long-term well-being. While there are clearly some problems, Schaafsma and Sweetman (2001) show that, on average, young immigrant children who enter the Canadian education system have very good outcomes that then translate into strong labour market outcomes. However, those who enter in their late teen years face much greater educational challenges, leading to lower average educational attainment, which in turn negatively affects lifetime earnings.[6] Aydemir and Sweetman (2008) show that second-generation immigrants do very well in the education system and on average have superior educational attainment than the Canadian-born, and higher earnings compared to workers of the same age without controlling for education. But once one controls for the immigrants' higher educational attainment, the earnings advantage dissipates (but does not become negative). Second-generation immigrants have high earnings, but those earnings are not as high as expected, given their educational attainment.

Looking at adult immigrants, Ferrer, Green and Riddell (2006) show that the distribution of English and French literacy scores, as measured by the International Adult Literacy assessment, is dominated by that of the Canadian-born. However, both groups receive the same (quite substantial) economic rate of return for literacy in terms of earnings, and the gap in literacy skills accounts for the observed discrepancy in the rates of return for education between immigrants who acquire their education outside of Canada and the Canadian-born. For university-educated immigrants, if their literacy levels were the same as that of the Canadian-born, then about two-thirds of the total earnings disadvantage of immigrants would be eliminated. (Interestingly, the literacy gap does not explain any of the low return for foreign-acquired experience, although the authors only had a cross-section of data and could not look at changes over time.) Overall, the message is clear: the translation of foreign educational credentials is strongly influenced by official language ability.

There is a need for the Canadian federal and provincial governments to continue to promote institutional structures to provide new school-age immigrants with opportunities to integrate into the Canadian education system, and for post-schooling immigrants to pursue French and / or English language training to a high level. Our impression is that the latter of these is the more pressing problem. Of course, governments can only provide opportunities to learn, and there are responsibilities on the part of those without sufficient French and / or English skills to pursue those skills with vigour. There is always also the issue of cost for this special language training, and it seems reasonable to apply the same norms to immigrants as are used for the rest of the population. Immigrants who are young, at the elementary and secondary level (with a strong focus on the higher end of secondary, which is where the economic need appears greatest), should receive the extra services at taxpayers' expense, whereas those who are post-secondary equivalent should face a cost-sharing arrangement akin to that faced by post-secondary students. That is, there should be both tuition and a government subsidy, with the tuition geared to income using a system of loans and / or grants.

Language / literacy training should be conducted in a strong and stable institutional environment, such as the provincial community college (or perhaps university) system, to promote quality outcomes. The funding structure needs to provide incentives to support the accumulation of skills and knowledge within that instructional system so that ongoing improvement in instruction is possible. Rolling short-term contracts that are demanding to administer can easily cause the system's attention to be diverted away from instructional service delivery towards government contract management. This is not to suggest that real accountability is not important—improved accountability would be a social benefit since it leads to improved operations—but all too often what goes under the label of "account-ability" is really the filling out of (many) forms, what is sometimes de-rogatorily called "busy work." Improved accountability should probably imply higher standards, but less administrative overhead, than is cur-rently the case.

Ethnic and Related Forms of Discrimination

There is a need to continue to fight ethnic and related forms of dis-crimination in the labour market as well as in pre-labour market environ-ments. For policy purposes, it is useful to distinguish between labour market and pre-labour market ethnic discrimination, both of which can have similar labour market outcomes. For example, if a person is sub-ject to discrimination in the education system such that s/he receives a lesser amount or quality of education, then this disadvantageous edu-cational outcome will likely be reflected in earnings. However, this is a pre-labour market effect *if* the labour market appropriately prices the skill. Although there is relatively little research in this area, it appears that the labour market may be very poor at undoing pre-labour-market discrimination. In practice, it is often difficult to distinguish between these two, but the policy prescriptions differ markedly.

Pendakur and Pendakur (1998, 2002, 2007) show important and sys-tematic differences in labour market outcomes across ethnic groups. Dicks and Sweetman (1999) show that gaps at the ethnic group level in education and earnings appear to take more than two generations to converge for many groups; further, the economic rates of return for schooling vary systematically across ethnic groups. This demon-strates a need to address issues of discrimination within the educa-tion system as well as the labour market, and is discussed at greater length below.

Immigrant Sponsorships

Sponsorship is an area of responsibility particular to immigration and to the pre-existing population (including established immigrants), rather than to new immigrants. Sponsorship is typically required for family class immigration and for some categories of refugee claims. Sometimes the federal government itself serves as a sponsor (for government as-sisted refugees); other times there are private non-family or family spon-sors. Sponsors clearly have the first responsibility when immigrants face financial difficulties in the sponsorship period. This is an area where little is publicly known about outcomes, and providing data for research would be advantageous.

Unfortunately, there appears to be a misalignment of responsibilities in cases where sponsorships break down. Ultimately, the federal government should bear responsibility for sponsorships, since it is the regulator and operator of the immigration system. It should not fall to municipal and/or provincial governments to support sponsorships that are not successful, since they have no role in establishing them.

In the United States, Smith and Edmonston (1997) found that the collection of taxes from immigrants and expenditures on immigrant-related services do not match jurisdictionally. Most funds accrue to the federal government, but the immigrant-specific costs are local or state responsibilities. This implies that non-immigrant-receiving states have the greatest fiscal benefit from immigration. Of course, the Canadian context differs very appreciably from the United States on this issue, but there appears to have been no research on this topic in Canada. Equalization payments and other transfers to the provincial governments from the federal one in Canada affect these issues in ways that do not exist in the United States; but it is not clear that the current situation is equitable, even though direct links of responsibility to issues such as sponsorship help the governance.

Courage

There is a need for both sides of the immigration two-way street to have the courage to take responsibility for asking and answering the hard questions so that the best solutions can be worked out. The economic poverty faced by many in the immigrant community is more politically incorrect than is the fear of asking and discussing questions that some may think of as difficult or sensitive. Hopefully, addressing the issues and making them better understood can allow for the formulation of good policy and community responses.

Measures

The measures available to examine immigration policy issues in the economic domain matter both because there is normally a focus on what we can measure, and because policy solutions are more successful if properly targeted. Immigration is also an issue worth pursuing in depth, since it is one of the larger social and economic issues facing Canada today.

Sources of Data

Undoubtedly, the most widely used source of data for examining the labour market outcomes of immigrants in Canada is Census data. Taken every five years, the census provides a picture of how economic outcomes change over time. However, while the census is endowed with rich information on demographic characteristics, it lacks information on immigration class, and there are appreciable delays in data preparation. Given that immigrants from different classes are admitted based on different criteria, adding a question asking the entry class would allow for a much richer analysis of immigrant outcomes. This could be done in the 2011 census or, even better, as a supplementary survey following up on the 2006 census using the census as a survey frame. A supplementary survey would allow a full set of immigrant-specific questions, and perhaps even a literacy measure, to complement the census data and would be of great value.

The Labour Force Survey (LFS) recently introduced an immigration question, which makes it an excellent source of extremely timely information. The LFS will produce a series of monthly indicators of immigrant labour market outcomes so that trends can be followed in real time.

Another data source, the longitudinal Immigration Database (IMDB), provides detailed information on immigration class. The IMDB links immigrant landing files with tax files. Starting in 1980 and currently covering up to 2004, the IMDB provides a limited amount of demographic information at the time of landing, including education, intended occupation, industry of employment, country of origin, and mother tongue. However, there is no additional demographic information collected after the time of landing. As well, another major drawback of the IMDB is that given its administrative nature, it is inaccessible to most researchers. Making it more available to researchers, along with some standardized coding for selected derived variables, would be a major step forward.

The Longitudinal Survey of Immigrants to Canada (LSIC) is a new addition to the sources of data on immigration. It contains information on immigration class and a wide range of information on both sending country characteristics and host country characteristics. The LSIC surveys respondents at six months, two years and four years after arrival, and the sample includes immigrants aged 15 years and older who immigrated between October 1, 2000 and September 30, 2001. While the LSIC has a very rich set of questions not asked in any other data source, the sample size is often too small (and there are issues with response rates and attrition); and for some unknown reason, it seems particularly ill-suited for addressing many current key economic questions. For example, the full set of points a skilled-worker principal applicant received cannot be inferred from the data; pre-immigration labour market experience is not measured; and pre-immigration temporary foreign-worker status can only be ascertained for those who resided in Canada prior to immigration and whose entry is not covered by an international treaty (such as NAFTA) that obviates the need for a visa. As well, the current cycle of LSIC surveys only immigrants who applied through a Canadian Mission Abroad. To obtain a more accurate representation of immigrant outcomes (and especially refugee outcomes), immigrants who applied within Canada should also be included in any subsequent surveys. This being said, the LSIC may be the best tool to study the outcomes of new immigrants. Whether another wave eight or ten years after landing is warranted remains an open question. An alternative is an immigrant over-sample in an ongoing or new longitudinal survey.

Language ability and the decline in returns to pre-immigration potential labour market experience have been highlighted as major reasons for the deteriorating labour market outcomes. However, most studies contain little information that can address these issues. For example, most rely on self-reported language skills: it would be helpful to have a more objective measure of language ability, such as the International Adult Literacy assessment. Similarly, information on the pre-Canadian labour market experience of immigrants (or pre-immigration, since some immigrants have Canadian experience prior to immigration) would permit a better understanding of the source of the decline and better policy development.

Better data to assess the role that discrimination plays on the poor economic outcomes would also be helpful. There has been a large amount of research into the earning differentials between immigrants and the Canadian-born, as well as between different ethnic groups (see, e.g., Pendakur and Pendakur 1998, 2002, 2007). But, since measures of, for example, ethnic discrimination are usually estimated by what is left over after observable characteristics are accounted for (that is, as a residual or a gap), their interpretation can be controversial. Digging a bit deeper to identify the effects of labour market versus pre-labour market factors in explaining these gaps in earnings and other outcomes would likely be a worthwhile area for future work.

Employers play a crucial role in immigrant integration, and research and data would be useful to better understand, for example, hiring decisions and practices. Information on how employers evaluate the foreign human capital and labour market experience of immigrants could help researchers and subsequently policy-makers design better policy.

Data also needs to be collected on temporary foreign workers and other non-permanent residents. Canada currently admits a large number of temporary foreign workers, and several recent policy changes have made it easier for employers to hire temporary foreign workers. (Although the census provides some demographic and economic information, as is the case for immigrants, the program that the non-permanent resident enters Canada through is not included.) Administrative data on temporary residents provides information on the program under which they have entered Canada. But, besides the lack of access to this administrative data for academic researchers, the data also lacks information on earnings.

Other sources of data are needed to further examine the emigration of immigrants documented by Aydemir and Robinson (2008). Given the large amount of emigration found in their study, the question of who decides to stay can have large implications for the success of immigration policy. However, they used the IMDB, which provides little to aid in understanding why many of these immigrants left. Although such a survey might be difficult to administer, interviewing people who left Canada would be very important for this analysis. For example, it is important to learn if immigrants are emigrating because of a lack of success in the Canadian labour market or because they had originally not planned to stay permanently in Canada.

New Indicators

New measures or indicators implemented based on the abovementioned data need to reflect the fact that many labour market and immigration issues are equilibrium outcomes of two (or more) interacting sets of economic agents. It is difficult to envision many indicators that reflect the actions of only one "side" of an interaction. Hence, measures should in general not be attributed to only "one side of the street," although they may be interpreted as affecting (or being affected by) one side more than another.

A first set of indicators should reflect the operation of the immigration system. In part, this process has already started in Citizenship and Immigration Canada's annual *Facts and Figures* publication. Further, the operation of the various stages of the process should be monitored by annual counts (by detailed immigration category) of new applications, applications processed, applications withdrawn, approvals, and approvals taken up (landings). Hopefully all these counts currently exist since they are needed to efficiently operate the system; but as far as we know, they are not publicly available. Combining them with the *Facts and Figures* publication should be straightforward. It would also be valuable to have information on processing times (for those landing each year, and the average and percentiles of time since application) and measures of the distribution of points awarded.

Beyond the current data published, the admissions system could make the following indicators available: (i) the fraction of cases where points system characteristics such as language and education were validated / assessed prior to landing; (ii) measures of pre-Canadian education converted to Canadian equivalents; and (iii) the prevalence of pre-arranged employment. There is also very little information on the emigration from Canada of immigrants. An annual indicator by immigration class could be produced to provide the count of immigrants who file a tax return (or who are the spouse / dependent of a filer) at two, five and ten years after landing. This is not asking for a count of those who pay taxes, or the value of taxes paid, but only to verify residency.

Some follow-up on the immigration system inputs could also be monitored, especially for skilled-worker principal applicants. Indicators of the fraction of sponsored immigrants not claiming social services during the sponsorship period (i.e., sponsorship success) would be useful. Also, a measure addressing the impact of the potential "cliff" at the end of the sponsorship period would be worthwhile. Similarly, a follow-up on business-class compliance, and on the occurrence and duration of jobs for which points for pre-arranged employment were provided, could be produced. For example, how many new immigrants are still with points-awarded employers two years after landing? Is the person still in the same job? A "better" job? No job?

In terms of more general labour market outcomes, measures such as those produced by Statistics Canada on an occasional basis looking at immigrant (relative) poverty rates, employment rates, and the like could be regularized. They could be generated annually using the IMDB.

Finally, explorations of issues related to the economic impact of immigration would be of high relative value, since so little work has been done. Much could be done with existing data, especially administrative data; but some of the work will need to look at broad general issues related to externalities, spillovers, and the various marginal costs and benefits of immigration. This is a relatively new research area, and some in-depth studies would be required prior to any indicators being developed.

Conclusion

Economic issues regarding immigration continue to be a policy priority, given the observed decline in labour market outcomes of the past two or more decades and the increase in poverty among new immigrants. The improvement that many had hoped for following the turn of the millennium appears not to have occurred; hopefully, relative outcomes will improve once the "IT bust" has dissipated, although the poor performance in the 2000s has not been restricted to that sector.

In contrast to how much we know about immigrant economic outcomes, little is known about the economic impact of immigration. Several fiscal, trade and economic development issues are ripe for analysis. However, even if future studies find that there are short-term financial costs to new immigration for the pre-existing population and it is financially neutral in the long term (which is plausible, but somewhat pessimistic), immigration remains economically beneficial since economics is about maximizing utility (sometimes called "happiness of life satisfaction"), rather than merely financial benefit. There are great non-monetary social and cultural benefits to immigration.

It is clear that both sides have responsibilities to aid in immigrant economic integration, and those responsibilities start before landing and are ongoing. Most arise from the integrated nature of the Canadian economy, relying on each member to consider the needs of others, so that all benefit from the economies of scale and specialization that underpin Canada's remarkably high standard of living. Part of the joint responsibility includes more research and ongoing monitoring of the economic outcomes of new immigrants so that we can develop, execute, and monitor policy changes to reduce poverty and increase the standards of living of new immigrants and all of society.

Notes

1.   There are also differences according to community characteristics. See, for example, Warman 2007.
2.   The selection of the sample for analysis (e.g., some studies focus only on full-year workers), and the definition of the variables (e.g., some studies

consider earnings to include only employment, and not self-employment, income) can also matter appreciably.

3. Lin (1998) shows that immigration likely has an impact on internal migration, making wage impacts at the sub-national level difficult to estimate.
4. In contrast, there were substantial economies of scale and beneficial skills transfer in much earlier periods (Green and Green 2004).
5. The policy change away from occupational targeting also reflected a shift from a focus on short-term concerns to longer-term ones, although it is not clear that longer-term concerns are actually better served under the newer regime.
6. For an international perspective on these issues see work by the Education Directorate of the OECD on their web page.

References

Antecol, H., P. Kuhn, and S. Trejo. 2006. "Assimilation via Prices or Quantities? Labor Market Institutions and Immigrant Earnings Growth in Australia, Canada, and the United States," *Journal of Human Resources* 41(4): 821–40.

Aydemir, A. 2003. "Effects of Business Cycles on the Labour Market Participation and Employment Rate Assimilation of Immigrants," in *Canadian Immigration Policy for the 21st Century*, eds. C. Beach, A. Green, and J. Reitz. Kingston, ON: McGill-Queen's University Press, pp. 373–412.

Aydemir, A., and G.J. Borjas. 2006. *A Comparative Analysis of the Labor Market Impact of International Migration: Canada, Mexico, and the United States*. NBER Working Paper No. 12327. Cambridge, MA: National Bureau of Economic Research.

Aydemir, A., and C. Robinson. 2008. "Global Labour Markets, Return, and Onward Migration," *Canadian Journal of Economics* 41(4): 1285–1311.

Aydemir, A., and M. Skuterud. 2005. "Explaining the Deteriorating Entry Earnings of Canada's Immigrant Cohorts, 1966–2000," *Canadian Journal of Economics* 38(2): 641–72.

Aydemir, A., and A. Sweetman. 2008. "First- and Second-Generation Immigrant Educational Attainment and Labor Market Outcomes: A Comparison of the United States and Canada." *Research in Labor Economics* 27: 215–70.

Beach, C., A. Green, and C. Worswick. 2008. "Impacts of the Point System and Immigration Policy Levers on Skill Characteristics of Canadian Immigrants," *Research in Labor Economics* 27: 349–401.

Beaudry, P., and D. Green. 2000. "Cohort Patterns in Canadian Earnings: Assessing the Role of Skill Premia in Inequality Trends," *Canadian Journal of Economics* 33(4): 907–36.

Beaujot, R. 2003. "Effect of Immigration on Demographic Structure." *Canadian Immigration Policy for the 21st Century*, eds. C. Beach, A. Green, and J. Reitz. Montreal and Kingston: McGill-Queen's University Press, pp. 49–91.

Betts, J., C. Ferrall, and R. Finnie. Forthcoming. "The Role of University Characteristics in Determining Post-Graduation Outcomes: Panel Evidence from Three Recent Canadian Cohorts," *Canadian Journal of Economics*.

Borjas, G.J. 1995. "The Economic Benefits from Immigration," *Journal of Economic Perspectives*, Spring: 3–22.

———— 1999. "The Economic Impact of Immigration," in *Handbook of Labor Economics*, 3A, eds. O. Ashenfelter and D. Card. Amsterdam: North-Holland, pp. 1697–760.

Citizenship and Immigration Canada. 2007. *Facts and Figures 2005: Immigration Overview Permanent and Temporary Residents*, Cat. no. Ci1-8/2003E. Ottawa: Government of Canada.

Coulombe, S., F. Hou, and G. Picot. 2007. *Chronic Low Income and Low-income Dynamics Among Recent Immigrants*. Analytical Studies Research Paper No. 294. Ottawa: Statistics Canada.

Denton, F., C. Feaver, and B. Spencer. 2001. "Alternative Pasts, Possible Futures: A "what if" Study of the Effects of Fertility on the Canadian Population and Labour Force," *QSEP Research Report* No. 367. Hamilton, ON: McMaster University.

Dicks, G., and A. Sweetman. 1999. "Education and Ethnicity in Canada: An Intergenerational Perspective," *Journal of Human Resources* 34(4): 668–96.

Dustmann, C., F. Fabbri, I. Preston, and J. Wadsworth. 2006. "The Local Labour Market Effects of Immigration in the UK." *Home Office Online Report*, March. London: Research Development and Statistics Directorate, Home Office.

Econtech Pty Ltd. 2006. "The Economic Impacts of Migration: A Comparison of Two Approaches." Canberra: Australian Department of Immigration and Multicultural Affairs.

Ferrer, A., and W.C. Riddell. 2008. "Education, Credentials, and Immigrant Earnings," *Canadian Journal of Economics* 41(1): 186–216.

Ferrer, A., D.A. Green, and W.C. Riddell. 2006. "The Effect of Literacy on Immigrant Earnings," *Journal of Human Resources* 41(2): 380–410.

Frenette, M., and R. Morissette. 2003. "Will They Ever Converge? Earnings of Immigrant and Canadian-born Workers over the Last Two Decades," *Analytical Studies Branch Research Paper* No. 215. Ottawa: Statistics Canada.

Grant, H., and A. Sweetman. 2004. "Introduction to Economic and Urban Issues in Canadian Immigration Policy," *Canadian Journal of Urban Research* 13(1): 1–24.

Green, A.G., and D.E. Green. 1999. "The Economic Goals of Canadian Immigration Policy: Past and Present," *Canadian Public Policy* 25: 425–51.

Green, A.G., and D. Green. 2004. "The Goals of Canada's Immigration Policy: A Historical Perspective," *Canadian Journal of Urban Research* 13: 102–39.

Green, D., and C. Worswick. 2004. "Earnings of Immigrant Men in Canada: The Roles of Labour Market Entry Effects and Returns to Foreign Experience." Ottawa: Strategic Research and Statistics, Citizenship and Immigration Canada. At http://www.cic.gc.ca/english/research/papers/earnings/earnings-toc.html.

Hou, F., and G. Picot. 2003. "The Rise in Low-Income Rates among Immigrants in Canada," *Analytical Studies Research Paper Series* No. 198. Catalogue no. 11F0019. Ottawa: Statistics Canada.

——— 2007. "Immigrant Economic Assimilation: Focusing on Experiences in Late 90s/2000s." Paper presented at the Queen's International Institute on Social Policy, Queen's University, Canada.

Lin, Z. 1998. "Foreign-Born vs. Native-Born Canadians: A Comparison of Their Inter-Provincial Labour Mobility," *Analytical Studies Research Paper Series* No. 114. Catalogue no. 11F0019. Ottawa: Statistics Canada.

Lowenstein, R. 2006. "The Immigration Equation." *The New York Times Magazine,* July 9, pp. 36–43 and 69–71.

Marr, W.L., and M.B. Percy. 1985. "Immigration Policy and Canadian Economic Growth," in *Domestic Policies and the International Economic Environment, Studies of the Royal Commission on the Economic Union and Development Prospects for Canada*, Vol. 12, ed. J. Walley. Toronto: University of Toronto Press.

McBride, S., and A. Sweetman. 2003. "Immigrant and Non-Immigrant Earnings by Postsecondary Field of Study," *Canadian Immigration Policy for the 21st Century*, eds. C.M. Beach, A.G. Green, and J.G. Reitz. Montreal and Kingston: McGill-Queen's University Press, pp. 413–62.

Organisation for Economic Co-operation and Development (OECD). 2005. "The Economic Impact of Immigration," in *Economic Survey of Italy 2005,* Chapter 4. At http://www.oecd.org/document/61/0,2340,en_2649_33931_34740925_1_1_1_1,00.html.

Pendakur, K., and R. Pendakur. 1998. "The Colour of Money: Earnings Differentials among Ethnic Groups in Canada," *Canadian Journal of Economics* 31: 518–48.

——— 2002. "Colour My World: Have Earnings Gaps for Canadian-Born Ethnic Minorities Changed Over Time?" *Canadian Public Policy* 28(4): 489–512.

——— 2007. "Minority Earnings Disparity Across the Distribution," *Canadian Public Policy* 33(1): 41–62.

Picot, G. 1998. "What is Happening to Earnings Inequality and Youth Wages in the 1990s?" *Analytical Studies Research Paper Series* No. 116. Catalogue no. 11F0019. Ottawa: Statistics Canada.

Picot, G., and A. Sweetman. 2005. "The Deteriorating Economic Welfare of Immigrants and Possible Causes," *Analytical Studies Research Paper Series* No. 262. Ottawa: Statistics Canada.

Poot, J., and B. Cochrane. 2004. "Measuring the Economic Impact of Immigration: A Scoping Paper." Immigration Research Programme, New Zealand Immigration Service, and Population Studies Centre, University of Waikato.

Reitz, J.G. 2007. "Immigrant Employment Success in Canada" including "Part I: Individual and Contextual Causes," and "Part II: Understanding the Decline," *Journal of International Migration and Integration* 8(1): 11–62.

Schaafsma, J., and A. Sweetman. 2001. "Immigrant Earnings: Age at Immigration Matters," *Canadian Journal of Economics* 34(4): 1066–99.

Simon, J.L. 1999. *The Economic Consequences of Immigration*, 2nd ed. Ann Arbor: University of Michigan Press.

Smith, A. 1759. *The Theory of Moral Sentiments*. Reprinted 2002. Ed. Knud Kaakonssen, New York: Cambridge University Press.

Smith, J.P., and B. Edmonston. 1997. *The New Americans: Economic, Demographic, and Fiscal Effects of Immigration*. Washington, DC: National Academy Press.

Swan, N., et al. 1991. *Economic and Social Impacts of Immigration: A Research Report*. Ottawa: Economic Council of Canada (Supply and Services Canada).

Sweetman, A. 2004. "Immigrant Source Country Educational Quality and Canadian Labour Market Outcomes," *Analytical Studies Branch Research Paper Series* No. 234. Ottawa: Statistics Canada.

———— 2005. "Immigration as a Labour Market Strategy: Canada," in *Immigration as a Labour Market Strategy: European and North American Perspectives*, eds. J. Niessen and Y. Schibel. Brussels, Belgium: Migration Policy Group, pp. 13–46.

Trefler, D. 1998. "Natives and Immigrants in General Equilibrium," in *The Immigration Debate: Studies on the Economic, Demographic, and Fiscal Effects of Immigration*, eds. J. P. Smith and B. Edmonston. Washington, DC: National Academy Press.

Warman, C. 2007. "Ethnic Enclaves and Immigrant Earnings Growth," *Canadian Journal of Economics* 40(2): 401–22.

Warman, C., and C. Worswick. 2004. "Immigrant Earnings Performance in Canadian Cities: 1981 through 2001," *Canadian Journal of Urban Research* 13(1): 62–84.

Chapter 2

The Political Integration of Newcomers, Minorities, and the Canadian-Born: Perspectives on Naturalization, Participation, and Representation

CHRISTOPHER G. ANDERSON AND JEROME H. BLACK

Introduction

The proposition that immigrants, minorities, and Canadian society in general bear major responsibilities for ensuring that newcomers become politically integrated into the host country has a strong normative quality. Such a "two-way street" approach holds, on the one hand, that newcomers should become full members of the national political community by first naturalizing and then exercising their democratic rights while fulfilling their obligations to be interested and engaged citizens politically. On the other hand, Canadian society and its institutions must facilitate the incorporation of immigrants by putting into place policies that encourage and assist in the process of political integration. It turns out that the notion of a two-way street as an optimal way to enhance integration is both an ideal and an actual characterization of the Canadian approach that has been in place, in some form or another, for more than thirty years.

In the late 1960s and early 1970s, as the Canadian state grappled to find a way to forge a new national identity in reaction to the challenges and concerns associated with, among other developments, a declining British connection, a stronger continental pull, Quebec nationalism, and growing immigration diversity, the successful integration of immigrants became a key component of the state's response. As part of a renewed nation-building effort, a "unity through diversity" approach, legitimized by multiculturalism, provided the basis for turning immigrants into

Immigration and Integration in Canada in the Twenty-first Century, eds. J. Biles, M. Burstein, and J. Frideres.
Montreal and Kingston: McGill-Queen's University Press, Queen's Policy Studies Series.

Canadians. While newcomers were expected to embrace Canadian institutions and values and to integrate themselves into the political sphere, there was also recognition and indeed a commitment that the receiving society and its political institutions would assist in this process. The desired results—a more effective integration process and a more cohesive national community—required that both the Canadian-born and immigrants fulfilled their obligations.

This chapter identifies some of the rights and responsibilities that define this two-way street approach to political integration, assisted by a review of the relevant literature concerning the extent to which immigrants (and minorities) and the Canadian-born have succeeded in meeting their obligations, and suggests indicators to measure progress in this regard. To do so, it examines three main dimensions of political integration—naturalization, political participation, and representation—that collectively generate a set of indicators of political integration that can be traced over time. First, however, two immediate questions must be addressed: (i) whose integration, and (ii) what standard of integration?

First, in keeping with the two-way street theme, the political integration of Canadian citizens by birth and by naturalization constitutes the central focus of this study.[1] It is important, however, to keep in mind non-Canadians (especially those within the country's borders) who might one day be granted citizenship, since their experiences could influence their subsequent political behaviour should they naturalize, while their actions might shape prevailing ideas about the political rights and responsibilities of new, old, and potential citizens. Moreover, responsibilities are generated between such non-citizens and the receiving country (Carens 2005; Goldston 2006). Special attention must also be paid to patterns along ethnoracial lines, especially between majority (i.e., those with British and/or French ancestry) and minority populations. Furthermore, the experiences of the children of immigrants need to be considered in light of evidence that second-generation visible minorities are much less socially and politically integrated than their non-visible minority counterparts (Reitz and Banerjee 2007).

Second, as Li (2003) suggests, the term "integration" is popular but problematic, because it is "often based on a narrow understanding and a rigid expectation that treats integration solely in terms of the degree to which immigrants converge to the average performance of native-born Canadians and their normative and behavioural standards" (11). As a result, differences between Canadian-born and foreign-born Canadians may be interpreted narrowly as indicating that the latter have not integrated adequately. With respect to political integration, this concern is partially offset in several ways. First, one of the main general conclusions drawn from the literature is that there are, in fact, relatively few gaps between Canadian-born and foreign-born in most areas of political behaviour. Second, by probing the responsibilities of the former towards the latter, the analysis explores the question of the extent to which the Canadian political system exhibits sufficient "institutional openness" (Li 2003) towards new citizens. Third, by taking ethnoracial aspects into account, the analysis is sensitive to the potential for racial discrimination and disadvantage to have a negative effect on the political participation—and thus the political integration—of the foreign-born *and* Canadian-born minority populations.

Even so, identifying the rights and responsibilities that define the two-way street of political integration between the Canadian-born and foreign-born remains a complicated endeavour. As Galloway (2000) observes, there is "the failure of the Citizenship Act to identify the responsibilities and rights that attach to the status" of Canadian citizenship (87). As a result, this question of rights and responsibilities is perhaps even more infused by a normative discourse of competing ideals than it might otherwise be. As well, the meaning of the rights and responsibilities involved—and thus the meaning of integration—clearly changes over time (Jenson and Phillips 2001): these concepts are forged and reforged through political contest and co-operation, with periods of relative fluctuation and stability. Thus, although the responsibilities identified and discussed below are firmly rooted in Canadian history and tradition, they are to some degree open to debate.

Challenges also extend from the empirically-oriented task of setting out appropriate indicators of the exercise of responsibility. One problem, as noted, is that using the Canadian-born levels of participation may say more about *their* limited engagement than the integration of immigrants. As well, in the case of representation, only *summary outcome* indicators seem feasible. For example, the incidence of MPs who are foreign born and/or have minority origins is offered as a key indicator of integration in that domain. But increases or decreases over time depend upon two different sets of (albeit interconnected) phenomena: varying efforts that newcomers and minorities make to enter the political elite and developments that occur within the mainstream political institutions (especially, the political parties) that facilitate or inhibit their access. It would be ideal to gauge the efforts of each separately with direct measures (say, the number of minority candidates who offer themselves as nomination contestants, on the one hand, and the proactive recruitment efforts of local parties, on the other), but such "quantities" would be quite difficult to establish with any reliability. Thus, an increase in minority MPs can index greater integration but cannot reveal the source of the increment. Moreover, as discussed in this chapter, some seemingly straightforward indicators require contextual explanation for their proper application.

The chapter is organized as follows. The analysis begins with naturalization, which is an essential aspect of political integration, because a citizen possesses political rights that are denied to non-citizens. In particular, under the *Charter of Rights and Freedoms*, Canadians have "the right to vote in an election of members of the House of Commons or of a legislative assembly and to be qualified for membership therein" (s.3), and "the right to enter, remain in, and leave, Canada" (s.6.1). Other political rights, however, extend to all who are present within the country's borders, regardless of their citizenship status, such as Fundamental Freedoms (s.2), as well as Legal (ss.7-14) and Equality (s.15) Rights. Thus, the question of rights and responsibilities that arise in the process of naturalization encompasses not just citizens but also those who are on a trajectory towards Canadian citizenship.

The rights and obligations that revolve around, and the practices that are indicative of, immigrant and minority political participation in Canada are discussed after the section on naturalization. Although all citizens possess the same rights in this domain and therefore arguably have an equal responsibility to participate, the Canadian-born (and, by extension, the Canadian state) can be said to possess additional responsibilities towards new citizens—responsibilities that are rooted in the comparative advantages they possess as a result of their continuous socialization within the political system. At the same time, the Canadian-born themselves have their own varied experiences and differ with regard to the incentives and resources that influence participation.

All citizens have the right to seek and hold office and therefore the opportunity to play an elite-level role in the Canadian system of representational government; for this reason, the analysis specifically addresses political representation as a distinct aspect of political participation. Such forms of political behaviour carry with them the potential to exercise direct power within the political system, including actions on behalf of minority and newcomer communities. To characterize the responsibilities that arise due to political representation, this analysis is framed by two stylized philosophical positions—liberal individualism and collectivism—that posit different sets of obligations on the part of mainstream as well as newcomer and minority entities.

The indicators of political integration generated from this analysis are presented collectively in the conclusion, in conjunction with a table.

The conclusion also sums up the main points advanced in this chapter and indicates areas of additional research which would, in the future, lead to the refinement of both the suggested indicators and new ones.

Naturalization

Naturalization formally incorporates non-citizens into the national political community by recognizing in them certain political rights and responsibilities. The acquisition of legal citizenship status is therefore a fundamental feature of political integration that can influence the course that it takes.[2] Although the process is at present structured by the *1977 Citizenship Act*, three recent efforts have been made to replace this law with new legislation, introduced (but not passed) in 1998 (C-63), 1999 (C-16), and 2002 (C-18). All three bills were investigated extensively by the Standing Committee on Citizenship and Immigration, which also wrote two additional reports on citizenship in 2005. Many analysts suggest that these attempted revisions constitute a new phase in the history of Canadian citizenship policy since the enactment of the 1977 law (Galloway 2000; Wong 2002; Garcea 2006).

Although the acquisition of citizenship through naturalization is often seen as a privilege granted by the state, rather than as a right demanded from it, the question of rights nonetheless arises. Indeed, the *1977 Citizenship Act* was created, in part, to recognize the rights of non-citizens in the naturalization process: in the absence of an absolute right to receive Canadian citizenship, applicants would possess "a qualified right" "upon compliance with certain specific statutory requirements."[3] Thus, the legislation outlined criteria for acceptance (s.5) and provided applicants with an appeal against an unfavourable outcome (s.14.5). While the privilege aspect can be seen to foster responsibilities on the part of the foreign-born, the rights-based features of naturalization generate responsibilities for the Canadian-born and the state.

On the foreign-born side, the primary issue revolves around whether landed immigrants fulfill a responsibility to become citizens.[4] While there is nothing illegal in their not assuming Canadian citizenship, and while such individuals can obviously still contribute to the country in numerous ways, it is sometimes argued that they ought to naturalize soon after becoming eligible in order to demonstrate their commitment to the country. Thus, while there is no consensus on whether such a responsibility exists, the question remains prevalent within naturalization debates in Canada and therefore worth considering.

The propensity for immigrants to naturalize can be measured statistically, using data collected by the Canadian government. For example, Tran et al. (2005) scrutinized census information and data from both the Longitudinal Survey of Immigrants to Canada (LSIC) and Citizenship and Immigration Canada (CIC), and found that most immigrants become Canadian citizens, with 84 percent of those eligible having done so as of 2001. The results for 1981, 1991, and 1996 are 77 percent, 82 percent, and 84 percent, respectively (Bloemraad 2004). Tran et al. also noted that 92 percent of those arriving between October 2000 and September 2001 signaled an intention to naturalize,[5] and observed that "recent groups of newcomers are taking less time to become citizens than previous groups" (11).[6] In general, they find that immigrants who are younger, have been in the country longer, or come from Africa or Asia are more likely to do so. Americans are particularly less likely to naturalize, while the opposite is true of refugees. In comparative perspective, the authors reveal that the naturalization rate of those eligible in Canada exceeds that of Australia (75 percent), the United Kingdom (56 percent), and the United States (40 percent). Thus, if the responsibility to naturalize exists for immigrants (and it is worth repeating that there is no consensus on this point), then it seems that it is largely being met.

For the Canadian-born, responsibility revolves around the conditions under which naturalization is granted, which can be further broken down in two ways. First, there is the responsibility to facilitate citizenship acquisition. As a country of immigration, Canada has committed itself to integrating non-citizens into the national community, and so the question is not whether but how this is to be accomplished. At present, under the *1977 Citizenship Act*, applicants must be 18 years or older, must not be under a removal order, and must have lived in the country legally as a permanent resident for three of the previous four years (s.5).[7] Applicants must also pass knowledge and language tests aimed at preserving the "value" of Canadian citizenship—at ensuring that it is not "for sale at bargain prices and for bargain requirements."[8] The question here, then, involves the fairness of such eligibility and test criteria.

Second, the Canadian-born have a responsibility to ensure that naturalized Canadians are treated equally with their Canadian-born counterparts with respect to their legal citizenship status. The recognition of the equality of all Canadians in the current law (s.6) has been maintained in the government's recent legislative efforts. For example, one of the declared purposes of C-18 was "to reaffirm that all citizens, no matter how they became citizens, have the same status" (s.3.d). The core issue here, then, is whether such equality is maintained in practice.

In order to assess the extent to which these responsibilities are being met on the Canadian side, the naturalization system anchored in the *1977 Citizenship Act* is taken as a baseline that reflects a general consensus on the conditions under which naturalization ought to occur. Given that immigrants have largely fulfilled their responsibility to naturalize under this system, and that—as discussed below— they generally participate at levels equal to or exceeding those of the Canadian-born, any efforts to make citizenship more difficult to acquire would seem to indicate that the commitment to facilitate political integration has decreased.[9]

Recently, politicians have expressed some interest in changing the residency requirement for naturalization by requiring immigrants to prove physical residency for three of the six years prior to their application. Such a move has been justified on the grounds that "a deep commitment to the adopted country...is possible only if the person is physically present in the country."[10] However, others argue that a six-year requirement is excessive and should be removed, and that a more flexible test of residency should be employed (Standing Committee 2005b). Both sides agree, however, that the proposed changes would make naturalization more difficult. In comparative terms, the Canadian standard is slightly higher than that of Australia (which requires a four-year residency, with no more than 12 months absent, but only 12 months as a permanent resident) but lower than that of the United States (which requires a five-year presence as a permanent resident, with at least 30 months in the country, and no absence greater than 12 months).

The eligibility criteria can also be examined in terms of particular categories of non-citizens. For example, live-in caregivers (Langevin and Belleau 2000) and refugees who do not possess adequate documentation to prove their identity to officials (Goodwin-Gill and Kumin 2000) are prevented from becoming permanent residents for a duration, thereby increasing the length of time before they can apply for citizenship. In contrast, legislation was passed in 2007 to ensure that foreign-born adopted children are treated equally as Canadian citizens with Canadian-born children, rather than having to first acquire permanent residence status (Library of Parliament 2007). Nonetheless, gaining citizenship remains more difficult for some categories of non-citizens than others, and recent proposals would make it more difficult for immigrants across the board.

As for the naturalization test, applicants must demonstrate their facility in English or French, knowledge of Canadian history and geography, and understanding of "Canada's system of government and the rights and responsibilities of citizenship" (CIC 2006b, 5). This knowledge is supposed to ease the integration process and aims to ensure that new citizens possess values such as "civic responsibility, respect for the law and understanding among peoples."[11] More generally, it is assumed that "someone who is born a Canadian presumably believes in all those things because those values are inculcated from birth, whereas a new Canadian has to adopt those values when they adopt this country."[12] However, a 2007 Ipsos Reid-Dominion Institute study found that "More than half (60 percent) of Canadians today would not be granted citizenship on the basis of having failed the citizenship exam," an increase from 45 percent in 1997 (2007, 2). In contrast, 70 percent of foreign-born Canadians surveyed in the 2007 study passed. Aside from what this might say about the quality of Canadian citizenship, it raises the question as to whether such a test is an appropriate measure of citizenship potential, with some arguing that "whether you know the name of the longest river in Canada really has nothing to do with citizenship."[13] Most policy-makers who commented on this issue before the Standing Committee from C-63 onwards, however, felt that these examinations served a useful integration purpose, as long as discretion was retained to make exceptions for the elderly and those with learning disabilities, for example (Standing Committee 2005b). An example of such can be seen in the recent decision to bring Canada's policies in line with Australia and the United States by reducing the age at which knowledge and language tests are waived, from 60 to 55 years (CIC 2005a).

This change can be viewed as an indication of the more general and positive role that the Canadian state has played in encouraging naturalization. For example, Bloemraad (2006) concludes that the discrepancy between citizenship acquisition rates (despite similarly liberal approaches) in Canada and the United States can be explained in large part by the positive interventionist approach that Ottawa has taken in promoting integration. This commitment was made more explicit in C-18: one of the expressed purposes of the legislation was "to encourage the acquisition of citizenship by all who qualify" (s.3.b). Moreover, the bill would have created a new cadre of Citizenship Commissioners, who would—during citizenship ceremonies—"underline the importance of the ceremony as a milestone in the life of new citizens" and "encourage citizens to give expression to their civic pride by respecting the law, exercising their right to vote and participating in Canadian society" (s.33.2). Furthermore, when application processing times increased from 10–12 months to 15–18 months, the government allocated

$69 million in 2005 to re-establish the former time frame,[14] and it has recently translated citizenship applications into Braille and initiated broad campaigns to promote citizenship and denounce racism in Canada (CIC 2005b).

As for legal citizenship equality, the major issue in recent years has been that of citizenship revocation. The central debate since C-63 has revolved around the questions of whether it should be "exclusively a judicial process" and which due process protections ought to be incorporated into the process (Standing Committee 2005a, 4). Critics argue that revocation is so serious that very high standards ought to prevail within a judicial setting, while the government maintains that adequate protections exist and that it can be trusted to use due discretion to ensure that only the guilty are targeted. Although C-18 addressed certain concerns raised with respect to C-63 and C-16, it retained a relatively unfettered power of annulment that would apply to those who acquired Canadian citizenship during the previous five years. It also introduced restrictions on foreign-born citizens against whom a security certificate had been issued. Thus, the debate was far from resolved when the Standing Committee released its most recent report on the issue (2005b); but clearly the proposals would have widened the gap between Canadian-born and foreign-born citizens considerably with respect to citizenship retention (Anderson forthcoming).

Although the responsibilities of the Canadian-born towards the foreign-born regarding naturalization remain very much in the eye of the beholder, it is possible to comment on changes and proposals since the enactment of the *1977 Citizenship Act*. Thus, while the government's proactive approach in encouraging naturalization has probably had a positive effect on naturalization rates, recent efforts to replace the 1977 law have included attempts to make it more difficult for immigrants to apply and to render it easier for the state to revoke or annul their citizenship after the fact. These changes reflect a larger trend amongst liberal democracies of "revalorizing" citizenship, in part by instituting more restrictive ways of rationing it (Feldblum 2000). As well, for certain categories of non-citizens, controversial barriers remain to obtaining Canadian citizenship. For such reasons, Wong (2002) argues that "The citizenship regime in Canada is shifting to [a more] exclusive one focusing on the soil, allegiance and loyalty" (181). Indeed, some of the proposals would constitute "a conceptual change from the current law, under which citizenship is a right, not a privilege, providing that objective criteria have been fulfilled" (Library of Parliament 2002, 10). At the same time, however, the government continues to take a proactive approach towards political integration by initiating new campaigns to promote citizenship, both in terms of naturalization and broader notions of civic engagement.

Political Participation

Citizens have the right to vote and to stand as candidates in federal, provincial, and territorial elections, but political participation encompasses, of course, a much wider array of activities. Along its most formal dimensions, political participation incorporates basic modes of electoral participation, such as voting in electoral events, campaigning (e.g., working for a party/candidate/side, donating money), and running for office. It can also include less formal aspects, such as contacting elected and nonelected officials and undertaking a range of protest activities (e.g., signing a petition, joining a boycott, demonstrating, striking illegally, and participating in sit-ins and occupations). Furthermore, political participation can include activities such as engaging in political discussions and following elections or politics more generally—typically antecedents of more concrete behaviour.

According to some analysts, political participation—conceived as a dimension of a broader process of civic engagement—also comprises activism in voluntary organizations and the community. For example, Frideres (1997) illustrates that participation can be measured "using such indicators as cleanup and beautification programs, home repair and improvement, building projects, provision of services (joint or with government agency), voting, political action, and other forms of membership in voluntary associations" (34). This inclusive approach captures the multifaceted nature of political engagement and facilitates empirical and theoretical perspectives on the interrelationship among the different forms of involvement (Saloojee and Siemiatycki 2003; Tolley 2003; Tossutti 2003). It is also useful for understanding how some minority categories (e.g., minority women) can gain contacts and experience in the voluntary sector to use as a springboard for seeking office (Black 2000a). Furthermore, a civic engagement perspective informs the government's understanding of the responsibilities of citizenship. For instance, in *A Look At Canada* (CIC 2006b), a booklet produced to assist naturalization applicants, citizens are said to have a responsibility to vote, help others in the community, care for and protect the country's heritage and environment, obey the law, express opinions freely while respecting the rights and freedoms of others, and eliminate discrimination and injustice, as well as to get involved in the community and in community groups.

While this suggests that the responsibilities of all citizens are equal with respect to political participation, in reality, the significant and time-consuming adjustments that immigrants must undergo during their resettlement in Canada, as they establish themselves economically and socially and/or acquire the requisite participation-connected knowledge and skills, make their situation more complex. As a result, their participation levels are expected to be lower, at least initially. In this context, two different types of responsibilities appear to be relevant.

First, although all citizens have a responsibility to participate politically, as a group the Canadian-born can be expected to do so more than the foreign-born, at least in the short term. Thus, they have a responsibility to play a leadership role by demonstrating to new citizens (and perhaps even to recent immigrants) the meaning and value of exercising an active form of Canadian citizenship.

Second, if significant participation gaps exist between recent immigrants (or particular communities among them) and the Canadian-born, then a responsibility may arise concerning the creation and implementation of measures to reduce or eliminate such differences. On the one hand, the Canadian state has a responsibility to encourage participation by decreasing the constraints on and increasing the opportunities for political action. On the other hand, minority communities and their leaders have a responsibility to be proactive in engendering active citizenship among the newcomers within their ranks.

To assess the political participation of immigrants, their participation rates or patterns need to be compared to those of the Canadian-born. A host of surveys over the years have included questions about participation. However, comparisons based on these surveys—to repeat the point—must bear in mind that the Canadian-born (or key categories among them) may be participating at levels that do not reflect citizenship ideals. Indeed, declining voter turnout rates and more broadly a general disengagement from the political system (Gidengil et al. 2004) have become part of recent Canadian political culture. As well, most of the relevant surveys have not been designed to explore ethnoracial distinctions along with foreign-born/Canadian-born differences, even though, as noted below, there is evidence of inter-group variability. For its part, the one major survey with a large enough sample size to permit examination of such distinctions—the 2002 Ethnic Diversity Study (EDS)—includes no measures of political behaviour beyond voting and involvement in voluntary organizations.[15]

The message that the available information conveys, however, is unequivocal: taking immigrants and the Canadian-born as two broad categories, the former are as politically active as the latter, certainly in the

long term. Indeed, after a period of adjustment, the participation rates
of new citizens converge with—and in some instances even exceed—
the "standards" set by the Canadian-born. For example, the 2004 Canadian National Election Study (of eligible voters) shows that immigrants
participate as much as the Canadian-born in voter turnout, contacting
government officials, engaging in boycotts, and participating in illegal
strikes: for instance, 85 percent of the foreign-born voted in the election
and 41 percent had contacted officials, compared to 87 percent and 37
percent (respectively) for the Canadian-born. For four other activities
where there were noticeable differences, newcomers actually participated more in three of them—communicating views to government
through protest (20 percent vs. 12 percent), doing so through "working
together with people who shared the same concern" (43 percent vs. 32
percent), and engaging in lawful demonstrations (30 percent vs. 22 percent). Canadian-born participation was only somewhat higher in the
case of signing petitions (83 percent vs. 73 percent). Moreover, immigrant participation rates generally increase for virtually all activities
with more time spent in the country. For voter turnout, the participation rates for those in the country ten years or less, between 11 and 20
years, and for 21 or more years are 71 percent, 68 percent, and 92 percent, respectively. In the case of contacting elected officials, the
corresponding percentages are 14 percent, 29 percent, and 44 percent.

Published results show the same patterns. In the *Citizens* volume of
the recent Canadian Democratic Audit project, Gidengil et al. (2004),
working mostly with the 2000 Canadian National Election Study, conclude that "Recent arrivals are less likely to be informed about Canadian politics, they are less likely to vote, and they are less likely to be
actively involved in voluntary associations." However, "Once
established,...immigrants typically display levels of political engagement similar to their native-born counterparts," with a few exceptions
(176). Foreign-born Canadians were less likely to take up party membership or engage in protest activities, but they actually displayed higher
levels of election (2000) and political interest (see also Tossutti 2003).
White et al. (2006) examined voter turnout more broadly. Pooling data
from the five election studies spanning the 1988–2004 interval, they
found a "somewhat anticlimactic" result, namely, parity in the participation rates of the Canadian- and foreign-born. They also show that
education, income, and political interest—major correlates of participation for the general population—only modestly influence turnout
differences among immigrants, leading them to speculate that the
foreign-born overcome a "steep political learning curve" because of a
strong sense that voting is a civic duty and/or a desire to "fit in" in "an

active effort to integrate" (14–15). Bilodeau and Kanji (2006) similarly combined national election survey data (1993–2004) to examine Canadian- and foreign-born differences with regard to interest in politics, attention to media-supplied political information, and knowledge of Canadian politics. Distinguishing between immigrants originating from traditional as opposed to non-traditional source countries[16]—the latter "with political cultures that are very different, most even non-democratic" (43)—they find that while the former displayed the highest levels of interest and attention, those from non-traditional countries were still more interested and attentive than the Canadian-born. No differences across the three categories were discerned in connection with political knowledge.

This conclusion about essential parity in participation rates between the foreign- and Canadian-born is not new and, in fact, is received wisdom, backed by a 25-year-old history.[17] Some older studies, moreover, took into account origin distinctions among immigrants. An analysis by Black (1982) using the 1974 Canadian National Election Study found that both British and non-British immigrants participated as much as the Canadian-born across a variety of participation activities. Similar patterns were uncovered in connection with a 1983 Toronto-area survey that included subsamples of the Canadian-born, immigrants from Britain, from Northern, Southern, and Eastern Europe, and from the British West Indies. The broadest inference is that all categories participated substantially in Canadian politics and that immigrants increasingly participated as they became established (Black 1987, 1991). Subsequent work by Chui et al. (1991) using the 1984 Canadian National Election Study data showed that the Toronto results were not idiosyncratic.

The older studies also uncovered variability in political engagement along ethnoracial lines. For example, Black (1991) found in that same Toronto survey that West Indian immigrants voted less and were less involved in campaigning, even after taking length of residence into account. Chui et al. (1991) discovered that Asians (and, to a lesser extent, Southern Europeans) were less likely to vote. Lapp (1999) also found significant differences by ethnicity in her aggregate-data analysis of voter turnout rates among five ethnic communities in Montreal (above-average voting within the Greek community, average levels among Italians and Portuguese, and below-average voting for the Chinese and Jewish communities).

More recently, several studies have exploited the large subsamples in the 2002 EDS to examine nativity and ethnoracial (especially visible minority) variations in connection with voter turnout for the 2000 election (Jedwab 2006; Tossutti 2005). Reitz and Banerjee (2007) employed turnout as one of several indicators (including voluntary organization involvement; see below) of the "social integration" of visible minorities relative to Whites. Their comparative matrix comprises immigrants resident for less than ten years, those in Canada for ten or more years, and second-generation Canadians; and their analysis further adjusts for age and, for the foreign-born, year of immigration. Among recent arrivals, they found no statistically significant differences in turnout between visible and non-visible minority immigrants, nor across the four visible minority categories specifically considered (Chinese, South Asians, Blacks, and Others). For earlier-arrived immigrants, only the "Others" voted less. In fact, the most striking differences occur among the Canadian-born, where the voting rates of visible minorities (overall and in each category) lag far behind those of their White counterparts. At least in the case of voting, then, political integration would appear to be less of a relevant concern for immigrants than it is for this segment of the Canadian-born.

Tossutti (2003) examined the civic engagement of immigrants undifferentiated by origin (along with participation more generally) using the 2000 election study. This survey asked respondents whether they had joined certain voluntary associations within the previous five years, with the list including community service, business, professional, environmental, women's, ethnic, sports and religious associations, as well as labour unions. Membership levels on the part of immigrants generally either matched or exceeded those of the native-born. In connection with ethnic and religious groups, the edge held by immigrants is not surprising; but newcomers were also much more likely to be members of professional associations. Moreover, over time the familiar pattern of convergence appeared: only for ethnic and religious associations was there less membership with more time spent in Canada.

Reitz and Banerjee (2007) used "volunteer activity"[18] (in the EDS) to index another facet of social integration. They found evidence of ethnoracial variation, as in the case of voting, though the gaps are fewer and more muted and, moreover, lean towards indicating more volunteer activity by visible minority categories. Among recent arrivals, only individuals of Chinese origin volunteered less relative to the other categories but Blacks actually volunteered the most. A similar picture emerges in connection with the more established immigrants, though South Asians were also more likely to volunteer more than non-visible minorities. For the Canadian-born (second generation individuals), the only significant result is that South Asians also volunteer more. In short, there is some variation in volunteering by origin group, but only for Chinese immigrants is there a deficit.

Thus, as a general pattern, immigrants act as responsible citizens insofar as they are politically engaged as much as or even—at times—more than the Canadian-born. Of course, more research is needed to provide greater understanding of the differences that arise in political activities across the nativity and origin divides. Such work would, first, allow for awareness of changing conditions that might affect the political integration of the more recent and future waves of immigrants; and, second, add to knowledge about the extent to which immigrant communities, their leaders, and the Canadian state are meeting their responsibilities to promote the involvement of newcomers.

What evidence there is indicates that ethnic communities do play such a role. Using the 1983 Toronto-area survey, Black and Leithner (1988) found that the ethnic media introduced newly-arrived immigrants to information about Canadian politics; and consumption of the media (especially print media) correlated with moderately higher levels of political engagement. In other research based on that survey, Black (1994) found that the social networks of the newly-arrived also contributed to their politicization. Political discussions about Canadian politics with friends and family (typically, individuals of the same origin group) took place more than might have been expected and were correlated with other indicators of political involvement. In her Montreal-based study, Lapp (1999) interviewed elites from the five communities and noted how leaders in some communities (e.g., Greek) found it easier to mobilize voters than leaders in other communities (especially, the Chinese). More recently, Bloemraad (2006) detailed the positive impact that leaders and community organizations play in encouraging both naturalization and participation within the Portuguese and Vietnamese communities in Toronto.

For its part, the Canadian state also plays a role in promoting political participation among the citizenry, including newcomers. For example, the efforts to promote naturalization noted earlier are certainly undertaken with an eye towards the encouragement of responsible citizenship. A broader commitment to promote citizenship in recent years can be seen through such campaigns as "Canada: We All Belong," which provides teachers and youth leaders with resources "to promote an understanding of active citizenship, social engagement and the shared values that have shaped Canada" (CIC 2005b, 45). For its part, Elections Canada has for the longest time taken steps to render the electoral process more accessible, in part by reaching out to new citizens; this includes such activities as producing electoral process material in multi-ple languages, and targeting minority communities through outreach programs (e.g., with respect to voter registration). More generally, Bloemraad (2006) relates the Canadian state's interventionist posture in supplying material and non-material support for immigrant com-munities to higher levels of participation.

In sum, the record shows that the participation levels of immigrants as a general category are at least comparable to those of the Canadian-born, and thus they appear to be fulfilling their responsibilities in this respect. From the perspective set out earlier in this chapter—that the Canadian-born might be expected to display a leadership role in set-ting high standards of political and civic engagement—the evidence suggests a responsibility deficit. At the same time, some of this deficit is tied to ethnoracial concerns—the limited involvement of second gen-eration visible minorities standing out most of all—implying that main-stream Canada has a responsibility to promote participation on the part of both sides of the street.

Political Representation

Office-seeking and office-holding are important considerations in the study of political integration because they are constitutionally protected rights that lie at the very centre of the exercise of representational govern-ment. The specific kinds of responsibilities that arise along the two-way street in this context, however, very much depend upon whether the philosophical point of departure taken is weighted towards a lib-eral individualist or a collectivist perspective. In their idealized guises, the former conceptualizes citizens more as autonomous actors who bring individual preferences to bear on the political system, while the latter additionally acknowledges that social groups often pursue objectives in the political arena on the basis of their distinctive collective identi-ties and interests.

There are several different ways of conceptualizing representation; but for present purposes, it suffices to examine the individualist and collectivist perspectives in terms of symbolic (or descriptive) and sub-stantive representation—the former emphasizing the personal charac-teristics of office holders, the latter the concrete actions that legislators undertake (Pitkin 1967). The individualist and collectivist perspectives both value, as symbolic statements, the presence of legislators from tra-ditionally underrepresented social categories, including immigrant and minority groups. For liberal individualists, this reflects the ideal that these men and women have "made it" on their own and, as role models, may inspire others to seek similar success in a system that rewards personal initiative. For collectivists, the symbolism is thicker: group legislators are a matter of group pride, allowing for the celebration of, and identification with, "their own" representatives.[19]

As for substantive representation, which is ultimately of more importance, liberal individualists believe that legislators need not necessarily share the characteristics of a particular group in order to represent its interests effectively; moreover, such interests are understood as being best expressed by individuals *qua* individuals. Collectivists, in contrast, argue that meaningful representation requires not only responsiveness to group members who have interests in common with their fellow citizens but also sensitivity to specific group-related interests. A stronger type of collectivism justifies group-based legislators because they uniquely understand the group's particular experiences and empathize with its aspirations and needs.

These different vantage points on substantive representation are associated with different ideas of what responsibilities exist for Canadian society, on the one hand, and immigrants and minorities, on the other. The individualist perspective would contend that all those in possession of the requisite resources and skills have a responsibility to be involved in such high-level engagement as office-seekers and office-holders. Those in the mainstream have a more specific obligation to ensure that the democratic process does not unfairly inhibit immigrants and minorities from making their way into the political elite. Significantly, this merit-based approach includes taking steps to ensure that candidate recruitment processes are free from bias and prejudice. Further, representatives of all backgrounds have a responsibility, at least in principle, to take into account the views of all individual citizens.

In contrast, the collectivist perspective implies that minority individuals who possess the requisite office-seeking resources and skills have a responsibility to ensure some measure of immigrant/minority-oriented representation. This includes making sure that the public agenda includes policy matters of particular importance to their communities (or minority communities in general). In turn, those dominating the established political order need to open up the candidate selection process, by eliminating overt forms of discrimination and by countering manifestations that are more subtle or correlative in nature (e.g., the holding of nomination meetings during religious holidays). This responsibility could even include the use of proactive measures to overcome the effects of past discriminatory practices, including, for example, financial incentives for parties to nominate more minorities.

There is also an obligation to ensure that the legislative environment does not inhibit minority-oriented representatives from promoting group concerns, for example, through either overly restrictive party discipline or stigmatization of those who champion relevant issues.

Thus, a collectivist perspective entails a more far-reaching set of obligations for all concerned. As a result, considerable weight should be given to the group-oriented approach in discussions of representation and responsibilities, though not necessarily exclusively so. Three lines of reasoning that draw upon various literature sets and some empirical material can be outlined in support of this position. First, key groups among the foreign-born and minorities are significantly under-represented among the legislative elite, which implies *at the very least* a deficit in symbolic representation. Second, biases appear to play some role in this underrepresentation, suggesting that the largely liberal individualist emphasis in mainstream politics comes up short in ensuring equitable representation. Third, presence does appear to matter, meaning that the absence of group-oriented legislators contributes to the neglect of minority interests.

With regard to underrepresentation of key groups, while Parliament has clearly become more diverse in recent years, with increasing numbers of both foreign-born and minority MPs, the changes have been uneven, and deep gaps in representation persist. Bloemraad (2006, 56–62) reports that in 1988, 9.8 percent of the MPs elected were foreign-born, while this was true of 15 percent of the MPs elected in 2000. Independent calculations for the 1993, 1997, 2004, and 2006 elections produce figures of 15.3 percent, 15.6 percent, 12.7 percent, and 13.3 percent, respectively. Apart from the fact that these numbers indicate a drop in foreign-born parliamentarians in the last two elections, they are all consistently below the corresponding population figures— the 2001 census counted 18.4 percent of the Canadian population as having been born abroad.

A similar pattern emerges in connection with ethnoracial status, which is probably a more appropriate overall indicator of the extensiveness of diversity, given that many questions of representation have an ethnoracial rather than birthplace foundation (including matters related to integration of the second generation), and given that some foreign-born MPs have majority backgrounds. In the 1993 election, enough MPs of ethnic (European) descent won seats to achieve rough parity with their relative population incidence. Visible minority representation also increased (from a handful in 1988 to 13 MPs); however, their percentage of seats remained far below their corresponding population share. While more were elected in the ensuing elections, the increases were modest and irregular, and the increments have only kept pace with growth of visible minorities among the population at large. For example, 19 visible minority MPs were elected in 1997, but in 2000, their numbers actually fell back to 17 (Black 2000b, 2002). In the 2004 election, the 22 visible minorities who won their seats constituted 7.1 percent of the total membership of the House; at the same time, visible minorities comprised 14.9 percent of the general population (Black forthcoming). For 2006, the figures are 7.8 percent and 15.9 percent, respectively (Black 2007). There are also important variations in representation across visible minority categories, most particularly, a sharp underrepresentation of MPs of Chinese or Black origin, especially compared to those of South Asian background (Matheson 2006).

The limited overall presence of visible minority MPs can be explained, in part at least, by their relative absence among parliamentary candidates. Over the 1993–2000 period, visible minorities comprised only 4–5 percent of candidates running for the main parties (Black 2000a; Tossutti and Najem 2002); and while the 2004 election results show a clear increase to 9.3 percent, this figure remains far removed from the population benchmark (Black and Hicks 2006b). On the positive side, there is growing evidence that visible minority candidates are not being relegated to less competitive ridings (Tossutti and Najem 2002; Black and Hicks 2006b).

Still, enduring biases in the recruitment process no doubt play some role in limiting their candidacies—the second concern that justifies paying heed to the collectivist approach. In particular, fewer candidates overall could mean that insufficient numbers of visible minorities are winning candidacies, and/or it could mean that they face an indifferent, or even unwelcoming, reception in some local parties at an earlier stage in the process. Certainly, a dominant thrust in the literature is that the playing field for majority and minority candidates has traditionally been quite uneven (e.g., Stasiulis and Abu-Laban 1991). Even if it is acknowledged that the parties, motivated by electoral incentives to recruit visible minorities, have been making *some* progress in this regard, there is plenty of room for improvement. One indication of a continuing lack of fairness is the way that visible minority candidates (and MPs) have tended to have stronger credentials (e.g., higher levels of education) than their White counterparts, implying the need to compensate for recruitment biases (Black 2000a, 2003). This suggests that responsibilities on the Canadian side of the two-way street are not being met. For example, parties need to examine how their recruitment processes and practices may inhibit, even inadvertently, minorities. Moreover, the mass media needs to treat the playing out of ethnic politics, including the oft-noted nomination battles in key ridings, not as aberrations but as part of traditional party politics in Canada (Stasiulis and Abu-Laban 1991; Canada 1991).

The third concern of the collectivist perspective is that presence does matter. Three points can be made with regard to this claim. First, issues and policy concerns specifically animate minority and newcomer communities—or at least key elements within them. Included in what might be called the "minority agenda" are numerous aspects of immigration and refugee policy, social acceptance and race relations policy considerations, diversity and cultural recognition, economic opportunities (including employment equity), and political representation itself. While in some instances the links between minority communities and particular policy stances are quite evident and supported by strong evidence (e.g., visible minorities are most likely to report discrimination; Statistics Canada 2003), in other instances there has been less empirical inquiry, but the relationship might be inferred on an intuitive basis or as a result of the public positions adopted by community leaders. One limited study of these links is by Blais (2005) who, using the 2004 election study, found that Canadians of non-European origin (i.e., effectively visible minorities) were more likely than others in the population to assert that Canada should allow in more immigrants, do more for racial minorities, and increase aid to developing countries.

A second point concerns whether minority legislators bring distinctiveness to the representation of ideas and interests in Parliament. If minority members of the political elite simply replicate the policy orientations of majority members, then the case for group-based representatives is weakened. More work on this question needs to be done, but what evidence there is suggests that minority politicians have distinctive attitudes. For example, a study of candidates who ran in the 1993 election found that visible minority contestants were most likely to endorse the idea of having many more racial minorities in Parliament, and generally held left-liberal positions on broader socio-economic issues, even controlling for party affiliation (Black 2001a).

Results from a survey of candidates who ran in the 2004 election point in the same general direction; visible minorities were more likely to regard their underrepresentation in Parliament as problematic, to find the current single-member plurality system as unacceptable, and to favour electoral reform initiatives (Black and Hicks 2006c). Unpublished results indicate that visible minority candidates were also much more likely to prefer the admission of more immigrants, in each of the major categories, and to moderately favour multiculturalism more than majority candidates (though the results significantly depended upon party affiliation).[20] Finally, interviews with minority and majority MPs in the mid-1990s by one of the authors also led to the conclusion that minority MPs are more preoccupied with the minority-relevant issues.[21]

As a third point, in the absence of more systematic research into the impact of presence in the political process, researchers can appeal to studies of other relevant social categories that have uncovered evidence that presence matters. There is, in fact, an abundance of "parallel" work on women in Canada (and beyond), as well as on minorities in other countries, especially the United States, that generally concludes that diversity candidates and legislators tend to think and act somewhat, if not radically, different from mainstream groups.[22]

Broadly speaking, then, minority politicians tend to have distinctive preferences, often rooted in community concerns, that they bring to bear on the political process; and they do so in spite of numerous barriers. This characterization validates the need to give serious weight to the collectivist perspective. It implicates responsibilities on both sides of the street but appears to lay the larger burden with majority politicians and the Canadian political process. Mainstream officials and institutions ought to allow for the full or at least proportional expression of concerns that are salient for minority communities. This would include the obligation for majority legislators who represent diverse ridings to give expression to such policy preferences and to facilitate the presence of minority MPs, who also may have a responsibility to give voice to such preferences. Minority MPs should not, however, have to incur costs, such as lost opportunities to climb the parliamentary hierarchy because they champion minority causes. Research also needs to gauge representation by considering the numbers of minorities in more prominent positions within Parliament, such as committee chairs, parliamentary secretaries, and cabinet ministers.[23]

A collectivist approach is certainly not inconsistent with Canadian integration policies in the modern era. Thus, while minority communities carry a responsibility to push for greater representation of their interests both individually and collectively, the institutions that structure Canadian political life—especially, the political parties inside and outside of Parliament—bear a particular obligation to reflect the pluralism of Canadian society.

Conclusion

The broadest conclusion reached in this chapter is that immigrants generally carry out their responsibilities in the three domains of political integration considered—naturalization, participation, and representation. In fact, there is evidence and several lines of argumentation that point to the larger onus resting with the Canadian-born and the Canadian political system to reduce their responsibility deficits. The Canadian mainstream needs to assume a greater leadership role in demonstrating to newcomers the substance and practice of good citizenship. This chapter suggests that more research and analysis are required to develop a more comprehensive picture of the intricacies of the responsibilities on the two sides of the political integration street. This includes greater understanding of the impact of ethnoracial distinctions, not only among immigrants, but also among the Canadian-born. Such an analysis would also prepare for research into remedial measures that might be adopted especially by the Canadian state to specifically deal with disadvantaged groups.

Moreover, while the three dimensions of political integration have been separated here for analytical purposes, they are interrelated in ways that should also be the focus of further investigation. For example, the state's efforts to politically integrate non-citizens on a path towards naturalization may very well shape their subsequent behaviour as Canadian citizens. As well, the responsiveness of the political system to the needs and interests of new immigrants may shape their political socialization as they move from non-citizen to citizen status. Further, the potential effects of group-based candidates and legislators on empowering ordinary community members and increasing their participation need to be investigated. As well, the analysis of participation and representation needs to be expanded to address in a more direct fashion the country's federal character by considering other levels and arenas of political activity.

Carrying out such research will no doubt point to new indicators of integration and provide the basis for refining those proposed here. Still, those offered for present purposes go a long way towards indexing and tracking over time the responsibilities on the two sides of the street. In the case of naturalization, the propensity of immigrants to naturalize can be traced by drawing upon state-generated data, which ought at least to be broken down according to origin and time of immigration. As for the responsibility held on the Canadian side, a much thicker analysis is required, one that assesses changes over time in the conditions under which Canadian citizenship is offered, as well as those under which it might be taken away.

As for participation, three indicators of political participation, operationalized using survey research methods, are suggested for both the foreign- and Canadian-born: (i) voting in the latest federal election, (ii) at least one additional form of participation, and (iii) activity in at least one voluntary organization. Voting, as the primordial act of political citizenship, is an obvious choice, while additional involvement captures a modest amount of participatory breadth; for its part, organizational activism taps the larger dimension of civic engagement. The specific questions (indicated in Table 1) that generate these measures come from the academic-oriented series of Canadian National Election Studies (e.g., 2004, 2006 studies). Their use in future election surveys promises continuity of analysis and an extended dynamic perspective. At a minimum, these engagement levels should be determined for survey respondents who are Canadian- and foreign-born (the basis for the primary comparison) and by length of residence intervals for immigrants (to assess convergence). With a longitudinal vantage point, participation rate changes both in absolute and relative terms can be tracked. Since the national election surveys typically do not have large enough samples to allow for evaluations that also factor in generation and ethnoracial differences, it would be valuable to carry out an EDS-type (large sample) survey every once in a while. The questions used with regard to voting and volunteering can be repeated to assure continuity.

With regard to representation, as already suggested, it is not possible to derive reliable indicators for the representation dimension of integration that uniquely capture the separate exercises of responsibility by minorities/newcomers and mainstream Canada. Thus, summary or "conflated" outcome measures have to suffice; and it probably makes the greatest sense to concentrate on visible minorities, though some consideration could be given to foreign-born status. Four measures are suggested, all involving the percentage of visible minorities (and subcategories): (i) candidates nominated in ridings where their party is competitive (major parties only); (ii) MPs elected in the general election; (iii) committee chairs and parliamentary secretaries; (iv) cabinet ministers. The latter two items are designed, of course, to measure enhanced status and the exercise of greater power within the parliamentary setting. Visible minority background can be determined through a variety of measurement approaches (e.g., Black and Lakhani 1997), while candidacies and legislative positions are easily established using party and government sources. The "counting" of visible minorities should also include breakdowns within the major subcategories in order to track the breadth of representation and in reference to visible minority (sub)population benchmarks.

Table 1: Proposed Outcome Measures

Naturalization Indicators (1 for the Canadian-born, 1 for the foreign-born)

A straightforward measure of the responsibility of the foreign-born is naturalization rates. These rates can be tracked statistically using state-generated data. Analysis should at least include distinctions according to time of immigration and origin. On the Canadian side, changes in government policy with respect to the conditions under which naturalization is offered and those under which it can be removed can be traced over time using the *1977 Citizenship Act* as a benchmark. This requires a contextual analysis of legislative and policy initiatives and practices as well as the debates that they generate.

Political Participation Indicators (3 for the Canadian-born, 3 for the foreign-born)

Three for the Canadian-born and three for the foreign-born, based on survey-derived questions (asked in national election studies). Analysis should include length of residence breakdowns for immigrants. Second-order comparisons should adjust for age and socio-economic status. Election series (past and present) should provide longitudinal vantage points.

1) Voting

    Did you vote in the election? (ELECTION SPECIFIED; ASKED FOR CITIZENS ONLY)

    Measure: Voted (yes, no)

2) Other Participation

    Over the past five years have you expressed your views about something the government should or should not be doing by:

    • Contacting a politician or government official either in person, or in writing, or some other way?
    • Taking part in a protest, march or demonstration?
    • Working together with people who shared the same concern?

    Measure: Participated in at least one of the three ways (yes, no)

3) Civic Engagement

    Please circle any voluntary association(s) in which you have been active during the past five years. (LIST PROVIDED)

    Measure: Active in at least one association (yes, no)

Representation (Summary Outcome) Indicators (4)

The percentage of visible minorities in four categories, starting from the 1993 election/35th Parliament with ongoing updates. Candidacy information from party sources and Elections Canada should be determined for each general election (1993 onwards). Legislative positions established from government sources should be determined at the outset of each session for each Parliament (35th Parliament, first

... continued

Table 1 (Continued)

session onwards). Visible minority background should be determined using a multi-method approach (e.g., Black and Lakhani 1997) and population benchmark data taken from census data and Statistics Canada visible minority projections. Analysis should include consideration of major visible minority subcategories.

Percent visible minorities (and subcategories) among:

1) Candidates nominated in ridings where their party is competitive (won the riding or lost it by 10 percent or less) (MAJOR PARTIES ONLY: Bloc Québécois, the Conservatives, the Greens, the Liberals, and the NDP)
2) MPs elected in general elections
3) Committee chairs and parliamentary secretaries
4) Cabinet ministers

Notes

1. The analysis is conducted with primary reference to federal politics. This provides focus in this study and, in any event, most of the relevant literature deals with national politics. As is noted in the conclusion, a much more comprehensive exploration of political integration ought to incorporate other levels of governance and facets of political life.
2. *Legal* citizenship—"the juridical status of membership held by an individual in relation to a territorial nation-state"—can be distinguished from *substantive* citizenship—"the rights, entitlements, obligations, duties, and other legal, social, and political practices that constitute the individual as an active, participatory, and functional political subject within a nation-state" (Macklin 2006, 22–23).
3. Secretary of State James H. Faulkner, in Canada, *House of Commons Debates* [hereafter *HCD*] (May 21, 1975), 5983.
4. Given recent academic (e.g., Hansen and Weil 2002; Martin and Hailbronner 2003) and political (e.g., the 2006 case of Lebanese-Canadians in war-torn Lebanon) interest in dual citizenship, consideration was given to the question of whether new citizens have a responsibility to renounce their previous citizenship(s). However, it proved difficult to make a sufficiently clear case that such a responsibility exists, while both the Canadian and comparative data are sketchy. For an examination of the Canadian experience, see Bloemraad 2004.
5. Following the release of the 2005 LSIC update, it was found that 15 percent had already become citizens, 56 percent had started the process, and

22 percent still intended to do so, leaving only 7 percent uncertain or not intending to apply (Schellenberg and Maheux 2007, 15).

6.   There has been a considerable increase in the number of applications for citizenship during the past few years, both because of higher levels of immigration since the mid-1990s and also because more long-term residents are coming forward (CIC 2006a, 33).

7.   An applicant can also be deemed ineligible on national security grounds (see ss.19–20), among other reasons (see s.22).

8.   Bob Brisco, in Canada, *HCD* (January 27, 1976), 10365.

9.   This does not preclude the possibility that by making it more difficult to naturalize, the Canadian state might be fulfilling other responsibilities.

10.   Immigration Minister Lucienne Robillard, in *HCD* (February 3, 1999), 1525.

11.   *Ibid.*, 1530.

12.   John Bryden, in Canada, *Minutes and Proceedings of the House Standing Committee of Citizenship and Immigration* (March 11, 1999), No. 52, 1120.

13.   Charles Caccia, in Canada, in *HCD* (December 8, 1975), 9807.

14.   By 2006, the timeframe had been reduced to 12–15 months (CIC 2006a, 33).

15.   Altogether the sample size is 41,695 (Statistics Canada 2002).

16.   The authors take traditional source countries to include Western, Northern, and Southern European countries (the prevalent areas of origin up to the 1960s) and non-traditional countries to be associated with Eastern and Central Europe, Asia, Africa and Latin America.

17.   For overviews of the earliest of studies, which tended to draw negative conclusions about immigrant political participation, see Black (2001b) and Tossutti (2003).

18.   Respondents were asked whether they had volunteered their time for an organization that they were members of or active in.

19.   Such enthusiasm would be tempered by low levels of group representation and a concern over token representation.

20.   This is work in progress; for an overview of the survey, see Black and Hicks (2006a).

21.   This is unpublished work; contact Black for more details.

22.   A good listing of this vast literature can be found in Ogmundson (2005).

23.   It would also be useful to examine the discourse and behaviour of minority MPs in connection with parliamentary debates, oral questions and private members' bills.

References

Anderson, C.G. Forthcoming. "A Long-Standing Canadian Tradition: Citizenship Revocation and Second-Class Citizenship under the Liberals, 1993–2006," *Journal of Canadian Studies*.

Bilodeau, A., and M. Kanji. 2006. "Political Engagement Among Immigrants in Four Anglo-Democracies," *Electoral Insight* 8(2), December: 43–49.

Black, J.H. 1982. "Immigrant Political Adaptation in Canada: Some Tentative Findings," *Canadian Journal of Political Science* 15(1), March: 3–27.

——— 1987. "The Practice of Politics in Two Settings: Political Transferability Among Recent Immigrants to Canada," *Canadian Journal of Political Science* 20(4), December: 731–53.

——— 1991. "Ethnic Minorities and Mass Politics in Canada: Some Observations in the Toronto Setting," *International Journal of Canadian Studies* 3 (Spring): 129–51.

——— 1994. "Political Discussions and Political Involvement: Capturing Personal Influence Effects in Dynamic Situations," *Working Papers in Political Science* No. 94-1. Montreal: Department of Political Science, McGill University.

——— 2000a. "Entering the Political Elite in Canada: The Case of Minority Women as Parliamentary Candidates and MPs," *Canadian Review of Sociology and Anthropology* 37(2), May: 143–66.

——— 2000b. "Ethnoracial Minorities in the Canadian House of Commons: The Case of the 36th Parliament," *Canadian Ethnic Studies* 32(2): 105–14.

——— 2001a. "Representation in the Parliament of Canada: The Case of Ethnoracial Minorities," in *Citizen Politics: Research and Theory in Canadian Political Behaviour,* eds. J. Everitt and B. O'Neil. Don Mills, ON: Oxford University Press, pp. 355–85.

——— 2001b. "Immigrants and Ethnoracial Minorities in Canada: A Review of Their Participation in Federal Electoral Politics," *Electoral Insight* 3(1), January: 8–13.

——— 2002. "An Update on Ethnoracial Minorities in the House of Commons," *Canadian Parliamentary Review* 25(1): 24–28.

——— 2003. "Differences That Matter: Minority Women MPs, 1993–2000," in *Women and Electoral Politics in Canada*, eds. M. Tremblay and L. Trimble. Don Mills, ON: Oxford University Press, pp. 59–74.

——— 2007. "The 2006 Canadian Election and Minority Representation in the 39th Parliament: More of the Same?" Montreal: Department of Political Science, McGill University.

——— Forthcoming. "Ethnoracial Minorities in the 38th Parliament: Patterns of Change and Continuity," in *Electing a Diverse Canada,* eds. C. Andrew, J. Biles, M. Siemiatycki, and E. Tolley. Vancouver: University of British Columbia Press.

Black, J.H., and B.M. Hicks. 2006a. "Strengthening Canadian Democracy: The Views of Parliamentary Candidates," *Policy Matters* 7(2). At http://www.irpp.org/pm/archive/pmvol7no2.pdf.

————— 2006b. "Visible Minority Candidates in the 2004 Federal Election," *Canadian Parliamentary Review* 29(2), Summer: 26–31.

————— 2006c. "Visible Minorities and Under-Representation: The Views of Candidates," *Electoral Insight*, 8(2), December: 17–23.

Black, J.H., and A.S. Lakhani. 1997. "Ethnoracial Diversity in the House of Commons: An Analysis of Numerical Representation in the 35th Parliament," *Canadian Ethnic Studies* 29(1): 1–21.

Black, J.H., and C. Leithner. 1988. "Immigrants and Political Involvement in Canada: The Role of the Ethnic Media," *Canadian Ethnic Studies* 20(1), May: 1–20.

Blais, A. 2005. "Accounting for the Electoral Success of the Liberal Party in Canada," *Canadian Journal of Political Science* 38(4), December: 821–40.

Bloemraad, I. 2004. "Who Claims Dual Citizenship? The Limits of Postnationalism, the Possibilities of Transnationalism, and the Persistence of Traditionalism," *International Migration Review* 38(2), Summer: 389–426.

————— 2006. *Becoming A Citizen: Incorporating Immigrants and Refugees in the United States and Canada.* Berkeley: University of California Press.

Canada. 1977. *Citizenship Act*, Statutes of Canada 1974–75–76, c. 108.

————— 1982. *Canadian Charter of Rights and Freedoms*, Part I of the *Constitution Act*, 1982, being Schedule B to the *Canada Act 1982* (U.K.), c. 11.

————— 1991. "Royal Commission on Electoral Reform and Party Financing," *Reforming Electoral Democracy, Vol. I.* Ottawa: Supply and Services Canada.

————— 2002. *Bill C-18, An Act Respecting Canadian Citizenship.* 2nd Sess., 37th Parl.

Carens, J.H. 2005. "The Integration of Immigrants," *Journal of Moral Philosophy*, 2(1): 29–46.

Chui, T., J. Curtis, and R. Lambert. 1991. "Immigrant Background and Political Participation: Examining Generational Patterns," *Canadian Journal of Sociology*, 16(4), Autumn: 375–96.

Citizenship and Immigration Canada (CIC). 2005a. "Citizenship and Immigration Minister Joe Volpe Announces New Measures to Improve the Citizenship Application Process" [News Release 2005-10]. Ottawa: Queen's Printer.

————— 2005b. *Annual Report to Parliament on Immigration 2005.* Ottawa: Queen's Printer.

————— 2006a. *Annual Report to Parliament on Immigration 2006.* Ottawa: Queen's Printer.

————— 2006b. *A Look At Canada.* At www.cic.gc.ca/english/resources/publications/look/look-20.asp.

Feldblum, M. 2000. "Managing Membership: New Trends in Citizenship and Nationality Policy," in *From Migrants to Citizens: Membership in a Changing World*, eds. T.A. Aleinikoff and D. Klusmeyer. Washington, DC: Carnegie Endowment for International Peace, pp. 475–99.

Frideres, J.S. 1997. "Civic Participation, Awareness, Knowledge and Skills." A discussion paper presented at the Heritage Canada Research Domain Seminar on Immigrants and Civic Participation, Montreal, November.

Galloway, D. 2000. "The Dilemmas of Canadian Citizenship Law," in *From Migrants to Citizens: Membership in a Changing World*, eds. T.A. Aleinikoff and D. Klusmeyer. Washington, DC: Carnegie Endowment for International Peace, pp. 82–118.

Garcea, J. 2006. "The Third Phase of the Canadian Citizenship Project: Reform Objectives and Obstacles," in *Continuity and Change in Canadian Politics: Essays in Honor of David E. Smith*, eds. H.J. Michelmann and C. de Clercy. Toronto: University of Toronto Press, pp. 195–224.

Gidengil, E., A. Blais, N. Nevitte, and R. Nadeau. 2004. *Citizens.* Vancouver: University of British Columbia Press.

Goldston, J.A. 2006. "Holes in the Rights Framework: Racial Discrimination, Citizenship, and the Rights of Noncitizens," *Ethics and International Affairs* 20(3), Fall: 321–47.

Goodwin-Gill, G.S., and J. Kumin. 2000. *Refugees in Limbo and Canada's International Obligations.* Toronto: Caledon Institute of Social Policy.

Hansen, R., and P. Weil (eds.). 2002. *Dual Nationality, Social Rights and Federal Citizenship in the U.S. and Europe.* New York: Berghahn Books.

Ipsos Reid and The Dominion Institute. 2007. *National Citizenship Exam: 10 Year Benchmark Study.* Ottawa: Ipsos Reid.

Jedwab, J. 2006. "The 'Roots' of Immigrant and Ethnic Voter Participation in Canada," *Electoral Insight* 8(2), December: 3–9.

Jenson, J., and S.D. Phillips. 2001. "Redesigning the Canadian Citizenship Regime: Remaking the Institutions of Representation," in *Citizenship, Markets, and the State*, eds. C. Crouch, K. Eder, and D. Tambini. Toronto: Oxford University Press, pp. 69–89.

Langevin, L., and M-C. Belleau. 2000. *Trafficking in Women in Canada: A Critical Analysis of the Legal Framework Governing Immigrant Live-in Caregivers and Mail-Order Brides.* At www.swc-cfc.gc.ca/pubs/pubspr/066231252X/index_e.html.

Lapp, M. 1999. "Ethnic Group Leaders and the Mobilization of Voter Turnout: Evidence from Five Montreal Communities," *Canadian Ethnic Studies* 31(2): 17–42.

Li, P.S. 2003. "Deconstructing Canada's Discourse of Immigrant Integration," *Journal of International Migration and Integration* 4(3), Summer: 315–33.

Library of Parliament [B. Dolin and M. Young, Law and Government Division]. 2002. *Legislative Summary – Bill C-18: The Citizenship of Canada Act.* Ottawa: Library of Parliament.

Library of Parliament [Elizabeth Kuruvila, Law and Government Division]. 2007. *Legislative Summary – Bill C-14: An Act to Amend the Citizenship Act (Adoption).* Ottawa: Library of Parliament.

Macklin, A. 2006. "Exile on Main Street: Popular Discourse and Legal Manoeuvres around Citizenship," in *Law and Citizenship,* ed. Law Commission of Canada. Vancouver: University of British Columbia Press, pp. 22–54.

Matheson, A. 2006. "Seeking Inclusion: South Asian Political Representation in Suburban Canada," *Electoral Insight* 8(2), December: 24–29.

Martin, D.A., and K. Hailbronner (eds.). 2003. *Rights and Duties of Dual Nationals: Evolution and Prospects.* The Hague: Kluwer Law International.

Ogmundson, R. 2005. "Does it Matter if Women, Minorities and Gays Govern? New Data Concerning an Old Question," *Canadian Journal of Sociology* 30(3), Summer: 315–24.

Pitkin, H. 1967. *The Concept of Representation.* Berkeley: University of California Press.

Reitz, J.G., and R. Banerjee. 2007. "Racial Inequality, Social Cohesion and Policy Issues in Canada," in *Belonging? Diversity, Recognition and Shared Citizenship in Canada,* Volume III, eds. K. Banting, T.J. Courchene, and F.L. Seidle. Montreal: Institute for Research on Public Policy, pp. 489–554.

Saloojee, A., and M. Siemiatycki. 2003. "Formal and Non-Formal Political Participation by Immigrants and Newcomers: Understanding the Linkages and Posing the Questions," *Canadian Issues,* April: 42–44.

Schellenberg, G., and H. Maheux. 2007. "Immigrants' Perspectives on Their First Four Years in Canada: Highlights from Three Waves of the Longitudinal Survey of Immigrants to Canada," *Canadian Social Trends* [Special Edition]: 2–17.

Stasiulis, D.K., and Y. Abu-Laban. 1991. "The House the Parties Built: (Re)Constructing Ethnic Representation in Canadian Politics," in *Ethno-Cultural Groups and Visible Minorities in Canadian Politics: The Question of Access,* ed. K. Megyery. Toronto: Dundurn, pp. 3–99.

Statistics Canada. 2002. *Ethnic Diversity Survey, User Guide.* Ottawa: Statistics Canada.

——— 2003. *Ethnic Diversity Survey: Portrait of a Multicultural Society.* September. Ottawa: Statistics Canada.

Standing Committee on Citizenship and Immigration. 2005a. *Citizenship Revocation: A Question of Due Process and Respecting Charter Rights.* Ottawa: Queen's Printer.

——— 2005b. *Updating Canada's Citizenship Laws: It's Time.* Ottawa: Queen's Printer.

Tolley, E. 2003. "Supplement, Substitute or Stepping Stone? Understanding the Electoral and Non-Electoral Participation of Immigrants and Minorities." Paper presented at the Sixth National Metropolis Conference, Edmonton, March 21–24.

Tossutti, L. 2003. "The Tripartite Model of Political and Civic Participation and Its Application to Social Capital in Multicultural Canada." Paper presented at the Sixth National Metropolis Conference, Edmonton, March 21–24.

———— 2005. "Electoral Turnout and Canada's Changing Cultural Makeup," *Canadian Issues*, Summer, 53–56.

Tossutti, L., and T.P. Najem. 2002. "Minorities and Elections in Canada's Fourth Party System," *Canadian Ethnic Studies* 34(1): 85–112.

Tran, K., S. Kustec, and T. Chui. 2005. "Becoming Canadian: Intent, Process and Outcome," *Canadian Social Trends*, Spring: 8–13.

White, S., N. Nevitte, A. Blais, J. Everitt, P. Fournier, and E. Gidengil. 2006. "Making Up for Lost Time: Immigrant Voter Turnout in Canada," *Electoral Insight* 8(2), December: 10–16.

Wong, L.L. 2002. "Home Away from Home? Transnationalism and the Canadian Citizenship Regime," in *Communities across Borders: New Immigrants and Transnational Cultures.*, eds. P. Kennedy and V. Roudometof. London and New York: Routledge, pp. 169–81.

Chapter 3

Creating an Inclusive Society: Promoting Social Integration in Canada

JAMES FRIDERES

Introduction

Although Canada has a strong and unique heritage as a nation of immigrants, the integration of newcomers has always presented a challenge for both the newcomers and the host communities. Moreover,
ethnic and immigrant integration of others to Canada—and the
multicultural questions surrounding it—have become major issues on
the political agendas of governments since the 1970s. With an estimated
200 million people worldwide (and the number increasing each year)
living outside their country of birth, the global migration phenomenon
shows no signs of abating. Canada has maintained an expansionist migration policy since World War II; and since 1960, it has pursued immigrants from non-traditional (non-European) sources. Moreover,
Canadian immigration policy over the past decade has directed the flow
of immigrants to serve the country's capitalist accumulation process,
in particular, the role of immigrant entrepreneurs in a globalizing
economy (Froschauer and Wong 2006). By 2002, immigrants accounted
for more than half of the total annual population growth, and this growth
is expected to increase to over 70 percent in the future. The treatment
and integration of immigrants is seen to be something that is a quintes-
sential trait of liberal democracy. As a result, the Canadian government
has generated considerable interest in the topic, and this in turn has
involved the media and the academy. However, to continue thriving as
a cohesive nation, immigrants must be woven into the fabric of society.
How well immigrants integrate into society has far-reaching implications for our current and future vitality.

Immigration and Integration in Canada in the Twenty-first Century, eds. J. Biles, M. Burstein, and J. Frideres.
Montreal and Kingston: McGill-Queen's University Press, Queen's Policy Studies Series.
© 2008 The School of Policy Studies, Queen's University at Kingston. All rights reserved.

Immigrant integration is a complex process that is tied to the ongoing debate about the role of immigrants in Canadian society. Until the mid twentieth century, immigrants were considered responsible for their own integration. Today, the Government of Canada has accepted some responsibility. Moreover, the concept of "integration" has a built-in vagueness, and yet its abstractness gives it a positive quality. As Favell (2001) notes, it suggests a comforting view of modern society, heading in a teleological direction with a progressive outcome. The opposite is "anomie," which implies "disintegration" or dysfunction, which in turn leads to societal breakdown. As such, many people argue that each society has to have some integration as a precondition of its being a society. As a result, political leaders and academics have adopted the same discourse and logic that focus on the social integration of diverse populations. At the same time, we can ask the question, Is Canada a reluctant country of integration?

The *State of World Population 2007* reports that by 2030, urban population will make up 60 percent of the world population. While mega-cities will continue to grow, most people will be living in cities of 500,000 or less, and most new urbanites will be poor. In Canada, since the urbanization process began nearly half a century ago, large cities are already places where cultural diversity flourishes (Ray 2003). However, efforts to minimize social polarization and manage diversity in cities must rely on public education and health care policies, usually the responsibility of the federal or provincial authorities. Nevertheless, municipal governments have a responsibility to develop local policies and programs that manage diversity and integrate immigrants. This is particularly true as cities become the centres of the growth of the knowledge-based economy.

As the demographic profile of Canada continues to change, we find that today, nearly one-fifth of the population is foreign born. In cities such as Toronto, the numbers have exceeded 50 percent. It is predicted that by 2017, nearly one-quarter of the Canadian population will be members of visible minority groups; and in some cities, this number may be higher (e.g., Toronto, Vancouver). Moreover, the ever-growing global economy will have profound impacts on all dimensions of Canadian society. Instead of a norm of permanent residency, more of the Canadian population will remain globally mobile, since they will be able to move around the world with ease. As such, social integration should be conceptualized not as constituting a "permanent" condition, but rather as a "circulation" process. If one looks at transnational social spaces, we can re-conceptualize integration as a network of ties and the unfolding of strong and dense circular flows of persons, goods, ideas, and symbols within a system (Faist 2000). Faist identifies three basic forms of transnational social spaces—transnational kinship groups, transnational circuits, and transnational communities. Each of these has an impact on the structure and organizational make-up of Canadian society, in addition to the permanent resident immigrant.

Integration as a Sociological Concept

At the macro level, the term "integration" refers to a society which is closely and intensely linked to its constituent parts, both groups and individuals. Today the term "social cohesion" has emerged to charac-terize an "integrated" society. However, social cohesion can be defined from the perspective of either a group or individual. That is, groups and individuals can display different degrees of integration within a given society (Entzinger and Biezeveld 2003). Additional dimensions of the concept "integration" imply a desirable outcome as immigrants become members of the host society (Li 2003). A desirable outcome is reflected by the two main goals of integration policies: (i) low conflict interaction between native-born Canadians and immigrants, and (ii) respect of immigrants' personal integrity (Ruspini 2005). These out-comes generally reflect a policy that assures safety and security for Canadians as well as ensuring that mutual respect and understanding are part of the Canadian ethos. In addition, under the guise of integra-tion, immigrants would have full rights as citizens of Canada after meeting the conditions for citizenship.[1] This suggests that integration refers to mutual interactions between treatment (perceived and/or real) and adaptation. It also suggests a two-way process of accommodation between immigrants and native-born Canadians (Dorais 2002).

Furthermore, integration is a process best conceived as multidimen-sional—social, cultural, political, identity, and economic. This means that one has to be careful when looking at the integration of immigrants, as they may be integrated in some dimensions but excluded in others (Phalet and Swyngedouw 2003).[2] This chapter focuses on only the social dimension of integration, although it notes the linkage with other di-mensions. The social dimension of integration focuses on the social con-tacts and group memberships of the individuals. However, even these contacts raise the question of whether these contacts/memberships are primarily within an ethnic group, a non-ethnic group, or a combina-tion of the two (Heckmann 1970).

Over the past two decades, the public discourse on integration of immigrants has been vastly more sensitive to and supportive of

differences. Today's discourse on issues such as autonomy of Aboriginal peoples, movements to preserve regional languages, Afro-centrist
or anti-assimilationist movements, and the general shift from an individualist, opportunity-oriented and colour-blind interpretation to a
collectivist, results-oriented and colour-conscious interpretation of civil
rights legislation and to a multiculturalist revision of school curricula—
all these changes reflect the sensitivity of "differences" in the current
understanding of integration. In short, these public debates now suggest that there is a shift from emphasizing universal interests to emphasizing the recognition of particularist identities (Brubaker 2001).

Integration of any form is not necessarily assimilationist in nature;
nor does it imply a global belief in the inevitability of assimilation, since
there is no "normative" thrust to the concept of social integration. Integration is segmented; and while most people agree that linguistic integration is preferable, integration does not suggest that other dimensions
of social life need to be integrated (e.g., religion). In other cases, if the
incomes of immigrants are similar to those of native-born citizens, social integration is considered to have taken place. However, the "segmented" integrationists have noted that resistance to integration by
some minority groups in certain dimensions of life is a good thing (Portes
and Zhou 1993); and thus, equal incomes must always be considered in
their context as a measure of social integration. While Canada eschews
multiculturalism as the centre piece of social legislation, there are genuine concerns about whether or not multiculturalism is the most viable
strategy for achieving social integration (Dib 2006). Nevertheless, Canadian multiculturalism has been recognized throughout the world as
a successful tool for the social integration and inclusion of immigrants.

At a more specific level, social integration is defined as the process
by which newcomers become a part of the social, cultural, and institutional fabric of the host community or society while at the same time
retaining their own cultural identity (Henry and Tator 2005). Integration involves two dimensions: a personal integration and a structural
integration. There are different ways in which immigrant groups integrate into a receiving society. The first is social integration into a social
system as individual actors (e.g., participation in labour market). The
second is the emergence of social structures related to social inequality
and social differentiation (Esser 2004). Favell (2001) argues that any discussion of integration that tries to measure it by evaluating the "degree" of state-institutionalized organization in the country assumes a
degree of coercive, state-powered pressure on immigrants to conform
to this framework. Others have argued that because of the one-way

direction of social integration pressures imposed on immigrants living in Canada, indicators of integration are generally indicators of state-organized assimilation pressures put on immigrant groups to conform to Canadian norms—the very opposite of what multiculturalism is supposed to do (Li 2003; Levitt 2004).

Policy-makers and service providers define integration as adding single elements to an existing structure and joining these to an interconnected "whole." This definition focuses on a process of connecting individual elements with the existing social/institutional structures. For immigration policy, this kind of integration means adding new and different populations to the existing social structures as well as ensuring the quality of connectedness of these new populations to the existing social system.

In the end, researchers have identified three dimensions of integration: social integration (sometimes referred to as institutional or structural integration), cultural integration, and identity integration. Social integration describes the participation of immigrants in the institutions of the host country. Cultural integration describes (i) the processes of value orientation and beliefs of immigrants, (ii) the process of learning the cognitive abilities and knowledge of the host culture, and (iii) the internalization of values, norms, and changes in belief systems. Identity integration (sometimes referred to as cultural integration by other researchers) describes the subjective feelings and definitions of belonging of the person or ethnic group (Heckmann 1997). The process of integration can last for several generations and may differ by dimension over time.

Social integration can give evidence of its existence through the incidence dimension on two levels—frequency and intensity. Frequency refers to the number of ties (contacts) with their surroundings that an individual or group maintains over time. Ostensibly, as an immigrant becomes more socially integrated, his/her contacts with others in the host society increase. The intensity dimension refers to the nature and quality of these contacts. Again, the quality (or meaningfulness) of these contacts is expected to increase over time.[3] However, successful integration is not only determined by the actions of the immigrants. The reception they receive from the host community also plays a critical role in the integrative process. Just as immigrant social integration is constrained by their human and social capital, host communities also are limited in the support they can provide immigrants. Moreover, most communities, with long traditions and values, do not always readily accept and value linguistic, cultural, and ethnic diversity quickly.

Nevertheless, the engagement of all stakeholders in the newcomer and receiving communities is critical to the successful social integration of immigrants.

In summary, we find that the old conceptualizations of social integration have come into question, and new conceptualizations of the process are needed to deal with the increasing complexity of Canadian society. Moreover, social integration has many spheres and phases, and an immigrant who is well integrated into one sphere might not have an equal degree of social integration in another sphere. Similarly, while linguistic integration can take place early in the immigration process, the incorporation of other values and beliefs may require much more time before they are balanced with those of the host community.

Review of the Literature

Three theoretical "integration pathways" have been identified in the literature (Haan 2007). The "Straight-Line Assimilation" pathway maintains that all immigrants become more like the native-born population over time. While the time frame for integration might vary between groups, the process and direction do not (Alba, Logan and Stults 2003). The Straight-Line theory also argues that an institutional Anglo-cultural core in the host society still acts as a kind of centripetal force on immigrants moving them toward assimilation (Esser 2004). Lee and Bean (2004) argue against this perspective, noting that no matter how long the time frame, some groups will never fully integrate in the host society.

This second integration pathway, "segmented assimilation," proposes that when immigrants face barriers (such as structural racism, a bifurcated labour market, or the ready presence of "counter-cultural" models such as street gangs and drug cultures), immigrant youth may engage in deviant behaviours so as to be accepted by these counter-cultures. While immigrant professionals and entrepreneurs have enough human and social capital to deal with the counter-forces, others do not. Portes and Zhou (1993) support such an argument, noting that some groups (e.g., Haitians) have been kept from a gradual and progressive transition into the mainstream through structural impediments, thereby prompting them to participate in "segmented assimilation" or what others might call "segmented social integration." Even if the immigrant group does not have sufficient human capital to deal with the counter-cultures, if they are part of a strong, cohesive community, they can create the necessary social capital to keep youth on the integrative track. Conversely, if the immigrants are poorly educated, lack strong community linkages, and do not have sufficient numbers, they will fall prey to the counter-cultural models and cease to integrate into mainstream society.

The third model, a deliberate non-integration pathway identified by Haan (2007), suggests that the lack of progression toward integration is a result not of external factors, but rather of voluntary efforts on the part of the ethnic group to remain outside the mainstream society. Moreover, rather than resulting in negative outcomes (as suggested by the segmented assimilation model), the results of such efforts by the ethnic collectivity are positive. For example, Cubans in Miami and some South Asian groups (most recently, Chinese groups) in Canada have taken this route (Fong and Ooka 2002; Myles and Hou 2004). In this model, the consequences of ethnic affiliation and community formation on social integration will depend on the neighbourhoods where the group members cluster, the size of the ethnic group, the degree of institutional completeness, and the human and social capital held by the community.

Overall, the literature suggests the following model (see Figure 1) of the interaction between the host society and the immigrant individual/ community, which in turn determines the nature and extent of social integration.[4] In this two-way process, immigrants must commit to becoming responsible, contributing community members and do their part to promote equal treatment and opportunity for all members. In turn, the host society must ensure that policies and programs reflect values of fairness and equal opportunity, protect civil rights and liberties, and create opportunities for immigrants to contribute to Canadian society. The model identifies the major components in the causal process.

Figure 1: Model of Integration

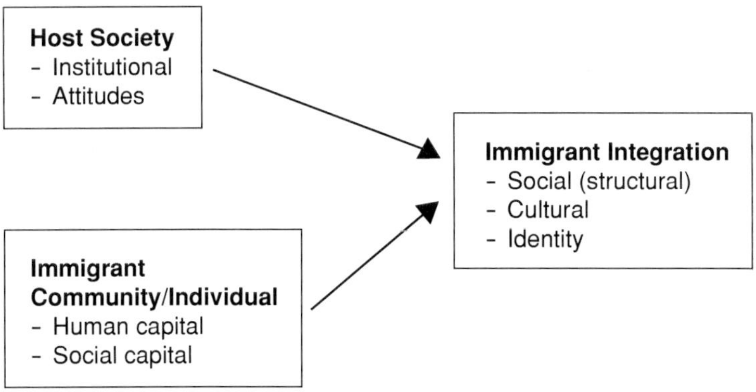

Transnational Communities

More recently, scholars have learned that immigration does not always result in permanent settlement in the host country. Policy-makers and scholars have recognized that migration produces a plethora of connections spanning "home" and "host" societies. While some immigrants do permanently settle in new societies, researchers in the area also have noted that many immigrants return home, engage in repeated migrations, or engage in circular migration. Even for those who engage in permanent migration to Canada, they can communicate with friends / relatives in their home country in any number of ways with speed and immediacy to remain "connected" with the home country (Waldinger 2007). While previous research regarded ties to home and host country as mutually exclusive, today with the gradual shift from Anglo-conformity to the melting pot to multiculturalism, immigrants enjoy a more relaxed political and ideological environment, diminishing the distance between nationals and immigrants (Alba and Nee 2003). It has become an empirical "fact" that even after several generations, cultural differences between some immigrant groups and their offspring are different from those intergenerational differences in the surrounding "host" society. Because transnational engagement varies over the life cycle, the social field for immigrants can vary.

As a result, researchers have become increasingly interested in the ties between immigrant diasporas and their respective sending countries. Transnationalism represents the obverse of the canonical notion of assimilation as a gradual but irreversible process of integration (Portes 2004). Transnationalism offers an alternative image, where there is continuous back-and-forth movement, enabling immigrants to sustain a presence in two societies and to exploit the economic and political opportunities created by such dual lives. The recent events in the Middle East (over ten thousand people resident in Lebanon were revealed to also hold Canadian citizenship) reflect this new image of who is a "Canadian." Moreover, transnational practices increase over time, so we can expect the numbers of "dual citizens" to increase over the next decade.

Scholars are now recognizing that some immigrants in Canada and their descendants remain influenced by their home country or by social networks that link them across national borders (Levitt 2004). As such, the lives of immigrants can no longer be fully understood by only looking at what goes on within the national boundaries. Levitt argues that our analytical lens must broaden and deepen because immigrants are often embedded in multi-layered, multi-contextual transnational social fields, including those who move to Canada as well as those who stay behind. Some nations have addressed this issue and have established protocols by which citizens of their country who have left may still participate in the political affairs of their home country. For example, Italian citizens living outside Italy have the right to choose twelve members of the Chamber of Deputies and six members of the Senate. This worldwide program is much like the extension of suffrage for citizens that other nations have implemented (e.g., Brazil, Mexico, and Poland). In the case of Morocco, citizens cannot "give up" citizenship, no matter where they live or what additional citizenship they take on. Thus, one can conceptualize the integration process of immigrants in the host society and a transnational connection to a homeland occurring at the same time that may reinforce each other.

Levitt (2004) also argues that prior research on immigration and integration equated society with the boundaries of a particular nation-state. As such, researchers took identity in the nation-state as the norm and considered transnational social identity and practices unusual. Levitt posits that while nation-states are important, social life is not confined by nation-state boundaries, particularly for immigrants. Thus, she prefers to research "social fields"—multiple interlocking networks of social relationships through which ideas, practices, and resources are exchanged, organized, and transformed. Moreover, these fields are multidimensional, encompassing structured interactions of differing forms by the nature of the organization of the society and the structure of its institutions. Evidently, social fields are not necessarily contingent with the boundaries of nation-states or any other traditional boundary. In short, individuals can and do live in transnational social fields. For example, citizens and policy-makers might mistakenly assume that the country is divided into two kinds of families—those composed of native-born (with their attendant rights and benefits) and those which are comprised of immigrants. However, Canadian families are far more complex than such simplistic conceptualizations: nearly 15 percent of Canadian families are "mixed" in the sense that one parent is an immigrant while the other is native-born. Adding to this complexity, siblings in the family may also be a mixture of immigrant and native-born.

When we review the best current data collection methods with regard to integration, we find there is a wide range of methodologies, perspectives, and findings. Major research projects have been supported in Europe (e.g., Haut Conseil à l'Intégration, Institut national d'études démographiques, Ethnic Minorities in Britain survey, and Eurobarometer), Africa (e.g., Afrobarometer) and the United States to assess the degree of immigrant integration. In Canada, the Metropolis Project has received modest support from the federal government (a variety of departments) to assess the nature and level of integration of immigrants. Much of the early research supported by Metropolis focused on economic and educational integration.[5]

As Citizenship and Immigration Canada notes, the goal of integration is to encourage immigrants to be fully engaged in the economic, social, political, and cultural life of Canada (Dorais 2002). Using occupational attainment and income of immigrants and a variety of data sources, several studies have analyzed differential labour market participation, access to higher occupations, and income (CIC 2001; Francis 2002; Li 2000; Sweetman 2001; Wang and Lo 2000). These measures of integration have assessed how immigrants differ from native-born Canadians in various dimensions (e.g., difference in annual income or difference in unemployment rates). This research concluded that if an immigrant has similar income, similar labour force participation, and speaks one of the official languages of Canada, then she/he is successfully integrated. Other foci of research carried out by Metropolis researchers have focused on cultural and/or identity integration and on topics such as linguistic retention, family structure, rates of endogamy, religious affiliation and residential segregation, and similarity of values/beliefs (de Vries 1999; Li 2001).

Joppke and Morawska (2003) have summarized the state of the art on integration research by concluding that integration assumes a society is composed of somatic individuals and groups integrated normatively by a consensus of the community and organizationally by the state institutions. They argue that a more realistic characterization of modern society is one comprised of multiple autonomous and interdependent fields. Each of these fields (similar to Levitt's 2004 conceptualization) engages the actors only partially but never completely. As such, immigrants are conceptually integrated with other individuals and groups with similar positions/values on some critical indicator(s). There is no one who is not linked to some group on any single indicator. Since individuals are linked to multiple groups by multiple values, Joppke and Morawska conclude that the "integration" of any person, including an immigrant, is fragmented in some fashion even though they contribute to the overall cohesion of society.

Integration as Policy

Freeman (2004) argues that efforts to integrate immigrants by host societies have varied considerably over the years. His analysis shows a clear trend toward a new form of integration that rejects permanent exclusion but does not require assimilation or multiculturalism on the part of the immigrant or host members. How this integration is implemented varies; Freeman concludes that no country possesses a truly coherent integration regime. Instead, he argues that one finds multifaceted, loosely connected sets of regulatory rules, policies, institutions, and practices in various spheres of society that together make up the frameworks within which immigrants and native-born work out their differences. As a result of this part-planned, part-accidental character of integration, it is difficult to characterize national models of integration strategies. Nevertheless, Entzinger (2000) has identified three spheres of integration policies. The first sphere is the legal-political that establishes citizenship rules. The second, the cultural sphere, identifies whether a society expects immigrants to accept the policy of assimilation or multiculturalism. And third, the socioeconomic domain is identified as the difference in the market rights of immigrants. Within these three spheres, policy-makers develop policy and programs that reflect the priority of the host society.

Post-1960 scholarship in the social sciences has delegitimized assimilation as a policy goal. Many countries of the world, including Canada, have accepted that conclusion and have introduced policies focusing on the multicultural dimension of immigrant integration. Nevertheless, today in some countries where there has been state-sponsored multiculturalism, such as Sweden, Denmark, and England, there seems to be some movement away from multiculturalism and back toward assimilationist policies.

Policy analysts have identified two barriers to successful integration: the inability of immigrants to adapt to the host society, and systematic discrimination in the host society (Wang and Lo 2007). Inability to speak the host language, lack of host country work experience, and lack of credentialization also are major impediments to social integration, although structural factors, such as the size of the ethnic community, level of institutional completeness, density of ethnic networks, and the availability of housing are all important mediating facilitators or barriers. Sex, age, and education also are important intervening variables that impact the level of social integration. The second barrier focuses on the extent of discrimination (perceived or real) actively engaged in by host members or defined by immigrants. While initial research focused on individual discrimination, it has quickly given over to a focus on systemic or structural discrimination (Henry and Tator 2005).

Today, the focus of research has been on immigrants, thereby suggesting that the reciprocal nature of social integration has not been well researched. There seems to be little research on the extent to which Canadian society and its institutions have changed. However, there is, at an anecdotal level, the existence of information that could inform us of the host institutional changes. An example is ethnic foods and restaurants. Clearly over the past two decades, the Canadian "surf and turf" restaurant has been phased out, and more grocery and eating establishments are ethnic in nature or have a substantial ethnic component. For those restaurants that have not been taken over by an ethnic "flavour," their fare generally includes a wide selection of both Canadian and ethnic-type foods. Grocery chains also have acknowledged the purchasing power of ethnic buyers and have increasingly stocked ethnic portions of their goods. The conservative banking system has now understood that to lure investors and clients to its institutions, it has to provide services to more than mainstream clients. As a result, banks have recruited multilingual staff who are now dealing with non-English and non-French clients. Even the medical establishment has given way to alternative medicines that a quarter century ago they referred to as "quack" medicine (e.g., acupuncture). Unfortunately, there has been little systematic research on how the host society and its institutions have changed as a result of the diversity of immigrants residing in the country.

Assessing successful integration means that researchers need to examine the degree to which institutions are open or closed to immigrants and whether communities are welcoming to new immigrants. Waldinger (1997) and Granovetter (2002) have asked the question what barriers Canadian social networks have established in society to deny immigrants the benefit of such networks. They conclude that the answer depends on whether the interrelations in such networks are characterized by "weak ties" (less exclusive and open to sharing with "outsiders") or whether the interrelations have "strong ties" (more exclusive) and thus create barriers for those outside the network so that they gain little benefits. Unfortunately, little research has been undertaken to assess these types of barriers to integration.

In summary, four elements of policy-making need to be taken into consideration with regard to integration. First, there is clearly a "problem" that needs to be dealt with but it is unclear what the problem is and how to define it. Researchers are called upon to give the "problem" a proper definition, which policy-makers may or may not accept. Second, once policy is made, how can the goals outlined be best attained? What programs will be funded? The third element focuses on what strategies are the most effective and/or efficient. The final element is the systematic evaluation of the programs/policy and the reformulation of those policies if necessary.

Measures of Social Integration

As noted above, several attempts have been made to assess the level of social integration of immigrants. Nevertheless, four problems have plagued the measurement process. First, researchers and policy-makers have used secondary data to measure integration. This means the iso-morphic fit between the concept of integration and the operationaliza-tion of the concept is loose at best. Second, control factors have not been introduced to assess the intervening and/or spuriousness of causal relationships between integration and various independent variables. Third, research has not established any "base-line" measures so that researchers and policy-makers can trace the level of social integration over time. Until we have base-line measures of social integration, it is difficult to assess policies and programs or to argue that immigrants are becoming less/more integrated into Canadian society. A fourth problem is that few research projects have had sufficient time and re-sources to expand their scope to a national level and thereby assess national and/or regional variations.

As noted in the introduction, one of the purposes of this volume is to identify key indicators that could be used to measure social integra-tion. The following list of indicators could be used to assess the level of social integration of immigrants in Canadian society. The list focuses on immigrants, native-born Canadians, and their communities. The selection of indicators reflects the use of both primary and secondary data collection, the need for pan-Canadian data, and the assurance that the data will be carefully analyzed. For example, the choice of crime rates must be interpreted in the context of understanding who is tar-geted by police, police bias, racial profiling, and a host of other factors that contaminate the actual crime rates. Our list of indicators is placed within three general categories: structural, community, and individual.

Structural

- Level of residential mobility
- Quality of services immigrants receive (e.g., health care, education)
- Labour market participation
- Occupational distribution
- Employment distribution
- Role of media in portraying immigrants and migration
- Use of social security, welfare and other social policy instruments
- Dependency measures

- Systemic discrimination
- Policies and programs that support fledgling immigrant communities and / or respond to their distinct needs and experiences (e.g., language programs)
- Percent of immigrants in Canadian organizations (e.g., police, educational, elected officials)
- Level of intermarriage
- Crime rates, delinquency rates
- Income levels
- Program evaluation (e.g., host programs)

Community

- Extent of "assimilation resistance" in community
- Civic participation
  - Knowledge about civic processes
  - Engaging in life of ethnic / larger community
  - Host community responsibility for promoting citizenship
  - Host community providing opportunities for immigrants
- Social climate of host community with regard to immigrants
- Quality of housing for immigrants
- Outreach services to immigrant communities (e.g., police)
- Degree of coordination of federal policies and programs
- Extent of partnership programs among various stakeholders

Individual

- Number of associations in which the individual is involved (all types)
  - Intensity of involvement in associations
  - Duration of involvement
  - Citizenship
- Immigrant understanding of Canadian institutional structure
- Host / immigrant community members feeling of security and belonging
- Individual levels of prejudice / discrimination
- Knowledge (formal and informal) of one of the official languages
- Participation in voting at all levels of government
- Public (both immigrant and native-born) attitudes—general and specific
- Number of contacts. This is a measure of immigrants who are well-connected and those who are ill-connected or marginalized

in either (immigrant/mainstream) society. For example, Dagevos (2001) constructed a scale for measuring social integration.

1. *Frequency of visits from "ethnic" neighbours*
2. *Frequency of visits from Euro-Canadian neighbours*
3. *Frequency of visits from "ethnic" friends*
4. *Frequency of visits from Euro-Canadian friends*
5. *Proportion of leisure time contacts with members of your own ethnic group*
6. *Proportion of leisure time contacts with members of the Euro-Canadian group*
7. *Degree of neighbourhood contacts with Canadian people*
8. *Degree of neighbourhood contacts with your own "ethnic" group*
9. *Attitude toward your children associating with Euro-Canadian friends*
10. *Attitude toward your children choosing a Euro-Canadian marriage partner*

- Affective and cost/reward measures of social integration

  I have a great love for Canada.
  I am proud to be a Canadian.
  I find the Canadian flag very moving.
  I would leave Canada to improve my life.
  I think Canada should increase/decrease the number of immigrants.
  I think that the government should spend more time and money on deporting illegal immigrants.
  I think that ethnic groups should be "distinct" or "blend."
  A variety of ethnic groups in Canada help/hurt life in my community.
  I favour/oppose bilingual education.
  I think that English/French should remain the only official languages.

The Future

It is important to remember that all of the various factors impacting upon the level of social integration may be interrelated. For example, low educational attainment may explain the low participation in the labour force and/or low incomes. However, systemic discrimination may be the actual cause of low participation. A third factor may be that immigrants in a particular community wish to remain outside the mainstream society (at least for some time) and thus do not participate in the mainstream labour market.

Moreover, the literature suggests that Canada needs to rethink its institutional structure with regards to promoting social integration. With the exception of implementing the policy of multiculturalism, little investment has been made in the structure and organization of government departments to co-ordinate and ensure policies and programs are adequately funded, implemented, and evaluated. For example, there might be an investigation into the organization of current ministries and sub-ministries in the federal government to determine if other organizational structures would be more effective and/or efficient. A role for the "third sector" (e.g., trade unions, immigrant NGOs, professional associations) and the private sector needs to be investigated (e.g., formally incorporated into the policies and programs leading to social integration). Perhaps a Commission for Integration Policies, a National Co-ordination Body and/or a special advisory council in the Prime Minister's Office might be established. Also, the creation of local immigration councils in each province/census metropolitan area (CMA) could ensure integration of policies and programs at different political levels. While all of these are just ideas to ponder, more research needs to be implemented in order to assess the value of such suggestions.

There is general agreement among scholars and municipal leaders that a majority of activity in the field of assistance and aid given to immigrants is provided by the NGOs. We also find that the federal government has shown little commitment to ensuring the input of the NGOs into social policies and strategies that they have recommended or carried out. At present, the majority of immigrants have not had to seek help from these private social organizations, since Canada has been successful in recruiting the "best and the brightest." However, with world-wide competition for immigrant workers, the continuation of such a strategy is not assured. In the past, many immigrants have often relied on their own resources (human capital) or on small groups formed through local networks or chains of support (e.g., along ethnic/national lines—social capital). Interestingly, the involvement of representative bodies of ethnic minorities has not been sought to identify good practices that assist ethnic minorities to socially integrate. In short, immigrants who benefit from the services offered by NGOs are not the poorest but are individuals who have already achieved a minimum degree of social integration with the host society (Ruspini 2005). Many of those immigrants who have few resources have not been served by any social agency. NGOs also have found it difficult to collaborate with other NGOs or to broaden their scope. With collaboration, immigrants may have a choice of services, since the funding basis of NGOs (from provincial or federal agencies) is based on their demonstrating no overlap with other NGOs and on their providing a "unique" value-added activity. In addition, government phases in and out integration programs without waiting long enough to assess their impact. While the point system ensures that immigrant selection is unbiased, there still remains a large gap between the formal criteria employed in the point system and the realities of the job market. For example, medical doctors from around the world would score high on the point system, but most find that they cannot enter the medical profession in Canada. A similar situation exists for immigrants trying to enter the upper management world of business. Unless contacts within the business community have been made prior to immigration, immigrants find it difficult to enter the managerial level of business in Canada.

In addition, until recently, the services and activities of NGOs have been of a predominantly welfare or humanitarian nature. They have not been aimed at encouraging emancipation and/or fighting against discrimination. The integration policies of Canada need to focus on a more "holistic approach" to social integration—that is, a comprehensive integration policy. These policies need to account not only for the economic and educational aspects of integration but also for issues related to cultural and religious diversity, citizenship, participation, and political rights.

Finally, immigrants and host communities require different support at different stages of the integration process (Geddes 2003). Each level of government is faced with implementing a series of provisions, policies, and social interventions that add up to form an "integration" policy. However, government officials need to see that integration is a process and that new (and different) policies and programs are required for each stage. A basic question that policy-makers tend not to ask is, Who or what is integrating whom and with what and when? For example, many policy-makers assume that immigration means permanent settlement, which, as pointed out previously, may or may not be the case. They also often assume that policy provisions are interventions, taken to be almost exclusively within the jurisdiction of the federal government.[6]

Researchers, government officials, the private sector, and NGOs need to meet to determine a common set of categories for identifying immigrants and integration, and then develop a set of official data. Their first activity would be to gather existing research on the topic of integration. Their second task would be to determine what they want to compare and explain. Traditional concepts such as "democracy" or "civil society" are bound up with normative ideas about nation-building and the progress of national societies: because they are ideologically loaded (Favell 2001), they do not lend themselves to a researchable question. On the other hand, narrower local studies undertaken by researchers can be too literal, reproducing a certain kind of perspective in their analysis (e.g., exploratory, qualitative). The answer lies somewhere between the two models. For example in studying social integration, the important focus should not just be on the quantity of participation that immigrants have, but rather on the quality—the degree to which immigrant groups actually manage to influence political outcomes and impact upon their quality of life.

The third task of research would be to measure the dependent variable (social integration) in different regional contexts. If we are interested in finding out what the "causes" of social integration are all about (the independent variables), we need to vary the explanatory factors. Taking a regional or city-wide approach would allow us to compare the efficacy of various independent variables impacting integration (our dependent variable). In this respect, using cities as the unit of analysis would be preferable. It would allow the researchers to study integration that enables both contextual specificity and structural comparisons that allow for the fact that immigrant integration could be influenced simultaneously by local, national, and global factors (Favell 2001).

A good first start in accomplishing the above would be to analyze existing data sets. For example, the Ethnic Diversity Survey, the General Social Survey (cycle 17 and 19) and the Longitudinal Survey of Immigrants in Canada are rich pan-Canadian data sets that have an enormous list of variables that could be used to assess the integration of immigrants. Other data sets not normally considered relevant might also be tapped (e.g., data from NGO immigrant and settlement service agencies). These data sets would be important sources of information, for information on both immigrants and host society members comprise the data sets, and the sample sizes are large enough to control for a variety of contextual, regional and other variables. However, these data sets would need to be made available to a large number of researchers, instead of the limited access now in place.

The following recommendations would ensure that research is carried out and placed within the context of evidence-based results on which to build policies and programs with regard to social integration of immigrants:

1. The public sector cannot be expected to solve the integration puzzle without relying on and leveraging the resources of the private sector and NGOs. These sectors have amassed extensive experience with immigrant integration and can serve as a crucial resource for identifying how immigrant social integration takes place (Papademetriou 2003).

2. Provide more support to volunteer and community groups through funding to provide frameworks, infrastructure and capacity building (e.g., host programs).

3. Undertake collaborative efforts between NGOs and ethnic/immigrant communities on various programs.

4. Make public service organizations (e.g., health services and education) more accessible to immigrants. A simplification of the bureaucratic process and the creation of mediation facilitators need to be put in place.

5. Educational institutions need to develop a culture of mutual exchange and reciprocal acceptance with immigrant communities, NGOs, and the private sector.

6. Each province/CMA needs to develop its own models of integration to fit the needs of its unique situation while at the same time adhering to a common standard.

7. The outward opening-up of Canadian citizenship should go hand in hand with the inward inclusion of immigrants.

8. Develop pan-Canadian efforts to credit foreign credentials and offer professional training to immigrants—both with low skills and educational levels and also to those who enter with high skills that are underutilized.

9. Expand integration programs to include not only the "settling in" but also the "recently settled."

10. While some integration policies/programs should be targeted to immigrant families and employ dedicated institutions, from an institutional and policy perspective, public service organizations should also be utilized. The public service institutions can help minimize differences in treatment between immigrants and native-born.

11. Create an office or institution whose sole purpose would be to monitor and shape immigrant integration policy. This office would also play a role in ensuring that mainstream policies take into consideration the specific needs of immigrants.

12. Host communities need to begin by assessing the needs of immigrants and then building the capacity of community organizations to respond to identified needs.

13. Host communities and immigrant communities must work together to identify barriers, develop policies, and implement programs that are related to immigrant adaptation.

14. Make policies and programs available to all immigrants to eliminate language barriers to services and provide opportunities to develop English/French proficiency.

Summary

The first objective of a social integration policy is to enable immigrants to get the fairest possible returns on the human capital they bring with them so that they can contribute as early and as fully as possible to community life in Canada (Papademetriou 2003). Moreover, social integration depends not only on the social policies of public education, health, and income, but also on the quality of the countless interactions that occur among the kaleidoscope of individuals, groups, and institutions within a city. In short, neighbourhoods are where social integration happens. Moreover, networks (social capital) are formed locally in neighbourhoods and in local and regional associations. As such, neighbourhoods have associational networks that can create across the country and develop further social capital for members of the community (Jentsch 2007). The emphasis on neighbourhood programming also acknowledges the fact that managing social integration can no longer be the sole concern for the federal government. NGOs, once seen as money-saving alternatives to public provision of services for immigrants, can no longer be viewed and financed with such a vision.

During the past quarter century of immigration, the cultural boundaries of the Canadian "we" have expanded to include all citizens of the state. As such, ethnicity is not "frozen" in time but is flexible and is respected. Immigrants are now freer to choose strategies of the mainstream society and/or the ethnic community through which they can socially integrate. However, the question remains whether or not national identity serves as a source of primary affiliation for immigrants and whether it is necessary for social cohesion. Data on the issue (Waldinger 2007) shows that over time, immigrants become more national in identity. Internal inclusion of immigrants and the acceptance of ethnic differences within the nation-state, such as continued ethnic group or language loyalties, have no long-term detrimental impact on social cohesion. Furthermore, immigrants may maintain those loyalties even as they become permanent residents and may also pass them on to their children (Waldinger 2007). The literature reveals that immigrants continue to get transformed into national life over time. Some immigrants are willing to quickly abandon their homeland culture in search of the good life in Canada; others find that the everyday demands of "fitting in" and the attenuation of home country loyalties and ties makes them increasingly similar to existing Canadians whose community they have joined; others again find the fit takes a much longer period of time. Immigrants find an appeal in the idea of a national community, and they begin to think of their new national community as theirs over time.

At the same time, evidence indicates that Canadians still wish to control the number and type of immigrants coming to their country as well as the activities they undertake. These wishes are revealed in the proactive integration policies of a more or less prescriptive kind (e.g., hate legislation), constitutional rights, and the more laissez-faire approach to integration (MacEiri 2007). Many immigrants believe that as they become part of Canada, they have a stake in what the new (future) Canada will look like, and their input should be considered. Moreover, they argue that as part of the Canadian "socialscape," they—not the dominant society—have the right to determine their own pace of social integration.

The globalization of communications and politics shows how there are complications in how "we" relate to "others." Today, this dilemma is contextualized into the question of "reasonable accommodation." Policy-makers argue that the process of reasonable accommodation prevents the development of a sense of alienation and hastens the process of social integration. Integration is important, because it intersects many important policy areas, such as education, the labour market, housing, and citizenship. With increased interaction between native-born and immigrants, the framework of integration has become crucial to the social cohesion of Canadian society.

Social integration is not an option; it is a vital component of current Canadian society and a building block for its future. Moreover, the state's role is crucial in providing leadership and vision in the process of integration. Nevertheless, Kazemipur (2006) has found that social networks of immigrants are inferior to those of the native-born in many important aspects, and they yield smaller pay-offs. Moreover, he has found that social capital is not a panacea for social ills and may not be useful in immigration settlement and integration. Academics, policy-makers, and the private sector are concerned about the social integration of immigrants into Canadian society. Unfortunately, they have not set aside their differences, allocated funds to engage in pan-Canadian research, nor developed a strategic set of indicators to establish a base-line for measuring social integration. Until this occurs, substantial work will take place in the field, but the results will not be of practical relevance to many of the stakeholders.

Notes

1. Canada has chosen to take a legal position with regard to immigrants known as the *jus soli* system, based on the principle of territoriality. Under this system, all residents have the same rights irrespective of their ancestry or length of residence—after a short transitional period when immigrants first arrive.
2. Nevertheless, there is a tension between the stated goals of our immigration policy and the expectations for immigrants. Adherence to distinct cultural and normative values (relative to Canadian norms and values) by immigrants is not expected, while conformity and compliance to Canadian values and norms is expected.
3. These two dimensions do not always correlate with each other perfectly. For example, if an individual has contacts with his/her work colleagues more than with his/her family, this does not mean that the intensity of those work contacts exceeds those of his/her familial linkages. This raises questions about the larger context into which an individual should be integrated. Is it at the society level or the local community/neighbourhood level?
4. Others have chosen to realign the factors and see the model as more linear. In their model, the immigrants entering the country (the independent variable) and impact on the host society (the intermediate variable) with the resulting social integration (dependent variable).
5. The reader is encouraged to review the working papers published by the five Metropolis centres across the country (Vancouver, Prairie, Toronto, Montreal and Atlantic). See www.canada.metropolis.net/main_e.html.
6. The province of Quebec is one case where the provincial government has taken control over immigration. Some other provinces, such as Alberta and Manitoba, have worked out agreements with the federal government in the recruitment of immigrants.

References

Alba, R., and V. Nee. 2003. *Remaking the American Mainstream: Immigration and Contemporary Immigration.* Cambridge: Harvard University Press.

Alba, R., J. Logan, and B. Stults. 2003. "Residential Inequality and Segregation in an Immigration Era: An Analysis of Major U.S. Metropolitan Regions in 1990," in *Host Societies and the Reception of Immigrants,* ed. J. Reitz. La Jolla, CA: Center for Comparative Immigration Studies, pp. 119–48.

Brubaker, R. 2001. "The Return of Assimilation? Changing Perspectives on Immigration and its Sequels in France, Germany, and the United States," *Ethnic and Racial Studies* 24(4): 531–48.

Citizenship and Immigration. 2001. *Performance Report.* Ottawa: Minister of Public Works and Government Services Canada.

Dagevos, J. 2001. *Perspectief op Integratie. Over de Sociaal-Culturele en Structurele Integatie van Ethnische Minderheden.* The Hague: Netherlands Scientific Council for Government Policy.

De Vries, J. 1999. "Language and Ethnicity: Canadian Aspects," in *Race and Ethnic Relations in Canada,* ed. P. Li. Toronto: Oxford University Press, pp. 231–50.

Dib, K. 2006. "Canada's 150th Anniversary. Multiculturalism and Diversity: Vehicles for Sustainable Socio-Economic Progress," *Canadian Ethnic Studies* 38(3): 143–59.

Dorais, M. 2002. "Immigration and Integration Through a Social Cohesion Perspective," *Horizons* 5(2): 4–14.

Entzinger, H. 2000. "The Dynamics of Integration Policies: A Multidimensional Model," in *Challenging Immigration and Ethnic Relations Politics,* eds. R. Koopmans and P. Statham. Oxford: Oxford University Press, pp. 97–118.

Entzinger, H., and R. Biezeveld. 2003. *Benchmarking in Immigrant Integration,* Rotterdam: European Commission.

Esser, H. 2004. "Does the 'New' Immigration Require a 'New' Theory of Intergenerational Integration?" *International Migration Review* 38(3): 1126–59.

Faist, T. 2000. *The Volume and Dynamics of International Migration and Transnational Social Spaces.* Oxford, UK: Clarendon.

Favell, A. 2001. "Integration Policy and Integration Research in Europe: A Review and Critique," in *Citizenship Today: Global Perspectives and Practices,* eds. T. Aleinikoff and D. Klusmeyer. Washington, DC: Brookings Institute, Carnegie Endowment for International Peace, pp. 349–99.

Fong, E., and E. Ooka. 2002. "The Social Consequences of Participating in the Ethnic Economy," *International Migration Review* 36: 125–46.

Francis, D. 2002. *Immigration: The Economic Case.* Toronto: Key Porter Books Ltd.

Freeman, G. 2004. "Immigrant Incorporation in Western Democracies," *International Migration Review* 38(3): 945–69.

Froschauer, K., and L. Wong. 2006. "Understanding Immigrants' Initiatives in the New Economy: The Case of Western Canada," *Canadian Ethnic Studies* 38(2): 86–103.

Geddes, A. 2003. *The Politics of Migration and Immigration in Europe.* London: Sage Publications.

Granovetter, M. 2002. "Theoretical Agenda for Economic Sociology," in *New Directions in Economic Sociology,* eds. M. Guillen, R. Collins, P. England, and M. Meyer. New York: Russell Sage Foundation.

Haan, M. 2007. "The Homeownership Hierarchies of Canada and the United States: The Housing Patterns of White and Non-White Immigrants of the Past Thirty Years," *International Migration Review* 41(2): 433–65.

Heckmann, F. 1970. "National Modes of Immigrant Integration." Paper presented at the University of Eriangen-Numberg, Germany.

———— 1997. "Patterns of Immigrant Integration in Germany," *Europaisches forum migrationsstudien*. Paper Number 14. Davis, CA: University of California.

Henry, F., and C. Tator. 2005. *The Colour of Democracy: Racism in Canadian Society*. Toronto: Thomson Nelson.

Jentsch, B. 2007. "Migrant Integration in Rural and Urban Areas of New Settlement Countries: Thematic Introduction," *International Journal of Multicultural Society* 9(1): 1–12.

Joppke, C., and E. Morawska. 2003. "Integrating Immigrants in Liberal Nation-States: Policies and Practices," in *Toward Assimilation and Citizenship: Immigrants in Liberal Nation-States*, eds. C. Joppke and E. Morawska. Houndmills, New York: Palgrave, pp. 1–36.

Kazemipur, A. 2006. "The Market Value of Friendship: Social Networks of Immigrants," *Canadian Ethnic Studies* 38(2): 46–71.

Lee, J., and F. Bean. 2004. "America's Changing Colour Lines: Immigration, Race/Ethnicity and Multiracial Identification," *Annual Review of Sociology* 30: 221–42.

Levitt, P. 2004. "Conceptualizing Simultaneity: A Transnational Social Field Perspective on Society," *International Migration Review* 38(3): 1002–39.

Li, P. 2000. "Earning Disparities Between Immigrants and Native-Born Canadians," *Canadian Review of Sociology and Anthropology* 37(3): 289–311.

———— 2001. "The Economics of Minority Language Identity," *Canadian Ethnic Studies* 33(3): 134–54.

———— 2003. "Deconstructing Canada's Discourse of Immigrant Integration," *PCERII Working Paper Series*, Edmonton: PCERII.

MacEiri, P. 2007. "The Challenges of Migrant Integration in Ireland," *International Journal of Multicultural Society* 9(1): 75–90.

Myles, J., and F. Hou. 2004. "Changing Colours: Neighbourhood Attainment and Residential Segregation Among Toronto's Visible Minorities," *Canadian Journal of Sociology* 29(1): 29–58.

Papademetriou, D. 2003. "Policy Considerations for Immigrant Integration," *Migration Information Source*. Washington, DC: Migration Policy Institute.

Phalet, K., and M. Swyngedouw. 2003. "Measuring Immigrant Integration: The Case of Belgium," *Migration Studies* 40(152): 773–803.

Portes, A. 2004. "A Cross-Atlantic Dialogue: The Progress of Research and Theory in the Study of International Migration," *International Migration Review* 38(3): 828–51.

Portes, A., and M. Zhou. 1993. "The New Second Generation: Segmented Assimilation and Its Variants," *Annals of the American Academy of Political and Social Science* 530: 74–96.

Ray, B. 2003. "The Role of Cities in Immigrant Integration," *Migration Information Source*. Washington, DC: Migration Policy Institute.

Ruspini, P. 2005. *Public Policies and Community Services for Immigrant Integration: Italy and European Union*. Milano, Italy: Initiatives and Studies on Multi-Ethnicity.

Sweetman, A. 2001. "Immigrants and Employment Insurance," in *Essays on the Repeat Use of Unemployment Insurance*, eds. S. Schwarts and A. Aydemir. Ottawa: The Social Research and Demonstration Corporation, pp. 123–54.

Waldinger, R. 1997. *Social Capital or Social Closure?: Immigrant Networks in the Labor Market*. Working paper #26, Lewis Center for Regional Policy Studies. Los Angeles: School of Public Policy and Social Research.

———— 2007. "The Bounded Community: Turning Foreigners into Americans in Twenty-First Century L.A.," *Ethnic and Racial Studies* 30(3): 341–74.

Wang, S., and L. Lo. 2000. "Economic Impacts of Immigrants in the Toronto CMA: A Tax-Benefit Analysis," *Journal of International Migration and Integration* 1(3): 273–303.

———— 2007. "What Does It Take to Achieve Full Integration? Economic (Under) Performance of Chinese Immigrants in Canada," in *Interrogating Race and Racism*, ed. V. Agnew. Toronto: University of Toronto Press, pp. 172–205.

Chapter 4

Immigration and Cultural Citizenship: Responsibilities, Rights, and Indicators

MARJORIE STONE, HÉLÈNE DESTREMPES, JOHN FOOTE, AND M. SHARON JEANNOTTE

One of the "most striking developments in recent political discourse," according to Gerard Delanty, is "the increasing confluence of culture and citizenship" (2002, 1).[1] While traditional citizenship theories founded on civil, political, and social rights often omit the sphere of culture entirely (Shafir 1998, 14; Delanty 2002, 1), the contemporary emergence of the "politics of recognition" (Taylor 1992) and of "cultural citizenship" as a dynamic concept underscore the need to analyze culture as a primary rather than secondary sphere of citizenship.[2] Seyla Benhabib (2002) observes: "*Culture* has become a ubiquitous synonym for *identity*, an identity marker and differentiator....[D]iverse groups engaged in the name of this or that aspect of their cultural identity have become contestants in the public sphere of capitalist democracies . . . in characteristic struggles for redistribution and recognition" (1). Many such contestations are associated with immigration, since disagreement affects citizenship rights and responsibilities, whether the debates concern reparation claims of Japanese- and Chinese-Canadians for historical injustice, responses to the Air India tragedy, the Danish cartoon controversy, or the murder of the Dutch filmmaker Theo Van Gogh by Mohammed Bouyeri, a self-described Muslim ideologue.

Understanding the causes and ramifications of the "confluence" Delanty describes is bedevilled by the fact that "culture," as Raymond Williams (1976) observed, is "one of the two or three most complicated words in the English language" (76).[3] The first section of this chapter therefore specifies our operative definitions of "culture" and surveys related concepts of "cultural citizenship," "cultural capital," and "cultural rights" within both English- and French-speaking contexts. We

Immigration and Integration in Canada in the Twenty-first Century, eds. J. Biles, M. Burstein, and J. Frideres.
Montreal and Kingston: McGill-Queen's University Press, Queen's Policy Studies Series.

also wish to emphasize at the start the special problems this volume's emphasis on integration poses from the perspective of culture, given the deep relations of cultural "memories, events, and narratives" to identity (Lowe 1996, 2). While an "integration" model has compelling claims,[4] cultural integration can easily be interpreted as a euphemism for assimilation, or as a term that implicitly denies immigrants agency in the performative enactments that constitute their own citizenship.

The second section of this chapter discusses responsibilities relating to immigration, integration, and citizenship, on the part of both host cultures and immigrants, addressing the need to balance immigrant responsibilities with cultural rights and recognition (or in French, "droits et devoirs"). Here we call for integration of a different kind—institutional integration—in the form of bridging policies and programs to overcome silos within and among levels of government, as well as gaps between government and community organizations, and between immigrant settlement agencies and the arts and culture sector.

The third section discusses the degree to which responsibilities are currently being met in Canada by host societies and immigrants. It draws on emerging work on "cultural indicators" or evidence-based measures for the social effects of culture and their impacts on citizenship and identity (Foote and Smith 2005). This section presents indicators for measuring cultural diversity, cultural participation, and intercultural communication, noting the need for research and policy development in this area that can capture subjective, dispersed, yet far-reaching impacts in the cultural sphere. How, for example, does one measure the impact of a novel such as Joy Kogawa's *Obasan* on public attitudes towards immigrants, their histories, and host society responsibilities in Canada? As Austin Cooke (2002) observes, together with Ken Adachi's community history and "the gently overwhelming advocacy of Art Miki and other members of the National Association of Japanese Canadians," it "turned around an entire country's understanding of itself and its history" (45).

Defining Culture, Cultural Citizenship, Cultural Capital, and Cultural Rights

Culture: A Definitional Jungle

Kroeber and Kluckhohn (1952) identify at least 164 definitions of culture, ranging from Matthew Arnold's "the best which has been said and thought in the world" (Arnold 1961, 6) to UNESCO's "the whole complex of distinctive spiritual, material, intellectual and emotional features that characterize a society or group" (UNESCO 1997, 12). Raymond Williams' (1976) discrimination among three principal senses of the word offers one useful map of this definitional jungle. He states that culture denotes (i) "a general process of intellectual, spiritual and aesthetic development"; (ii) "a particular way of life, whether of a people, a period or a group" (a usage derived from the German Romantic Johann Gottlieb Herder's influential theories on *Kultur* as the shared values, meaning, linguistic signs, and symbols of a people); and (iii) "the works and practices of intellectual and especially artistic activity" (80).

The three senses of "culture" that Williams describes overlap, to a degree, with Dick Stanley's (2005) "three faces of culture": "Culture H," the repository of past meanings and symbols, traditions; "Culture C," the making of new meanings and symbols through discovery and creative activity in the arts; and "Culture S," the set of symbolic tools from which individuals construct their "ways of living" (22–23). If the "making of a society is the finding of common meanings and directions," as Williams contends (cited in Stanley 2005, 23), then the integration of any member of a society would involve a process that works something like this:

- We use Culture S as a tool kit of meanings to understand our daily lives.
- We obtain this tool kit through education and socialization, which draws on Culture H, our traditions and heritage.
- We introduce new meanings into this mix through the creative arts and industries (Culture C) where they are tested to see whether they will be useful in adapting to new "ways of living". (Stanley 2005, 25)

In terms of immigrant cultural adjustments and contributions to a new country, key questions to ask include, first, how do newcomers make use of Culture H and Culture C to adapt their Culture S to a new environment and a new country? Second, how does the host society use Culture H and Culture C to help immigrants develop new symbolic landscapes (Culture S) that will ease their entry into their new environment? Finally, how might immigrants, through the agency of Culture C, contribute to the Culture H and Culture S of the host society, thereby adding new elements to and altering the tool kit that the host society uses to define itself?[5] Typically migration produces complex forms of "double consciousness," cross-cultural consciousness, and diasporic identity (Siemerling 1996, 2005). The Culture S, H, and even C of Stanley's theory thus exist in doubled forms and in hybridized formations. These complex formations are captured in theories of "polysystems" and in some emergent concepts of cultural citizenship.

Going beyond the conceptions advanced by Herder ("Volksgeist"),[6] Franz Boas, Ruth Benedict ("cultural configurations") and Lévi-Strauss ("symbolic systems"), all of which state that each culture obeys its own logic, Itamar Even Zohar has developed a concept of culture as a fabric of relationships, a complex of open, heterogeneous systems, each governed by its own independent set of laws and therefore capable of combining in multiform constellations (Robert 2002, 457). More specifically, Zohar's theory uses a semiotic approach which defines culture as an "inventory of possibilities" regulating daily life. It does so, says Ruth Amossy (2002) in her study of culture and polysystems, by constructing models for interpreting reality or producing sets of instructions that guide behaviours. The cultural inventory therefore provides a cohesiveness that grounds social group identity and enables groups to emerge and survive as collective entities. This inventory or these elements may be generated either by individuals or by social groups, either spontaneously or deliberately (Amossy 2002, 130).

Terry Eagleton (2000) and Pierre Bourdieu (1986) have developed a conception of cultural practices based on rivalries between classes or social groups, which give rise to conflicts over control of symbolic capital and cultural space. In their theory, the creation and transmission of knowledge as representations of Self and the Other remain the purview of dominant classes, leaving scant room for genuine dialogue between social or cultural groups; intercultural mediation is not readily compatible with overweening cultural hegemony.

The power relations Eagleton and Bourdieu describe are crucial to immigrants' relationships with their host societies, as well as to the formation of new concepts of cultural citizenship. As Diana Brydon (2005) comments, "citizenship cannot be disaggregated from the institutions that exercise regulative power, most especially the state" (2).

Cultural Citizenship: Locations, Definitions, Divergences

One obvious manifestation of the confluence of "culture" with "citizenship" is the emergence of the term "cultural citizenship" as a strategic, though variable, concept within a wide range of discursive sites. In his chapter on "Cultural Citizenship" in *A Handbook of Citizenship Studies*, Toby Miller (2002) identifies immigration as "the key crisis that has underpinned the clamour for cultural citizenship" (233). He identifies "three key sites for theorizing" immigration: the works of Renato Rosaldo and colleagues in U.S. Latino contexts; Tony Bennett and colleagues in Australian contexts; and Will Kymlicka and "fellow liberal political theorists" in the Canadian context (Miller 2002, 232–33). Miller's formulation itself reflects the marginalization of key aspects of culture that we have described—in particular, Culture C—as well as the pressure from disenfranchised cultural minorities aside from U.S. Latinos. Significantly, one early use of the term appears in a 1997 UNESCO report based on a 1997 global forum on indigenous peoples, which records a shift from "a policy of assimilation to a concept of *cultural citizenship*" (UNESCO 1997, 6).

In the studies and documents produced by UNESCO since that first report, the concept of cultural citizenship has normally been used in the context of adult education, specifically with respect to promoting Aboriginal culture. Cultural citizenship appears to be entertained only as a bulwark against the effects of marginalization and an argument for full recognition of individuals as citizens, a prerequisite for full cultural recognition and the creation of a social and political space for the expression of Aboriginal heritage in a global context.

In Canadian and Australian policy circles, cultural citizenship has been mobilized as a strategic concept, evident in *Towards Cultural Citizenship* (Mercer 2002) and *Accounting for Culture: Thinking Through Cultural Citizenship* (Andrew, Gattinger, Jeannotte, and Straw 2005). "Cultural citizenship" is also integral to the "Cultural Indicators" initiative of Canadian Heritage, and to research on "creative cities" by Nancy Duxbury (2005) and many others. In addition, at least three recent conferences, in Europe, the United States, and Canada, have focused on cultural citizenship.[7] The authors of a January 2006 Call For Papers for an issue on "Citizenship" in *Essays in Canadian Writing* rightly observe that "Recently, the term *citizenship* has migrated from its traditional home in political and legal discourses, and emerged as a highly conspicuous and powerful concept-metaphor in global debates on cultural belonging. We suggest that citizenship is supplementing or even replacing nationality or the nation as the dominant critical keyword in Canada's latest era of social change and security concerns" (Chariandry and McCall 2006, par. 1).

Since cultural citizenship encapsulates the complex roles that Culture S, II, and C play in the politics of identity, it is not surprising that definitions of the concept vary according to the location they emerge from. Like anthropologists, literary critics, or activists who write to validate the cultural claims of minorities such as U.S. Latinos, UNESCO documents addressing indigenous rights emphasize the transnational dimensions of cultural citizenship (Rosaldo 1997; Mirón, Inda and Aguirre 1998). In such contexts, the term is closely associated with new forms of citizenship produced by globalization, migration, and the Internet, variously articulated as "cosmopolitan citizenship" (Delanty 2000, 2002), "flexible citizenship" (Ong 1999), "nomadic citizenship" (Joseph 1999), "diasporic citizenship" (Cho 2005), and "global citizenship" (Bhabha in Mohanty 2005). In contrast, policy-makers within nation-states tend to stress the pivotal role of cultural citizenship in social integration—not across national borders, but within them. For example, John Foote and Marilyn Smith (2005) of the Department of Canadian Heritage define cultural citizenship as "an emerging concept that examines the formative role of culture in constructing and understanding citizenship practices such as identity formation and the altruistic behaviours that contribute to a collective's ability to 'live together'" (Executive Summary, par. 1).[8] These differences underscore the need for a cross-cultural, comparativist approach to cultural citizenship and its policy implications.

For example, in French and European contexts, different patterns of usage emerge that speak both to the politics of language and of location. While the concept of cultural citizenship enjoys wide currency in Canada, the term is only beginning to surface in European and French-language studies that are not attached to research projects connected directly or indirectly to the Canadian government or the North American Anglophone tradition. European reports, scientific papers, and even policy papers speak instead of "cultural policy," "civic or political citizenship" and "cultural diversity."[9] So it is not in policy papers or in documents published by the European Union or its various commissions that the term is found, but rather in petitions and letters from artistic associations that have taken a stand in favour of a new cultural policy or a new "cultural citizenship" allowing for more sensitive treatment of cultural values, goods, and services in international trade talks. This use of the term clearly betokens a fear of uniformization and/or an apprehension that cultural components of the political fabric will be neglected.

As another example, in Brazil, itself a hub of migration and cultural diversity, the use of the term cultural citizenship implies resistance to neo-liberal policies that heed only the laws of the market. From Brazilian perspectives, the point is not only to recognize the diversity of the cultural fabric and its rich symbolic capital, but also to provide funding for grassroots cultural practices through approaches that do not treat them as folklore. The concerted effort by some left-wing Brazilian economists and municipal and community organizations to make culture a factor of collective identity and push forward the development of a new political culture founded on integration and mutual recognition of Self and the Other is also worthy of note.

Social Capital and Cultural Capital: Refining the Policy Discourse

While many discussions of immigrants have explored the role of social capital in successful integration, they have not addressed how "social capital" relates to "cultural capital" or to the three "faces" of culture described by Stanley. Among various approaches, Robert Putnam's definition of social capital as "social networks and the norms of reciprocity and trustworthiness that arise from them" (Putnam 2000, 19) fits well within the context of this chapter. While not universally accepted, his conceptual approach is useful because it divides social capital into two types: *bonding social capital*, which refers to social networks that reinforce exclusive identities and homogeneous groups; and *bridging social capital*, which refers to horizontal networks that are outward looking and encompass people across diverse social cleavages.

Although there is much less consensus around definitions of cultural capital, the most widely-quoted derives from Pierre Bourdieu (1986), who characterizes it as the "disposal of taste," meaning types of cultural consumption that mark people as members of a specific class. Essentially, Bourdieu defines cultural capital as something that reinforces personal prestige and credentials. It consists of three elements: *habitus or embodied capital*—the system of lasting dispositions that form an individual's character and guide his or her actions and tastes; *objectified capital*—the means of cultural expression, such as painting, writing or dance, that are symbolically transmissible to others; and *institutionalized capital*—the academic qualifications that establish the social and economic value of the person (243).

Only recently have scholars begun to examine the possible collective (as opposed to personal) impacts of investments in cultural capital. In environmental studies, researchers have found that social capital in itself does not ensure a positive approach to sustainability and that cultural capital appears to determine the *quality* of social capital. In other words, how people view the world around them—their philosophy and ethics, their traditional knowledge and their symbolic relationship with each other and their environment—are critical factors in the sustainability of their communities (Berkes 1998, 27). Acquisition of such sensibilities is clearly a function of *habitus* in the Bourdieuian sense; but the *habitus* of individuals is beneficial not only to themselves but also to the environment around them. In the field of development, Helen

Gould (2001), similarly observes "when a community comes together to share cultural life, through celebration, rites and intercultural dialogue, it is enhancing its relationships, partnerships and networks—in other words, developing social capital" (71).

Karim (2005) points out that "[t]he citizen role involves a range of tacit knowledge, competence and taken-for-granted assumptions" and that this "has implications for a variety of state policies, including economic policy, since those citizens who do not have certain forms of *cultural* competencies are denied access to society's resources" (147). Jeannotte's (2005) review of the research literature to map both the personal and collective benefits being attributed to cultural capital identified four overall themes:

> Theme 1—Personal empowerment
> Theme 2—Cultural participation
> Theme 3—Cultural development and quality of life
> Theme 4—Cultural sustainability (127)

If full cultural citizenship is to be a goal of immigrant integration, policy-makers will need to develop answers to several key questions linked to these four themes. For Theme 1, they need to understand the role that cultural capital plays in helping individual immigrants get their credentials recognized, get better jobs, and strengthen their personal and professional networks. For Theme 2, they need to know whether immigrant cultural participation contributes to intercultural partnerships and understanding. Does it help build community connections (or "bridging" social capital) or is it primarily a mechanism to reinforce solidarity (or "bonding" social capital) within ethnic enclaves? For Theme 3, despite the growing literature on "creative cities" and the "creative class" (for example, the work of Florida and Gates (2001), linking vibrant city economies to the presence of diversity), research seldom examines whether cultural interventions attract investment or improve the quality of life in immigrant neighbourhoods. Perhaps the most challenging area of research relates to Theme 4, cultural sustainability. Does cultural capital promote identity, well-being, and social cohesion within immigrant communities? The answers to these questions require an understanding of the degree to which cultural capital in immigrant communities links to both social and economic capital. The final section of this chapter will return to the problem of developing more accurate indicators to measure the host society's success in linking immigrant cultural capital to full cultural citizenship.

Cultural Rights

A third concept integral to the confluence of culture and citizenship is "cultural rights," an underdeveloped area of both academic and policy study in Canada and elsewhere (Baeker et al. 2001), even though language rights have been central to Canada's official bilingualism policy, and the emergent discourse of "cultural rights" has been most compellingly deployed in relation to indigenous peoples. Robert Albro and Joann Bauer (2005) point out in a special issue of *Human Rights Dialogue* on "Cultural Rights" (Spring 2005) that "scholars and practitioners have paid surprisingly little attention to cultural rights, despite the fact that they have been enshrined in international law since 1966 when the United Nations adopted the International Covenant on Civil and Political Rights (Article 27) and the International Covenant on Economic, Social and Cultural Rights (Article 15)" (3). Cultural rights provide an important means for measuring participation in cultural life (Laaksonen 2005). In relation to immigrants and ethnic minorities, citizenship debates have focused most often on minority rights and multiculturalism, as in Kymlicka's argument for "group-differentiated rights or 'special status' for minority cultures" (1995, 5). Kymlicka's theory has been criticized, however, for faltering "on his definition of culture": that is, for relying on "essentialist" assumptions of ethnic groups as homogenous, when "culture is clearly fluid and ever changing" (Faulks 2000, 96–98).[10] Such homogenous notions of culture do not accommodate the complex overlapping identities and discourses of rights produced by new forms of diasporic and cosmopolitan cultural citizenship now emerging. Additional policy issues include investigating the extent to which cultural rights include provision of resources for maximizing cultural capital. They also include the need to assess the tension between cultural rights that maximize transnational identities and those that preserve national identities, a point we flesh out below in relation to the meanings of "cultural diversity."

Rights and Responsibilities: Governments, Host Societies, and Immigrants

Citizenship, Rights, and Responsibilities

As discussed above, citizenship means formal recognition of a person's status as a citizen and constitutes, in itself, a privilege granted to individuals by the state. Theoretically, citizenship guarantees the individual enjoyment of full political rights. In Canada, many of these rights are defined in the *Canadian Charter of Rights and Freedoms*, which is part of the Canadian Constitution. According to federal government documents, the constitution "legally protects the basic rights and freedoms of everyone in Canada" (CIC 2006, par. 1), such as, for example, the right to a fair trial and freedom of religion and peaceful assembly. The Charter also enshrines the equality of English and French in Canadian federal institutions, and this is reinforced by the *Official Languages Act.*

Clearly, the citizenship rights a state grants its citizens also constitute obligations of the state to its population, which is now entitled to demand those rights. Therefore, each right gives rise to a series of government duties and responsibilities: to safeguard the right and also to implement it. This correspondence or fit between rights and responsibilities could serve to ground any study of the responsibilities toward immigrants and minorities in Canada. With regard to culture and language, for example, it needs to be said that to promote better integration of immigrants and minorities into Canada's demographic fabric, the state must first fulfil its obligations under the *Charter of Rights and Freedoms* and the laws respecting immigrants.

Successful immigration policies require not only a dynamic interchange of rights and responsibilities but also nuanced definitions of "cultural citizenship," "cultural capital," and "cultural rights" rooted in the particularities of locations and in citizen participation. "Questions about the content of citizenship and the balance between rights and duties are always contingent upon the decisions of community," which cannot be codified in a static contract because these change over time. "Political participation is therefore central to uniting rights and responsibilities" (Faulks 2000, 81), much as responsive, well-functioning government institutions are.

Government Responsibilities

Most citizens would agree that governments have the responsibility to set in place the infrastructure for immigrant cultural citizenship. Equally important, however, are the mechanisms to ensure that this infrastructure works. Federally, both the *Charter of Rights and Freedoms* (1982) and the *Multiculturalism Act* (1988) have been instrumental in converting earlier "soft" rights compliance regimes into measures with some constitutional and legislative "clout" behind them. The *Multiculturalism Act* is, indeed, explicit about working to achieve the equality of all Canadians in the economic, social, political, and cultural life of the nation.

While contemporary cultural policies generally include an obligation to support cultural diversity, the term is used in two different ways in policy discourse: first, as plurality of cultural expression within Canada; and, second, as maintaining a national cultural "voice" within a global environment. At times, there is a tension between the two dimensions of diversity, as the "national voice" has become less "univocal" in the years since many cultural policies were established. *Multicultural* policy-makers in Canada tend to focus on the former definition of "cultural diversity" and link it to the notion of cultural citizenship that is concerned with integration *within* national borders; whereas arts and culture policy-makers—when they consider immigrants at all—tend to see them as part of a globalized threat to indigenous cultural citizenship—that is, as avid consumers of foreign content via the Internet and satellite television. In both cases, there appears to be a tendency to view cultural citizenship as an "either/or" proposition, instead of one that is now increasingly porous, negotiated, and subject to global cultural flows.[11]

Government thus needs to address these newer and more fluid forms of cultural citizenship and identity. At the federal level, responsibilities might be better met by working more effectively across the silos arising out of the historical genesis of the Department of Canadian Heritage (see Baeker et al. 2001), in order to ensure that cultural and citizenship policies are complementary and consistent, as well as to maximize the benefits of innovative initiatives across divisions.

While it has "unquestionably been the federal government that has set the tone and direction of Canadian cultural policy" (Baeker et al. 2001, 9), many key dimensions of immigrant cultural citizenship fall under provincial jurisdictions—through, for example, provincial responsibility for education, provincial arts councils, subsidies for cultural industries, and cultural diversity initiatives. Cities and municipalities also play a critical role in host society responsibilities, because it is at the regional and municipal level that immigrant and cultural diversity and integration services are delivered, through immigrant settlement agencies, multicultural associations, public libraries, museums, and other municipal agencies, as well as NGOs operating on a patchwork of federal, provincial, and municipal funding.

At the provincial level, immigration policy is often most closely linked to labour and economic policies. However, to foster full cultural citizenship for newcomers, all three levels of government need to take responsibility for maximizing the *institutional integration* of cultural policies and programs that relate to immigrants and cultural minorities across jurisdictional boundaries. Since the arts and culture sector has already developed structures and organizations for bridging some of these boundaries between levels of government, possibilities for building upon these in relation to immigrant cultural services should be investigated. A responsive federal government would also provide for the increased burden being met by provinces and municipalities in creating the infrastructure for second language, education, and credentialing programs, cultural capital networks, and exercise of cultural rights by newcomers. The provision of immigrant services and information in both of Canada's official languages is a primary area in which greater integration among levels of government is called for.

More than 20 years after the introduction of Canada's first language policies, restoring to Canada's francophone minorities the social and political status they are officially guaranteed under the *Charter of Rights and Freedoms* and the *Official Languages Act of Canada* is essential. English is not the lingua franca of all immigrants arriving in the country, and many settling outside Quebec need to be received in French. Outside of Quebec, services for refugees are almost all (if not all) in English; there is no one to counsel refugees in French, to help them integrate into the local French-speaking community, find French schools, and most importantly, give them a sense that it is worth becoming part of French Canada.

A fair and responsible approach to immigration should also guarantee equal rights and services in both languages to newcomers and members of ethnic communities who wish to avail themselves of such services. This policy would not only promote the integration of francophone immigrants but would also send French-speaking Canadians a clear political message that they are an asset to the country and full-fledged citizens who should not have to fight every day for recognition of the rights guaranteed under Canada's laws and Constitution.

Host Society Responsibilities

Multiple host society responsibilities are shared by the three levels of government, the private sector and communities. They include informing newcomers on their arrival of their rights as guaranteed by the Charter, including the right to freedom of expression and peaceful protest, and educating them in the Canadian values described above. Education in Charter rights is particularly vital for newcomers from countries without traditions of civil rights and free speech—or where there are gaps between official rhetoric and state practices—as is often the case, for example, for the persecuted writers (principally journalists) whom PEN Canada (www.pencanada.ca) is assisting to integrate into communities across Canada.[12]

Governments and host societies need to attend as well to the ways in which barriers for newcomers have differential impacts, based on race and country of origin, gender, class, age, and disability. For example, numerous studies have shown how the problems experienced by immigrant women can be compounded by systemic prejudices arising out of these factors operating in conjunction (see Dossa 2004; Tastsoglou and Dobrowolsky 2006).

Equally important is fostering awareness that *both* host societies and immigrant groups have distinctive cultures (in the sense of Stanley's Culture S), a point often overlooked. (Analogously, in the North American discourse on race, whiteness is assumed to be a neutral ground that is unmarked as a racial category, and "race" is instead associated with marked "visible minorities.") The negotiation of complex sets and subsets of rights and responsibilities becomes more complicated when the host society itself takes the form of a minority that may not be "visible," as in the case of Acadian communities in Atlantic Canada.

Canadian immigration policy needs to progress beyond "cultural competency" models aimed at integrating newcomers into the host society's values and practices to models of *intercultural competence*. Researchers in second language acquisition now increasingly employ such models (van Esch and St. John 2004). These models also underlie the innovative Clinician Assessment for Practice Program (CAPP; www.capprogram.ca) of the College of Physicians and Surgeons of Nova Scotia, which teams up international medical graduates (IMGs) with Canadian practicing physicians to promote the transfer of skills and medical culture. Designers of the CAPP program define intercultural competence as including "(1) knowledge of the effects of culture on the beliefs and behaviours of others; (2) awareness of one's own cultural attributes and biases and their impact on others" (Saunders and Fotheringham 2006, Slide 5).

Professionals in the host society with this type of intercultural competence are more likely to recognize how they benefit from their own forms of cultural capital, and thus are more likely to recognize how systemic cultural bias may enter into the credentialing assessments of newcomers. To address the cultural dimensions of credentialing, host societies have to integrate Culture S, H and C into settlement and newcomer services, working both through federal programs and immigrant service delivery by provincial and municipal governments and NGOs. While settlement agencies and organizations often work closely with private sector businesses and economic organizations on such issues,

as well as with multicultural associations, there are far fewer partnerships between these agencies and the arts and culture sector, even
though this sector makes up approximately 5 percent of the labour force
in Canada and is an important source of economic growth (Baeker et al.
2001, 19–20).

"Creative cities" research by Florida and Gates (2001) and others has
shown how important the arts can be to cities that attract clusters of
innovation. Government and private sector initiatives can also use arts
and culture to attract immigrants to rural regions facing depopulation
and to build sustainable communities. For instance, the arts are central
to an initiative to attract immigrants to the small francophone town of
Saint Leonard in New Brunswick. In the first two years of the model's
development, Saint Leonard's Carrefour d'immigration rurale set up a
collection of books on cultural diversity. It was made available to the
public at the municipal library, making it a focal point for raising awareness of the Other in the region. The acquisition was accompanied by
reading activities for children; and plays and discussion groups were
incorporated into the elementary and high school curricula. These efforts targeted primarily at a school-age audience also helped spur discussion in families, a factor which should not be neglected in a rural
environment. The initiatives are part of a more comprehensive strategy
for the economic and social integration of francophone immigrants in
the region.

The success of such ventures depends upon host society creation of
forums, both for newcomers' expressions of their culture, and for the
sharing of Culture S, H, and C between newcomers and the communities they are entering. Libraries, other cultural institutions (such as
museums and art galleries), and cultural events such as film, literature,
or music festivals provide vital means for this intercultural sharing that
goes beyond the folkloric displays of different ethnic cultures at many
annual multicultural festivals. As critics of certain forms of state-
sponsored multiculturalism point out, often the "essentialized search
for the authentic ethnic" in such official contexts breeds nostalgia, cul-
tivates purist doctrines of the motherland, and marks difference through
"religion, food, dress," rather than building "cross-ethnic alliances" and
coalitions (Sucheta Mazumdar, cited in Mishra 2005, 201).

Nevertheless, multicultural associations or councils that bridge cultural gaps between host society members and newcomers, as well as
among different immigrant groups and ethnic minorities undeniably
perform a critical role in integration. Such multicultural councils can
provide important venues for intercultural transfer among ethnic
groups, the sharing of cultural capital, the identification of civic

responsibilities, and the fashioning of new models of "multi-layered" forms of citizenship that connect the "local to the global" (Faulks 2000, 149).[13] Among the domains that could strongly benefit from an integrated approach, media, education, and cultural production play an especially critical role.

It is in fact vitally important to foster a sense of belonging and develop civic consciousness—which follows from collective consciousness—among minorities and newcomers if they are to feel that media, social, and government discourses truly speak to them.[14] It is equally important that minorities and recently arrived immigrants receive fair and in-depth coverage in print and electronic media so that they may obtain the most objective possible information and glean critical insights into the dominant values of Canadian society. Journalists must be better trained, the public better informed, and newcomers and minorities better integrated into the media. The same applies to the primary and secondary education systems.

Educational institutions are powerful instruments of integration that address both the host communities and newcomers or ethnic minorities, creating oppo ʾinities for intercultural communication and exchange. Schools ʾ ɪ the media should, among other things, promote the integratior discourses and cultural/artistic materials produced by newcom ʾ and members of ethnic minorities into the Canadian majority's ʾtural, educational, and media systems.

Cultu ʾ production can also be a powerful source both of discriminator ʾnstructions negatively impacting newcomers and of artistic exp ʾ ɜions that counteract these forms of oppression. Writers from d ʾ ɹent cultural backgrounds in the "new" canon of Canadian literaʾe—Wayson Choy, Hiromi Goto, Dionne Brand, Rohinton Mistry, and ʾlichael Ondaatje, among many others—indicate the transformative effect that literature can have on Canadian attitudes towards immigrants and their contribution to the fabric of national identity (see Cooke 2002; Kamboureli 1996, 2000; Siemerling 1996, 2002; Verduyn 1998).

Immigrant Responsibilities

While this chapter has thus far emphasized the responsibilities of the host society, the immigrants themselves have complementary responsibilities. If the Charter is the foundation of Canadian law, immigrants should be willing to respect the rights it articulates, such as the right to life, liberty, and security of the person, and the right to equal protection and equal benefit of the law without discrimination. The word "values" is often loaded with all kinds of cultural "freight"; but in the context of cultural citizenship, the Charter articulates a basic set of Canadian values—for example, freedom of conscience, expression and association—that immigrants should be expected to recognize and adhere to.

Certainly, the right to vote is matched by a responsibility to vote; but immigrants need to understand that this responsibility goes beyond such a basic civic duty. Just as governments are responsible for promoting diverse cultural expression and fostering participation, newcomers should feel a reciprocal responsibility to participate in Canadian cultural and civic life. One of the new forms of "flexible" citizenship that global migrations have produced, especially among economic elites, is a citizenship practice that seeks as many rights as possible and as few responsibilities as possible, mirroring the corporate trends of globalization (Ong 1999, 112–13). Clearly, this approach to citizenship imperils the creation of cohesive cultures and societies.[15]

Breton, Hartmann, Lennards and Reed (2004) have articulated how the interplay of rights and obligations contributes to the social covenant through four types of expectations that citizens, both native and foreign-born, have of their society: (i) fairness, (ii) recognition of their contribution to the society, (iii) trust that others will not take advantage of them, and (iv) a sense of belonging in the community. In return, individuals invest time, energy, and resources in a community if they feel that these expectations are being met. "[C]ontributing represents a commitment to a community since it is social reality that one is helping to maintain," generating a sense of "social ownership" (Breton et al. 2004, 15–16).

Little empirical research has investigated levels of social obligation among various groups within the Canadian population; but findings by Breton et al. from a survey of over 2,000 Canadians carried out in 1997 suggest that "immigrants generally and immigrants from non-European countries, in particular, are much more likely to express a strong sense of indebtedness than Canadian-born respondents: 48 per cent of those from non-European countries, 40 per cent of those from Europe, the United States and the United Kingdom, and only 29 per cent of those born in Canada" (128).

While the findings of Breton et al. on immigrants' sense of social indebtedness are intriguing, less research has examined the ways in which a functioning social covenant depends in turn upon a shared cultural reality, based on the recognition of cultural rights and the shared cultural capital that underlie emerging forms of cultural citizenship. To what extent can cultural policies that promote intercultural communication, inter-generational involvement, and collaborative artistic, social and economic synergies stimulate the exercise of citizenship responsibilities by newcomers? In what measurable ways are immigrants in Canada now able to contribute to and participate in the civic and cultural life of their communities? To what extent are governments and host societies meeting their respective responsibilities regarding the cultural adjustment and expression of immigrants? The cultural citizenship indicators outlined in the final section of this chapter outline a possible approach to developing the knowledge base needed to guide future policy and program development in this area.

Cultural Citizenship Indicators

While multiple quantitative and statistical indicators[16] exist for measuring economic and social immigrant integration, accurate and suitably nuanced methods for evaluating the extent to which governments, host societies, and immigrants are meeting the responsibilities we have outlined above are less well developed in relation to the cultural sphere. The reasons are numerous, arising from the definitional challenges "culture" poses, the complexity of the new forms of diasporic cultural citizenship now emerging, the tendency for existing surveys and data sets (such as the 1992 data contained in the *Ethnic Diversity Survey* 2003) to marginalize or overlook the cultural sphere (especially Culture C or creative expression), and the importance of the qualitative and subjective dimensions of culture that are difficult to capture at the macro level.

The search for cultural citizenship indicators entails developing practicable measures of overlapping concepts that apply both to culture and to citizenship. Linking socio-demographic variables (including, most notably, age, gender, education, ethnocultural ancestry, and language) facilitates the development of cultural citizenship measures. We have identified three basic categories of indicators for tracking the intersections of culture and citizenship—both the effects of citizenship on culture, and of culture on citizenship—in relation to immigrants in Canada: cultural diversity, cultural participation, and intercultural dialogue. This final section suggests how these indicators can be used to measure and verify the implementation of rights and responsibilities associated with immigrant integration in Canada. It also identifies policy issues and gaps in the available data.

While the range of domestic information and data regarding separate diversities in culture and citizenship is expanding, identifying trend lines in the amalgam of cultural citizenship has been difficult, given the lack of adequate overlap in key variables and comparable questions in many citizenship and culture surveys. Critical citizenship data can be found in public sources, such as Statistics Canada's *Longitudinal Survey of Immigrants to Canada* (Statistics Canada 2003b), *Ethnic Diversity Survey* (Statistics Canada 2003) and *General Social Surveys,* Cycles 17 and 19 (Statistics Canada 2003a, 2005a).[17] On the cultural side, Statistics Canada's annual cultural surveys focus predominantly on economic variables and less on social factors. The *Census of Population* for 2001 (Statistics Canada 2002) and the *Census of Population* for 2006 (Statistics Canada 2007) contain information on cultural variables, such as occupations, income and education, and citizenship variables such as self-declared ethnocultural ancestry. While going beyond domestic indicators to develop international comparative indicators is problematic for measuring cultural citizenship, valuable work has been done in Europe, through the Council of Europe and the European Union, in regard to cultural participation, social cohesion, and intercultural dialogue.[18]

Cultural Diversity Indicators

In the *Universal Declaration on Cultural Diversity* (2002), UNESCO broadly defined cultural diversity as "the set of distinctive spiritual, material, intellectual and emotional features of society or a social group...that encompasses in addition to the arts and literature, lifestyles, ways of living together, value systems, traditions and beliefs."[19] However, as noted above, differing national and international contexts and agendas often produce conflicting definitions of cultural diversity. Other definitions of diversity refer somewhat more narrowly to ethnocultural composition of populations, cultural sector attributes, or citizenship and cultural rights.

   Our conception of cultural diversity encompasses people and system diversity. It includes the following potential indicators:

1. Linguistic Diversity: Proficiency in official and non-official languages is the major indicator of integration of immigrants in Canada utilized to date in surveys and longitudinal studies.[20] While the majority of cultural programming in Canada is in either English or French, non-official language content is increasing, especially in broadcasting and print media. In the context of integration, indicators of immigrants' use and retention of both official and non-official languages are key variables in measuring social integration and cultural development. Indicators that document the effects of immigrant opportunities and incentives to use and retain non-official languages over time and across generations are especially important, given the risk of decline and ultimately the extinction of certain minority languages. Comparable indicators of use and retention of Aboriginal languages in Canada, especially those deemed to be at risk, are also available.

2. Diversity in Cultural Content Supply and Accessibility: The frequency and content share of immigrant issues in mainstream media and cultural production, along with time use and other measures of participation, are promising areas for cultural indicators affecting immigrant settlement. More precise and comprehensive measures for the diversity of cultural content in Canada need to be developed, including broadcasting and other audio-visual media (radio, television, film and video, sound recording, the visual arts), the print media (books, newspapers, periodicals, libraries) and new multi-media platforms (Internet, mobile phones).[21] Examples of areas for investigation include the analysis of the following:

- ethnocultural content in traditional and digitized media and the degree to which this content reflects and/or generates new diasporic and cosmopolitan forms of cultural citizenship;
- ethnocultural participation and representation in academic curricula and public sector literature, including cultural materials and resources available for use by immigrants and settlement agencies.

3. Creative Cities and Sustainable Communities: Many recent studies have emphasized the growing concentration of new immigrants in major urban centres (the "MTV" phenomenon of Montreal, Toronto, and Vancouver), along with the integration and settlement problems this has produced in relation to children, youth, and seniors at risk, economic and educational disparities, racism and discrimination especially felt by visible and other minorities, substandard housing, homelessness, crime, and unemployment/under-employment.[22] Yet, as noted above, immigrants are part of the nexus of urban factors attracting a creative population and a vital cultural infrastructure. Cultural citizenship in the cities is thus a crucible for change, if managed effectively. Ray (2005) notes that cities are "ideally suited to address many issues associated with the inclusion of newcomers" (7).[23] There is little doubt that urban indicators of cultural diversity, participation, and dialogue are or should be essential ingredients in city planning and urban development, as well as in the urban settlement and integration of immigrants. Culture is also increasingly recognized as a pillar of sustainable communities in rural settings, as the example of Saint Leonard in New Brunswick suggests. Culture transforms place into community and helps mould identity and belonging through cultural events and activities such as festivals, exhibitions and street culture, thereby bridging ethnocultural and ethnoracial boundaries and removing barriers to inclusion.

4. Ethnocultural Labour Force: In order to determine the extent of immigrant work in the cultural sector, studies need to identify professional artists and other members of the cultural labour force with diverse ethnocultural backgrounds. Using 1996 census data, Jack Jedwab (2003) measured the number of ethnic groups represented in the fine and applied arts, recreation and sports. He concluded: "While immigrants have a higher degree of post-secondary arts qualifications than the percentage they represent within the total population, they are underrepresented in the arts and arts-related occupations in Canada relative to the share of employees that they constitute within that sector" (14). This indicator could be developed further and updated by investigating more recent editions of the *Census of Population*, the monthly labour force, the relative distribution of immigrant groups in differing cultural occupations, and certain economic impact studies of culture.

Cultural Participation Indicators

Researchers have posited critical linkages between civic and cultural participation and the building of cultural and social capital, personal empowerment, and growth of collective belonging and identity or identities. Possible indicators include audience tastes and preferences (arts and film), visitor tastes and preferences (heritage, libraries), cultural donations and volunteerism, and cultural consumption behaviour (household spending).

Donations and volunteerism are traditionally considered participation activities, although, like other cultural indicators, they also have a profound impact on social cohesion and intercultural dialogue. Indeed, cultural donations and volunteerism act as a medium by which citizenship develops across ethnocultural lines. Charitable donations and volunteerism are therefore key indicators that give substance and weight to the rights and responsibilities of immigrants.

The Canadian Council of Social Development (CCSD) recently completed a report on the social and civic engagement among Canadian immigrants based on data and indicators derived from the *National Survey of Giving, Volunteering and Participation* (Statistics Canada 2000) and the *General Social Survey on Social Engagement* (Statistics Canada 2003a). Like many Canadians, immigrants are involved not only in bettering their economic inclusion through such means as the recognition of educational and professional credentials but also in ensuring their social inclusion through activities discussed herein. The study found that volunteering rates of immigrants increased above the benchmark figure for Canadian-born respondents the longer the former have lived in Canada. In addition, the higher the education and income of immigrants, the greater their participation rate in volunteering.[24] Greater proportions of immigrants (23 percent) than Canadian-born (7 percent) belong to community organizations in which members belong to a different ethnic group than their own.

While other cultural participation indicators are available, they are not always applicable to immigrants; nor are immigrant motivations and barriers to participation fully documented. To the extent that traditional surveys of cultural participation have examined immigrants at all, they have tended to focus largely on live arts attendance. Environics (2001) found that immigrants may be somewhat more interested in attending cultural events based on their own cultural background than non-immigrants and would like more exhibits or performances that connect with their cultural or ethnic background. Nine out of ten immigrants expressed an interest in seeing artwork and attending live performances based on different cultures, compared to 81 percent for respondents born in Canada (Jedwab 2003). In August 2005, Solutions Research Group surveyed 3,000 members of the six largest ethnocultural target groups in Montreal, Toronto, and Vancouver: Chinese, South Asian, Italian, Black, West Asian/Arab, and Hispanic. With the exception of Italian, all groups are strongly attracted to performances featuring their own cultural traditions at the possible expense of mainstream cultural events (Solutions Research Group 2005). General interest in other cultures is commonly felt across all target groups.

Trend lines can now be drawn on a variety of aspects of cultural participation using data collected in the *General Social Surveys on Time Use* in 1992, 1998, and 2005. With the exception of the arts, however, most cultural participation data do not extend to identifying audiences and participants by ethnic origin or immigrant status. Moreover, most cultural participation studies have not yet incorporated new media or new digital technology activities.

One important practicable area for research is participation of immigrants in local libraries, which fosters inclusion and participation in a highly cost-effective way. Library use by immigrants for education, information, enlightenment, or networking is a significant indicator of immigrant settlement and integration. For immigrants making use of the Internet for information searches and communications, libraries serve as a conduit for becoming and staying informed, as well as inter-acting across cultural lines. Research that correlates reading, literacy rates, and official language capacity with library visits by immigrants might be useful.

Intercultural Dialogue Indicators

Intercultural dialogue is the strategic linchpin between growing diversity and desired outcomes, such as cultural and social capital, or cultural and civic participation on the one hand, and social cohesion and quality of life on the other. According to a recent Council of Europe study, intercultural dialogue encompasses (i) dialogue between people of different cultures often but is not always enclosed within national boundaries; (ii) dialogue based on attitudes of non-violence; (iii) openness to others and a willingness to see solutions; and (iv) co-operation facilitated or occasioned by the dialogue (Bourquin 2003). Another report for the Council of Europe in 2003 referred to "inter-culturality" as the set of processes through which intercultural dialogue and relations between and among different cultures are constructed and maintained (Leclercq 2003).

Examples of possible indicators of intercultural dialogue include events or activities bringing cultures together. Other indicators include the degree of intercultural structures within government, intercultural education, hybrid artistic forms, and venues that mirror emerging forms of cultural citizenship. The diverse urban concentration of immigration in Canada opens up new vistas for cultural expression and belonging. Spoonley et al. (2005) describe settlement outcomes in New Zealand in the context of social cohesion. They propose a set of indicators that measures the impact of settlement policies on social cohesion in New Zealand, including socially cohesive behaviour (belonging and participation) for each of the migrant/refugee community and host communities. They also identify three conditions for a socially cohesive society—inclusion, recognition and legitimacy. Clearly, the internalization of the above cultural values through intercultural dialogue should also enhance social cohesion.

In 2005, the Solutions Research Group surveyed ethnic groups in Canada's three largest cities about their attachment to their respective ethnic groups and to Canada. Chinese and South Asian respondents in Vancouver and Toronto reported a stronger sense of attachment to their racial, ethnic, or religious group than the general populations of those cities. In Montreal and Toronto, West Asian/Arab, Black, Hispanic and Italian respondents indicated a stronger sense of attachment to their own groups than those cities' general populations. While generational differences and strong bonding among certain ethnocultural groups may account for some of these findings, in all cases, attachment to Canada appears to grow with age. Discrimination may also contribute to reduced attachment. According to Naeem Noorani, the Solutions Research Group of Toronto found that South-Asian, West Asian/Arab, Black and Hispanic respondents were significantly more likely to state that the media present negative stereotypes of minority groups (over 50 percent) than the general populations of Toronto, Vancouver and Montreal were (38 percent) (Solutions Research Group 2005, 1). Such findings underscore the reality of multiple attachments and identities and the expectation that one level of identity or belonging does not necessarily supersede or replace another or other(s).

Conclusions and Recommended Next Steps

This chapter has called attention to the importance of recognizing culture as a tool in immigration and citizenship. Some of the indicators identified here, especially those bearing on knowledge of prevailing cultural customs, values, and activities in Canada, are already being used at the federal level in certain citizenship and cultural policies and programs. However, there appears to be a need to reflect more closely on the detail of potential indicators of cultural citizenship. This is not surprising, given the rapid pace of demographic change in Canada, occasioned by continuing high levels of immigration. There is clearly a shortfall in data on immigrant cultural participation, as well as a need for the harmonization of different questionnaires designed to elicit such information. There is also a serious gap in the nature of public and private sector partnerships and structures intended to further intercultural dialogue in Canada among the diverse civic and cultural stakeholders in both the immigrant and host communities. Research on the differential between cultural policy goals and program implementation, with attention to inequities in power between many immigrants and their country hosts, is also lacking.

As a result, we make the following recommendations:

1. Work should continue on mining existing data sources and specifying practicable and evocative indicators of cultural citizenship, as well as applying them in policies and programs in support of the settlement and integration of immigrants in Canada.

2. Case studies of cultural and civic diversity, participation, and dialogue should be conducted to demonstrate how and with what effect culture and citizenship interact and what kind of linkages are required to foster a productive amalgam of cultural citizenship in Canada.

3. In order to develop a comprehensive cultural citizenship research agenda, the conceptual underpinnings and potential indicators or measures of cultural citizenship described in this article should be extended to other topics in future research.

4. To develop a cultural citizenship research agenda, governments at all levels should co-ordinate, interact, and integrate existing policies and programs affecting immigrant integration. This includes enhancing communications and joint projects between the cultural and citizenship sectors of the Department of Canadian Heritage, between departments and agencies at all relevant domestic and international levels, and among governments, immigrant settlement and related service agencies, and groups, individuals and organizations in the arts and culture sector.

5. It would be equally important to encourage initiatives that recognize writers and artists from minorities and works that bear witness to intercultural exchange in Canada. Such a strategy would give minorities more space and prompt greater receptiveness and tolerance for immigrants and visible minorities and—this should be underscored—for all of Canada's founding peoples, including those who are minorities in their regions.

Much of the research and analysis contained in this chapter has focused on the social impact of cultural citizenship, or perhaps more accurately, on the impact of culture on citizenship. Actively involved citizens are more likely to participate in and support a flourishing and diverse cultural sector. Indeed, the synergies between culture and citizenship may lead to enhanced cultural and social capital formation conducive to a high quality of life and a broader understanding and appreciation of the role of cultural and civic rights in the lives of both current and future citizens of Canada. Indicators designed to identify these synergies should also be incorporated in future reports on policy and program performance and public opinion monitoring of cultural citizenship.

Notes

We would like to thank Nancy Duxbury, James S. Frideres, Catherine Murray, and Winfried Siemerling for helpful comments on draft versions of this chapter, and Diana Brydon for her earlier input.

1. As this essay indicates, the confluence is more widespread than Delanty suggests, extending beyond political discourse to fields such as literature, cultural studies, and philosophy, as well as to policy circles.
2. As Delanty notes, traditional theories of citizenship often bypass the cultural sphere, as policy analyses do. Little explicit attention was given to culture at a 2005 Policy Forum organized by the Multiculturalism and Human Rights Branch of Canadian Heritage or at a Public Policy Forum on "Integrating Immigrants" held in Toronto in March 2006 (*Canada 2017 — Serving Canada's Multicultural Population for the Future* and *Integrating Immigrants*).
3. A 2001 report on Canadian cultural policies identifies "the lack of conceptual and definitional clarity" as a "major barrier to advancing a coherent policy agenda related to culture" (Baeker et al. 6).
4. Gershon Shafir (1998) argues that the model of *"differentiated citizenship* awarded to immigrant groups" advocated by Will Kymlicka and others might lead to *"dual citizenship,"* or "demands" by "national minorities" for "ever-increasing autonomy, sovereignty, and, eventually, secession" (20).
5. While Stanley offers a relatively neutral approach to the principal forms of "culture," Roy Miki (2005) distinguishes the "cultural as a matrix for the social imagination of embodied subjects" from "'culture' as an achieved state to be possessed, commodified, or otherwise treated as a privileged container that subordinates individual agency to pre-emptive frames of already constituted identities." Miki thus sees culture as more likely to "be found in complicity with political and economic regimes in power," while the cultural is a dynamic process permitting some agency by embodied subjects (1). Benhabib (2002) notes that "much contemporary cultural politics today" relies on "an odd mixture of the democratic equality of all cultural forms of expression," drawn from social anthropology and a "Herderian emphasis on each form's irreducible uniqueness" (3–4). "Whether conservative or progressive," she maintains, such conceptions rely on "faulty epistemic premises" that cultures are "clearly delineable wholes" which are "congruent with population groups." As a result, the "internal homogeneity of cultures" is privileged in ways that "potentially legitimize repressive demands for communal conformity" and "fetishize" cultures in ways that "put them beyond the reach of critical analysis."

6. For more information on the history of the concept of culture, see the excellent overview by Ruth Amossy in the article on "Culture" in *Dictionnaire du littéraire*.

7. These include "Cultural Citizenship" at the John F. Kennedy Institute for North American Studies in Berlin, in 2003; a symposium at the Radcliffe Institute in 2004—where the leading postcolonial scholar Homi Bhabha has been working on "global" or "cultural" citizenship (Mohanty 2005); and the 2005 TransCanada conference, organized by Smaro Kamboureli and Roy Miki (www.transcanadas.ca).

8. Delanty further distinguishes concepts of cultural citizenship drawn from "cultural sociology" from those drawn from political theory, noting that those drawn from the former tend to be more far-reaching in emphasizing the centrality of culture to understanding citizenship (Delanty 2002, 61).

9. In documents distributed by the European Union, the following passage is more the exception than the rule: [translation] "Forty years is not a long time for people who were recently in conflict and have no collective identity to build a cultural identity. European citizenship is not just an institutional conundrum or 'the last utopia'; it is a political and philosophical problematic for a post-national society. European citizenship is a compromise between a liberal conception and a voluntarist approach to citizenship, between political citizenship and cultural citizenship" (Withol de Wenden 2000).

10. On "cultural rights," see also Bryan Turner, reviewed in Delanty (2002), and Lurry (1993).

11. For an overview of the impact that global cultural flows are having on contemporary Canadian society, the reader is encouraged to go to the website of the Robarts Centre for Canadian Studies at York University at http://www.robarts.yorku.ca/projects/global/.

12. Since writers are often intellectual leaders, this PEN initiative offers potential for programs promoting intercultural awareness and cross-cultural competency through the activities of writers-in-exile.

13. Alexandra MacCallum, past Executive Director of the Multicultural Association of Nova Scotia, ran a Multicultural Council of this kind on Prince Edward Island, bringing together immigrant groups, until its small annual federal funding was cut. Interview with MacCallum by Marjorie Stone, March 2005.

14. According to numerous studies and the impressive report produced by the Media Awareness Network, television images of minorities, in both entertainment programming and news coverage, fail to reflect Canada's cultural diversity. In drama series, for example, minority women are significantly under-represented (women 4.55 percent and men 12.73 percent).

When minority women do appear, they are confined to bit parts or to stereotypical and generally poorly paid roles. The same applies to newscasts and current events programming: less than 8 percent of sources and 7 percent of reporters are members of ethnic minorities. The Media Awareness Network observes that, according to a number of analysts, the media still tend to portray members of visible minorities as foreigners and there is frequent racial bias in media coverage of crimes. The news media and the entertainment industry are helping to create or reinforce prejudices about ethnic minorities. (*Représentation des minorités ethniques et visibles dans les médias: introduction*, Media Awareness Network. www.media-awareness.ca/francais/enjeux/stereotypes/minorites_ethniques/index.cfm).

15. "Citizenship is always a reciprocal and, therefore, social idea. It can never be purely a set of rights that free the individual from obligations to others" (Faulks 2000, 4).

16. Indicators are forms of information that summarize the characteristics of systems or highlight what is happening in one or more systems. To be reliable, indicators require clear conceptual grounding, theoretical modeling and access to relevant sources of longitudinal data and information.

17. Cultural factors are occasionally addressed, albeit indirectly, through such variables as social networks, official language skills, education and employment.

18. For example, the EU's *Eurobarometer* (2003) measures cultural participation. The Council of Europe published *Concerted Development of Social Cohesion Indicators — Methodological Guide* (2005) and began work in 2006 on the development of a "White Paper on Intercultural Dialogue."

19. In the UNESCO *Convention on the Protection and Promotion of the Diversity of Cultural Expressions* (2005), which Canada was the first country to ratify, cultural diversity is referred to as "the common heritage of humanity" and "the manifold ways in which the cultures of social groups and societies find expression." (UNESCO 2005)

20. Data and indicators concerning both official language majorities and minorities in Canada are derived from the Canadian *Census of Population* and the Department of Canadian Heritage's Official Languages Program.

21. The cultural sector is measured in accordance with Statistics Canada's *Cultural Statistics Framework* (2005) based on existing data sources and internationally recognized data categories. Not included but arguably part of the cultural sector are crafts and new media.

22. According to the Canadian Council of Social Development, in its Urban Poverty Project 2007, and based on the data on 46 large Canadian cities

and the 2001 Census, the poverty rate in 2000 was 16.9 percent for Canadian-borns and 24.1 percent for immigrants. For immigrants who came to Canada prior to 1986, the poverty rate was 15.3 percent; for those who immigrated between 1986 and 1990, it was 21.8 percent; for those who immigrated between 1991 and 1995, the poverty rate was 27.8 percent; and for those who immigrated betwen 1996 and 2001, it was 44 percent.

23. Brian Ray in "The Role of Cities in Immigrant Integration" notes that cities can encourage "two–way integration between immigrants and receiving communities {and} opportunities for positive encounters between groups in public spaces" (*Metropolis World Bulletin*, September 2005).

24. Immigrants aged 55 to 64 were the most likely to volunteer, whereas for the Canadian-born population, the highest volunteer rates were among those 35 to 54.

References

Albro, R., and J. Bauer. 2005. "Abstract" and "Introduction." *Human Rights Dialogue: Cultural Rights*, Series 2 (12). At http://www.cceia.org/viewMedia.php/prmTemplateID/8/prmID/5131.

Amossy, R. 2002. "Culture," in *Dictionnaire du Littéraire*. Paris: Presses Universitaires de France, pp. 129–30.

Andrew, C., M. Gattinger, M.S. Jeannotte, and W. Straw (eds). 2005. *Accounting for Culture: Thinking Through Cultural Citizenship*. Ottawa: University of Ottawa Press.

Arnold, M. 1961. *Culture and Anarchy and Other Writings*. Cambridge, MA: Cambridge University Press.

Baeker, G., with contributions from J. Foote, M.S. Jeannotte, and M. Smith. 2001. *"All Talents Count": A Pilot Inventory of National Cultural Policies and Measures Supporting Cultural Diversity: Canadian Country Profile*. Ottawa: Strategic Research and Analysis Directorate, Department of Canadian Heritage.

Benhabib, S. 2002. *The Claims of Culture: Equality and Diversity in the Global Era.* Princeton: Princeton University Press.

Berkes, F. 1998. "Cultural and Natural Capital: A Systems Approach Revisited," in *Social Capital Formation and Institutions for Sustainability*, ed. A. Mendes. University of British Columbia: Workshop Proceedings: Sustainable Development Research Institute. At http://www.sdri.ubc.ca/documents/SocialCapitalFormation.pdf.

Bourdieu, P. 1986. "The Forms of Capital," in *Handbook of Theory and Research in the Sociology of Education,* ed. John G. Richardson. Westport, CN: Greenwood Press, pp. 241–58.

Bourquin, J-F. 2003. *Violence, Conflict and Intercultural Dialogue.* Strasbourg: Council of Europe.

Breton, R., N.J. Hartmann, J.L. Lennards, and P. Reed. 2004. *A Fragile Social Fabric? Fairness, Trust, and Commitment in Canada.* Montreal and Kingston: McGill-Queen's University Press.

Brydon, D. 2005. "Metamorphoses of a Discipline: Rethinking the Canadian Literary Institution," in *Trans.Can.Lit: Resituating the Study of Canadian Literature,* eds. S. Kamboureli and R. Miki. Waterloo, ON: Wilfrid Laurier University Press, 2007, pp. 1–16.

Canadian Council of Social Development. 2000. *Populations Vulnerable to Poverty: Urban Poverty in Canada.* At http://www.ccsd.ca/pubs/2007/upp/.

Chariandry, D., and S. McCall. 2006. "Citizenship and Cultural Belonging in Canadian Literature." Call for papers for a special issue of *Essays in Canadian Writing.* A TransCanada Project. Email circulation. 20 January.

Cho, L. 2005. "Diasporic Citizenship: Contradictions and Possibilities for Canadian Literature." Vancouver: Paper Delivered at the TransCanada I Conference, June 23-26. At www.transcanadas.ca.

Citizenship and Immigration Canada (CIC). 2006. "Regard sur le Canada: Les droits et les responsabilités des citoyens canadiens." At http://www.cic.gc.ca/francais/ressources/publications/regard/regard-20.asp.

Cooke, A. 2002. "Literary Studies and the Metropolis Project: Bridging the Gaps," in *Newsletter. Association of Canadian College and University Teachers of English,* eds. D. Brydon, A. Cooke, W. Siemerling, M. Stone, and C. Verduyn. June. ACCUTE, pp. 33–47.

Delanty, G. 2000. *Citizenship in a Global Age: Society, Culture, Politics.* Buckingham and Philadelphia: Open University Press.

———— 2002. "Two Conceptions of Cultural Citizenship: A Review of Recent Literature on Culture and Citizenship," *The Global Review of Ethnopolitics,* 1 (March): 60–66. At www.ethnopolitics.org/archive/volume_1/issue_3/delanty.pdf.

Dossa, P. 2004. *Politics and Poetics of Migration: Narratives of Iranian Women from the Diaspora.* Toronto: Canadian Scholars' Press.

Duxbury, N. 2005. "Cultural Citizenship and Community Indicator Projects: Approaches and Challenges in the Local/Municipal Context." Paper presented at the Canadian Heritage workshop, "Cities and Citizenship: Developing Indicators of Cultural Diversity." Toronto: 10th International Metropolis Conference, October 17–21.

Eagleton, T. 2000. *The Idea of Culture.* Oxford: Blackwell Manifestos.

Environics Research Group Ltd. 2001. *Arts and Heritage Participation Survey Among Canadians of Ethnic Minority Backgrounds.* Ottawa: Department of Canadian Heritage.

European Union. 2003. *Eurobarometer 2003.1: New Europeans and Culture.* At www.ec.europa.eu/culture/eac/sources_info/pdf-word/etude.pdf.

Faulks, K. 2000. *Citizenship*. Key Ideas Series. London and New York: Routledge.

Florida, R., and G. Gates. 2001. *Technology and Tolerance: The Importance of Diversity to High-Technology Growth*. Washington, DC: Brookings Institution Center on Urban and Metropolitan Policy.

Foote, J., and M. Smith. 2005. "Framing Indicators of Cultural and Shared Citizenship in Canada." Paper presented at the Canadian Heritage workshop, "Cities and Citizenship: Developing Indicators of Cultural Diversity." Toronto: 10th International Metropolis Conference, October 17–21.

Gould, H. 2001. "Culture and Social Capital," in *Recognising Culture: A Series of Briefing Papers on Culture and Development*, ed. F. Matarasso. London: Comedia, Department of Canadian Heritage and UNESCO, pp. 69–75.

Jeannotte, M.S. 2005. "Just Showing Up: Social and Cultural Capital in Everyday Life," in *Accounting for Culture: Thinking Through Cultural Citizenship*, eds. Andrew, C., M. Gattinger, M.S. Jeannotte, and W. Straw. Ottawa: University of Ottawa Press, pp. 124–45.

Jedwab, J. 2003. *Diversity, Demography and the Arts in Canada: the Possible Effects of Canada's Changing Population on Canadian Cultural Expression*. Gatineau: Minister's Forum on Diversity and Culture.

Joseph, M. 1999. *Nomadic Identities: The Performance of Citizenship*. Public Worlds series, Vol. 5. Minneapolis and London: University of Minnesota Press.

Kamboureli, S. (ed.) 1996. *Making a Difference: Canadian Multicultural Literature*. Toronto: Oxford University Press.

——— 2000. *Scandalous Bodies: Diasporic Literature in Canada*. Don Mills, ON: Oxford University Press.

Karim, K. 2005. "The Elusiveness of Full Citizenship: Accounting for Cultural Capital, Cultural Competencies and Cultural Pluralism," in *Accounting for Culture: Thinking Through Cultural Citizenship*, eds. Andrew, C., M. Gattinger, M.S. Jeannotte, and W. Straw. Ottawa: University of Ottawa Press, pp. 147–58.

Kroeber, A.L., and C. Kluckhohn. 1952. *Culture: A Critical Review of Concepts and Definitions*. Cambridge, MA: Harvard University Peabody Museum of American Archaeology and Ethnology Paper.

Kymlicka, W. 1995. *Multicultural Citizenship*. Oxford: Oxford University Press.

Laaksonen, A. 2005. *Measuring Cultural Exclusion through Participation in Cultural Life*. Paris: Presented at the Third Forum on Human Development: Defining and Measuring Cultural Exclusion.

Leclercq, J-M. 2003. *Facets of Interculturality in Education*. Strasbourg: Council of Europe.

Lowe, L. 1996. *Immigrant Acts: On Asian American Cultural Politics*. Durham and London: Duke University Press.

Lurry, C. 1993. *Cultural Rights*. London: Routledge.

Mercer, C. 2002. *Towards Cultural Citizenship: Tools for Cultural Policy and Development*. Hedemore, Sweden: Bank of Sweden Tercentenary Foundation and Gidlungs Forlag.

Miki, R. 2005. "'Inside the Black Egg': Cultural Practice, Citizenship, and Belonging in a Globalizing Canadian Nation," *Mosaic* 36 (September): 1–19.

Miller, T. 2002. "Cultural Citizenship," in *A Handbook of Citizenship Studies,* ed. E.R. Isin and B.S. Turner. London: Sage.

Mirón, L.F., J.X. Inda, and J.K. Aguirre. 1998. "Transnational Migrants, Cultural Citizenship, and the Politics of Language in California," *Educational Policy* 12(6): 659–81.

Mishra, V. 2005. "Multiculturalism." *The Year's Work in Critical and Cultural Theory*. The English Association, 3(1). Oxford: Oxford University Press, pp. 182–204.

Mohanty, S. 2005. "Towards a Global Cultural Citzenship." Interview with Homi K. Bhabha. *The Hindu*. 3 July.

Ong, A. 1999. *Flexible Citizenship: The Cultural Logics of Transnationality*. Durham and London: Duke University Press.

Putnam, R. 2000. *Bowling Alone: The Collapse and Revival of American Community*. New York: Simon and Schuster.

Ray, B. 2005. "The Role of Cities in Immigrant Integration." *Metropolis World Bulletin*, September.

Robert, L. 2002. "Polysystème," in *Le dictionnaire du Littéraire*, eds. P. Aron, D. Saint-Jacques, and A. Viala. Paris: Presses Universitaires de France, pp. 456–57.

Rosaldo, R. 1997. "Cultural Citizenship, Inequality, and Multiculturalism." *Race, Identity, and Citizenship: A Reader,* ed. R.D. Torres, L.F. Mirón, and J.S. Inda. Oxford, UK, and Malden, MA: Blackwell, 1999, pp. 253–61.

Saunders, P., and A. Fotheringham. 2006. "Intercultural Competence." Halifax: Presentation, Annual Medical Education Symposium, Dalhousie Medical School. 21 April.

Shafir, G. 1998. "Introduction: The Evolving Tradition of Citizenship," in *The Citizenship Debates: A Reader,* ed. S. Gershon. Minneapolis and London: Minneapolis University Press.

Siemerling, W. 2002. "Cultural Plurality and Canadian Literature," in *Encyclopedia of Literature in Canada,* ed. W.H. New. Toronto: University of Toronto Press, pp. 265–71.

———— 2005. *The New North American Studies: Culture, Writing, and the Politics of Re/Cognition*. New York and London: Routledge.

———— (ed.). 1996. *Writing Ethnicity: Cross-Cultural Consciousness in Canadian and Québécois Literature*. Toronto: ECW Press.

Solutions Research Group. 2005. *Diversity in Canada.* Toronto: Solutions Research.

Spoonley, P., R. Peace, A. Butcher, and D. O'Neill. 2005. "Social Cohesion: A Policy and Indicator Framework for Assessing Immigrant and Host Outcomes," *Social Policy Journal of New Zealand* 24: 85–110.

Stanley, D. 2005. "The Three Faces of Culture: Why Culture is a Strategic Good Requiring Government Policy Attention," in *Accounting for Culture: Thinking Through Cultural Citizenship,* eds. C. Andrew, M. Gattinger, M.S. Jeannotte, and W. Straw. Ottawa: University of Ottawa Press, pp. 21–31.

Statistics Canada. 2000. *National Survey of Giving, Volunteering and Participating.* At http://www.statcan.ca/english/Dli/Data/Ftp/nsgvp.htm.

——— 2002. *Census of Population: 2001.* At http://www12.statcan.ca/english/census01/products/standard/themes/Releases.cfm?M=3&Y=2002.

——— 2003. *Ethnic Diversity Survey: Portrait of a Multicultural Society.* At http://www.statcan.ca/bsolc/english/bsolc?catno=89-593-X.

——— 2003a. *General Social Survey on Social Engagement: Cycle 17.* At http://www.statcan.ca/bsolc/english/bsolc?catno=89-598-X.

——— 2003b. *Longitudinal Survey of Immigrants to Canada.* At http://www.statcan.ca/bsolc/english/bsolc?catno=89-615-X.

——— 2005. *Cultural Statistics Framework.* Ottawa.

——— 2005a. *General Social Survey on Time Use: Cycle 19. Ottawa. 1992, 1998 and 2005.* At http://www.statcan.ca/bsolc/english/bsolc?catno=89-622-X.

——— 2007. *Census of Population: 2006.* At http://www.tetrad.com/demographics/canada/census/cen2006.html?gclid=CJra3e3zqJICFQE8xwodB3spQQ.

Tastsoglou, E., and A. Dobrowolsky, eds. 2006. *Women, Migration and Citizenship: Making Local, National and Transnational Connections.* Aldershot, UK, and Burlington, VT: Ashgate Press.

Taylor, C. 1992. "The Politics of Recognition," in *Multiculturalism and the Politics of Recognition,* ed. A. Gutmann. Princeton: Princeton University Press, pp. 25–73.

UNESCO. 1997. "Cultural Citizenship in the 21st Century: Adult Learning and Indigenous Peoples." Hamburg: UNESCO Institute for Education. Follow-up to the Fifth International Conference on Adult Education. At www.unesco.org/education/uie/confintea.

——— 2002. *Universal Declaration on Cultural Diversity.* Paris: UNESCO. At http://unesdoc.unesco.org/images/0012/001271/127160m.pdf.

——— 2005. *Convention on the Protection and Promotion of the Diversity of Cultural Expressions.* Paris.

van Esch, K., and O. St. John. 2004. *New Insights into Foreign Language Learning and Teaching.* Foreign Language Teaching in Europe, Volume 9. Frankfurt: Peter Lang.

Verduyn, C. 1998. *Literary Pluralities.* Peterborough, ON: Broadview Press.

Williams, R. 1976. *Keywords: A Vocabulary of Culture and Society.* Fontana: Croom Helm.

Withol de Wenden, C. 2000. "Construire le mythe européen," in "La citoyenneté européenne en devenir," *Label France*, 40, juillet. Paris, Ministère des affaires étrangères. At www.diplomatie.gouv.fr/label_france/france/DOSSIER/presidence/05.html.

Part II

Chapter 5

Integration Policies in English-Speaking Canada

JOHN BILES

Integration of Newcomers to Canada: A Societal Project

As the introduction to this volume noted, Canada is a self-professed nation of immigrants. Consequently, the responsibility for overseeing the integration of newcomers in Canada is not limited to one department within one order of government; rather, it is a societal endeavour. Obviously, one chapter cannot do justice to the myriad of societal actors in this endeavour; instead I will explore four of the more active funders of integration programs in Canada: the federal government, the provincial governments, the municipal governments, and the so-called universal service providers, such as the United Way, along with other community partners.

This chapter will demonstrate that regardless of the funder, a lead department, agency, or program is essential to the success of these programs. These lead organizations must work with a cross section of their colleagues to ensure the effective integration of newcomers in Canadian communities. In addition, the major issues faced by newcomers require the various funders to work collaboratively to develop solutions and to dismantle barriers and obstacles that impede integration—a responsibility that goes beyond immigration and has been recognized at the highest level.

For example, the 2004 federal Speech from the Throne observed:

> Jurisdiction must be respected. But Canadians do not go about their daily lives worried about what jurisdiction does this or that. They expect, rightly, that their governments will co-operate in common purpose for

Immigration and Integration in Canada in the Twenty-first Century, eds. J. Biles, M. Burstein, and J. Frideres.
Montreal and Kingston: McGill-Queen's University Press, Queen's Policy Studies Series.

the common good—each working from its strength. They expect them to just get on with the job (GoC 2004a, 5).

To be sure, the jurisdictional challenge is especially present in the case of immigration. Section 95 of the *British North America Act*, which is a constituent element of the Canadian Constitution, defines immigration as a concurrent jurisdiction between the federal and provincial governments, with federal paramountcy (meaning that where provincial and federal approaches contradict one another, the federal approach is legally dominant). Accordingly, provincial involvement in immigration has ebbed and flowed since Confederation (Garcea 1994).

At the outset of the twenty-first century, provincial governments are the most active they have ever been: all ten have now signed individual agreements of varying complexity with the federal government. Interestingly, the vital role of municipal governments has also finally been acknowledged, and a process has begun to formalize their participation.[1] Similarly, organizations like the United Way, which used to provide integration support before governments became active in this field, are also once again seen as key players.[2]

Before exploring the current policies and approaches of these various funders, we should pause for a moment and revisit the frame within which all integration takes place in the Canadian context. That frame explicitly acknowledges the reciprocal obligations of both the host population and newcomers to adapt to take the shifting concerns of a diverse population into account. Indeed, section 3 of the *Immigration and Refugee Protection Act* (2001) includes under the objectives of the Act: "(e) to promote the successful integration of permanent residents into Canada, while recognizing that integration involves mutual obligations for new immigrants and Canadian society."

This mutual obligation has been part of the Canadian approach to diversity since at least the promulgation of an official multiculturalism policy in October 1971, but certainly since multiculturalism was finally formalized in legislation in the *Canadian Multiculturalism Act* (1988). As Garcea (2006) notes, every provincial government, with the exception of Quebec, has also created its own multicultural policy. While there is significant debate on whether there is actually a difference between multiculturalism policy as practiced by the federal government and nine provincial governments and the interculturalism policy of the Government of Quebec (Nugent 2006), I will not delve into this here. A later chapter in this volume focuses on integration policy in Quebec and describes its unique approach, so this chapter will focus on the rest of the country that operates through a decidedly multicultural frame.

Finally, contrary to many other immigrant-receiving nations, Canada provides the majority of services provided to newcomers through third parties, whether immigrant service provider organizations, multicultural/ethno-specific organizations, issue-based organizations, educational institutions, or partners in the private sector.[3] These organizations are critical players in the integration of newcomers to Canada. Although they have an important role in influencing the policies developed by funding organizations, generally they are not themselves funders; as a result, I will describe their role only briefly in this chapter.

Federal Government

Today, the federal government has the largest role in establishing integration policies in Canada. It does this through a wide range of departments and agencies,[4] but three in particular stand out: Citizenship and Immigration Canada (CIC), Canadian Heritage, and Human Resources and Social Development Canada (HRSDC). Other relevant departments and agencies provide services to all Canadians, and newcomers are just one sub-population of interest. Accordingly, I will focus solely on the three departments below.

Each of these three departments has a different focus. CIC is primarily responsible for the settlement of newcomers in their first three years. After that, responsibility for longer-term integration is passed over to the rest of the Government of Canada, with primary responsibility falling on Canadian Heritage.[5] HRSDC is an important player on a range of important cross-government initiatives; but it is also an exemplar of how a major department delivering services to all Canadians needs to view immigrants as a significant segment of the population that may require tailored outreach and service delivery.

Citizenship and Immigration Canada (CIC)

The federal government's Citizenship and Immigration (CIC) department provides funding and support to service provider organizations to deliver programs and services based on four major categories: (i) official language acquisition handled by the Language Instruction for Newcomers to Canada Program (LINC); (ii) the Immigrant Settlement and Adaptation Program (ISAP); (iii) the Host Program; and (iv) Refugee Programs. Several specific initiatives, such as enhanced language training and the Foreign Credentials Referral Office, started as HRSDC initiatives but are now managed under the aegis of CIC.

CIC was projected to spend $732.2 million on settlement and integration programs in 2007–08. This includes $224.4 million for Quebec, $97.5 million for other provinces, $173.6 million for ISAP, $174.7 million for LINC, $49.5 million for the Resettlement Assistance Program (RAP), and $10 million for the Host Program (GoC 2007). This may seem like an enormous sum;[6] yet if you divide integration expenditures by the approximate average of 250,000 immigrants who arrive in Canada every year, the result is less than $3,000 per immigrant. As Biles and Burstein (2003) note: "Having embarked on a course that entails large-scale immigration...it is essential that Canadians behave wisely and make the necessary investments, financial and personal, to ensure that integration is successful" (15).

Language Instruction for Newcomers to Canada (LINC)

The primary investment in settlement and integration by CIC is language instruction. Since 1992, the Language Instruction for Newcomers to Canada (LINC) program has funded basic language instruction in either one of Canada's official languages to adult immigrants as soon as possible after their arrival.[7] The program provides funding to service provider organizations that offer language instruction to adult immigrants for up to three years from the time they start training.[8] Each service provider organization must meet certain guidelines and benchmarks outlined by the program. Interestingly, in addition to language skills, participants in LINC report that the program also helps them to learn basic details about Canada and Canadian civics; and some organizations report that they feel participants are more prepared to interact in a culturally diverse environment because of LINC's multicultural classrooms (GoC 2004b).

One common criticism of LINC is that most of the training is for basic level English or French, and most immigrants need advanced or employment-specific language training in order to access employment (GoC 2004b). Recognizing this gap, CIC has recently sought and received an additional $20 million per year to fund enhanced language training as part of the Immigrant Settlement and Adaptation Program (ISAP).

Immigrant Settlement and Adaptation Program (ISAP)

The Immigrant Settlement and Adaptation Program (ISAP) funds organizations that provide programming designed to assist immigrants access services and to integrate into their community. These programs include reception and orientation services, translation and interpretation services, referrals to services, employment assistance, and counselling. ISAP also funds research projects, seminars, and conferences related to settlement and integration activities and provides training for settlement workers.

ISAP focuses specifically on the following:

- *Reception:* Meeting newcomers at points of entry or at their final destination, and taking care of their immediate needs (housing, clothing, household effects, transportation) during their first days in Canada.
- *Referral:* Putting newcomers in touch with community resources/ services (banks, shops, housing, health, cultural, educational, recreational and legal facilities).
- *Information and Orientation:* Giving clients practical guidance to help them cope with the problems of everyday living, introducing them to the community, and giving them information on their rights and obligations. This service could include advice on how to use public transit, how to find housing, and how to do taxes, daycare, school registration, shopping, budgeting, and food preparation. It may provide information about safety, the police, Canadian values, and the roles and responsibilities of landlords and tenants. These sessions may be given in groups or one-on-one.
- *Interpretation and Translation:* Providing interpretation to make it easier for newcomers to cope with day-to-day survival in the community. Translation must be limited to documents related to employment, health, education and legal matters that are necessary for immediate settlement.
- *Counselling:* Identifying newcomers' needs, determining how these should be addressed, and helping clients link up with specialized services if they are having problems adjusting to life in Canada. This does not include in-depth social or psychological counselling normally provided by professional counsellors.
- *Employment-related services:* Organizing job-finding clubs, which cover job search strategies, resume writing, interview techniques and telephone follow-ups. Newcomers may also be helped to obtain trade/professional certification or recognition of their academic credentials. Other job search support may also be provided.

Obviously, ISAP covers the widest range of services of the core settlement programs offered by CIC. To illustrate the important role of these programs, I will briefly describe four key initiatives undertaken within this program: (i) Canadian Orientation Abroad; (ii) Newcomer Information Centres; (iii) Settlement Workers in Schools; and (iv) Enhanced Language Training.

Canadian Orientation Abroad

The better prepared newcomers are to tackle the challenges migration poses, the better the results. As a result, CIC began the Canadian Orientation Abroad in 1998. It consists of modules lasting one, two, or three days, depending upon immigration class, and includes an introduction to Canada and information on "settling-in," employment, rights and responsibilities, climate, finding a place to live, living in a multicultural society, and the cost of living and education. In 2004–05, this orientation was offered to 9,056 people (GoC 2005a). A recent evaluation found that family class immigrants and refugees were generally very positive about the course, with convention refugees tending to be very enthusiastic about the course and the new information they learned.

Skilled workers were also positive but were clearly looking for different kinds of information (GoC 2005a). To broaden access to this information, CIC and HRSDC have launched an on-line immigration portal that builds on the work of several provinces and of CIC's integration-net.[9] I will return to this in the sub-section on HRSDC below.

Newcomer Information Centres

Clearly, not all immigrants need or are interested in some of the ISAP offerings on employment information. Instead, they want information that they can access themselves. Generally, these immigrants have some ability in English and are usually in the skilled worker class (GoC 2005a).

The Newcomer Information Centres fill this niche. These centres provide information and referrals, a self-directed resource library, and Internet access. They were first opened in 2001 at the YMCA of Greater Toronto and in Mississauga. Subsequent centres have been opened in Peel, Brampton, and Ottawa.

Settlement Workers in Schools

A third example of innovative ISAP programming is the Settlement Workers in Schools (SWIS) program. SWIS facilitates the integration of newcomer children into Canadian schools. Through this initiative, settlement workers operate in schools with high concentrations of immigrant children, providing services to the parents, children, and the school system. They act as cultural brokers and facilitators between students, parents, and administrators. They may orient newcomers to school rules, refer children to appropriate agencies in cases of domestic violence, act as intermediaries, and provide general information about Canadian society, culture and climate. This program is not national in scope: it remains an initiative of the Ontario regional division of CIC. Recently, this program has been expanded, with SWIS settlement workers relocating from the schools to the public libraries in Toronto and Windsor during the summer months (Quirke 2007).

Enhanced Language Training

As mentioned above in the section on Language Instruction for Newcomers to Canada (LINC), some highly-skilled immigrants have expressed concern that LINC training was not working effectively to prepare them for the labour market. To address this problem, the Enhanced Language Training Initiative was launched. It has funded 253 projects delivered through 140 service provider organizations. Projects are either development projects, which support labour market levels of language training, or delivery projects, which include both language training and bridge-to-work components. Results of a formative evaluation of the initiative in 2007 found that it has helped to improve language skills, increase knowledge/experience of Canadian work environments, increase job finding skills, prepare applicants for licensure exams, and establish mentors/contacts and other social capital networks (Goss Gilroy Inc. 2007).

Host Program

The Canadian approach to integration is based upon the premise of the two-way street, supported by an emphasis on ensuring cross-cultural connections. This emphasis on cross-cultural contact is a government articulation of Allport's (1954) "contact hypothesis." Simply put, the contact hypothesis states that social contact between majority and minority group members will reduce prejudice, providing it occurs under favourable circumstances. The importance of this kind of contact has also recently been emphasized with a renewed interest in social capital in Canadian policy circles (Li and Kunz 2004). The pre-eminent CIC program premised on the contact hypothesis is the Host Program.

The objective of the Host Program is to match immigrants with established Canadians to assist in successful integration. In this program, immigrants practice language skills, learn about Canadian society, and build a network of support and friends to aid in integration. Organizations receive funding to recruit, train, match, and monitor Canadians who volunteer to serve as hosts.

Volunteers do not have to make any financial contributions; instead, they are asked to act as friends and mentors to newcomers in the first few months of arrival. Types of activities outlined by the program include banking and grocery shopping, getting around the community, finding major services in the area, getting used to their new home, becoming familiar with English or French, enrolling in the local school, operating household appliances, and using the transit system.

Host delivery models include individual or group matches, including conversation circles as well as youth and professional matches (GoC 2004c). Interestingly, youth Host Programs remain unfunded at the federal level, but several provinces include variations in their funding arrays (Anisef et al. 2005). For example, conversation circles were added following a review of Ontario Host in 2001 (GoC 2004c).

While Host is the smallest of the core settlement programs managed by CIC, policy-makers and researchers recognize its importance. A recent evaluation found "all lines of evidence strongly support significant positive impacts of the Host Program, most notably with respect to providing social support/friendship and expanding the newcomers' social networks" (GoC 2004c, under "Overall Success of the Program"). In addition, several focus group participants have noted that the Host Program helped to reduce their feelings of stress and isolation. The evaluation also found that participants had increased opportunities to practice language skills and better awareness of Canadian society and values; volunteers reported positive impacts, especially awareness, understanding, and appreciation of other cultures (GoC 2004c).

Refugee Programs

The interaction between immigrants and Canadians of longer tenure is not limited to the Host Program. Immigrants have often had time to prepare for their migration, have been selected through the points system which ensures adequate human capital, and have often followed in the footsteps of families, friends, or neighbours in chain migration movements. In contrast, refugees, particularly government sponsored refugees, seldom have a choice in which country accepts them as refugees. As a result, they need significant assistance at first.[10]

Canadians demanded the creation of a Privately Sponsored Refugee Program in the 1970s in response to the so-called "boat people" of South-East Asia (Beiser 1999; GoC 2007a). Since 1978, this program has contributed to the resettlement of 195,000 refugees and persons in refugee-like situations. The federal government facilitates the refugee's arrival, and sponsors commit to providing care, lodging, settlement assistance, and financial support to the refugee for up to one year after arrival. With the sponsor's agreement, this period can be stretched up to three years in exceptional circumstances. Sponsors can either be a Sponsorship Agreement Holder, most of whom are faith-based organizations, ethnocultural groups, or humanitarian organizations, or a group of five or more Canadian citizens who agree to meet sponsorship obligations (GoC 2007a).

While a recent evaluation found the program to be a success—privately sponsored refugees typically enter the labour market faster than government-assisted refugees—it also found that sponsors faced challenges with unexpected needs and with finding adequate and affordable housing. In addition, during an evaluation, some focus group participants said that due to a reluctance to accept support from family members, some sponsored refugees immediately enter the labour market, rather than participating in settlement services or language training opportunities that would have improved their career prospects and long-term integration. Indeed, a survey showed that only half of the focus group participants had availed themselves of language training since arriving in Canada (GoC 2007a).

The alternative to privately sponsored refugees is the Government-Assisted Refugees. CIC has two programs to facilitate their integration, although neither program builds the same level of bridging social capital as the privately sponsored refugee program. The first, the Resettlement Assistance Program (RAP) provides immediate services, including financial assistance, to government-assisted refugees and humanitarian cases. Financial support is provided for one year (normally) or two years (in extreme cases, based on the welfare rates of the province of residence). Assistance may also include accommodation. The second, the Immigration Loans Program, assists government-sponsored or privately sponsored refugees based on need and ability to repay for the payment of costs associated with migration, including travel documents, medical examinations, transportation, and landing fees. The Immigration Loan Fund was established in 1951 and currently has a limit of $110 million. The recovery rate for repayment is 91 percent (GoC 2004d, 26).

Cross-Government Initiatives

In addition to these principal or "foundational" settlement programs (as CIC has begun to call them lately), CIC also contributes to other initiatives that cut across mandates of several government departments. Three of these include activities surrounding (i) r2ecognizing foreign credentials, (ii) attracting and retaining francophone immigrants, and (iii) combatting racism and discrimination.

HRSDC is the principal department involved with foreign credential recognition, although the Foreign Credentials Referral Office (FCRO), created under the aegis of CIC in May 2007, ensures that CIC continues to have an important role to play. The FCRO provides prospective newcomers to Canada with information about the Canadian labour market and credential assessment and recognition processes. Its initial five-year term has a budget of $32.2 million, which includes $18.5 million for Service Canada to deliver over-the-phone and in-person service. The remaining $13.7 million will be used to develop partnerships, like the on-going pilot partnership with the Association of Canadian Community Colleges to work with prospective immigrants in India, China, and the Philippines (GoC 2007g).

The other two major cross-government initiatives are led by Canadian Heritage (below). First, CIC has been provided with $2 million a year to encourage the attraction and retention of francophone immigrants; and second, it combats racism with its Welcoming Communities Strategy, as part of Canadian Heritage's *Canada's Action Plan Against Racism*. This strategy received $17.6 million over five years starting in 2005–06 and $4.4 million in on-going funding after that period.

Canadian Heritage

Unlike CIC, Canadian Heritage does not deliver integration programs specifically targeted at immigrants. Instead, its mission is to build a more cohesive and creative Canada with two specific strategic outcomes: (i) encouraging Canadians to express and share their diverse cultural experiences with each other and the world; and (ii) helping Canadians live in an inclusive society built on intercultural understanding and citizen participation.

On a simplified level, CIC's role in the first three years is focused primarily on the newcomers themselves to ensure successful integration, whereas Canadian Heritage works primarily with Canadian society, writ large, to ensure that the two-way street model of integration is a success.[11] For example, the bulk of CIC's expenditures are on language training for newcomers, whereas the majority of effort by Canadian Heritage is directed at heritage and cultural programs.

Nevertheless, three broad areas of Canadian Heritage are important to the integration of newcomers: (i) the Multiculturalism Program, (ii) the Official Languages Program, and (iii) the rest of the Department's activities that are integral to the development and evolution of Canadian identity, as expressed through arts, culture, heritage and national celebrations and commemorations.[12] I will only discuss the first two, since they have very specific programs and policies in place pertaining to immigrants. A later section will describe the cross-government *A Canada for All: Canada's Action Plan Against Racism.*

Multiculturalism Program

The Multiculturalism Program, the most important program in the Canadian Heritage portfolio for the integration of newcomers, tends to focus on effecting institutional change.[13] The Multiculturalism Program recognizes the diversity of Canadians as a fundamental characteristic of Canadian society and is committed to a policy of multiculturalism designed to preserve and enhance the multicultural heritage of Canadians while working to achieve the equality of all Canadians in the economic, social, cultural, and political life of Canada. For the past decade the Multiculturalism Program has pursued three overall policy goals:

- *Identity:* Fostering a society that recognizes, respects and reflects a diversity of cultures such that people of all backgrounds feel a sense of belonging and attachment to Canada.
- *Social Justice:* Building a society that ensures fair and equitable treatment and that respects the dignity of people of all origins.
- *Civic Participation:* Developing active citizens with both the opportunity and the capacity to participate in shaping the future of their communities and their country.

Within the three broad goals, the program's priority is to meet evolving needs. In the 2005–06 Annual Report, these priorities were articulated as (i) building the capacity of ethnocultural/racial minorities to participate in public decision-making; (ii) helping public institutions to break down systemic barriers to diverse populations; (iii) helping federal institutions to integrate diversity considerations into policies, programs, and services; and (iv) encouraging communities and the broad public to engage in informed dialogue and sustained action to combat racism (GoC 2007b).[14] At present the Multiculturalism Program receives $17.2 million a year, plus additional support for the Community Historical Recognition Program.

The Community Historical Recognition Program was announced in 2006 as part of the Government of Canada's apology to the Chinese-Canadian community for the Chinese Head Tax that was charged for decades at the outset of the twentieth century.[15] A total of $24 million was allocated to this initiative, which provides funding for community-based projects linked to wartime measures and/or immigration restrictions (GoC 2007b). At the same time, a National Historical Recognition Program received $10 million to support federal initiatives that educate Canadians about these measures and restrictions and the impacts they have had on present-day Canadians (GoC 2006b).

Canadian Heritage must also table a report every year in Parliament on the working of the *Canadian Multiculturalism Act*. The Annual Reports lay out both the activities of the program itself and those of other federal departments and agencies. Thus, they provide an interesting catalogue of multiculturalism-related initiatives undertaken in any given year across the Government of Canada. In the summer of 2005, Multiculturalism Champions were nominated within federal institutions both to act as the chief contact for the submissions for the Annual Report and to help departments meet their obligations under the *Canadian Multiculturalism Act* (GoC 2006c). For newcomer integration in Canada, two longer-term investments are of interest: (i) justice, security and policing; and (ii) foreign credential recognition.

Justice, Security, and Policing

Justice, security, and policing concerns took centre stage in the wake of the terrorist attacks of September 11, 2001. Canada experienced a short-lived upswing in hate crimes directed against minorities (Biles and Ibrahim 2002), and tensions between police and security forces and minority communities were exacerbated. To address these concerns, the Secretary of State for Multiculturalism held a Forum on Policing in a Multicultural Society in February 2003.[16] Law enforcement agencies, Aboriginal, ethnic and racial communities, academia and public institutions discussed and developed strategies in three areas: recognizing and embracing diversity; policing with a national security agenda at the forefront; and overseeing and governing civilians.

Follow-up work has included a conference in Winnipeg, the launch of the Law Enforcement Aboriginal Diversity Network (LEAD),[17] and *Embracing our Community Mosaic*, a three-year project of Saskatoon community leaders and police to engage the community, offer better diversity training to police officers, and develop recruitment strategies to make the police service more representative (GoC 2005b). To date, approximately 200 law enforcement organizations and 600 individual members have joined LEAD (GoC 2007b).

Foreign Credential Recognition

A key cross-government concern reiterated in the Speech from the Throne in early 2004 and in the Conservative election platform in the 2006 federal election was the importance of foreign credential recognition. While the federal lead for this file lies with HRSDC, Canadian Heritage has undertaken a number of these initiatives, including a policy development roundtable on the integration of internationally trained professionals and trades people, and the British Columbian network of associations for foreign trained professionals (GoC 2003a, 14). These initiatives have led to the creation of Capacity Canada, which, in turn, has scored some important successes. Capacity Canada has gathered and shared best practices from across the country and has been influential in drafting Ontario's *Fair Access to Regulated Professions Act* (Government of Ontario 2006; Buhel and Janzen 2007).

Official Languages Program

The second critical program at Canadian Heritage is the Official Languages Program. The bulk of the resources of this program are targeted at either teaching Canadians one of the official languages or providing services to official language minority communities. However, during the past five years, it has developed an expanded interest in the connection between francophone minority communities and immigration and diversity (GoC 2007c). In order to maintain francophone minority communities and enhance linguistic duality in Canada, newcomers and minorities must be both attracted to these communities and comfortable enough to remain members of them. To facilitate this connection, the federal government has started a variety of initiatives. In March 2003, it released its *Action Plan for Official Languages.* The plan focused on three major areas: education, community development, and an exemplary public service. A budget of $751.3 million over five years was allocated to implement the plan. The majority of these funds are earmarked to provide services to official language minority communities across the country, but $55 million is specifically targeted at immigrant integration: $9 million over five years, and $2 million on-going in order to initiate activities aimed at attracting, settling, and integrating immigrants within francophone communities outside Quebec.

This plan was updated in September 2006, with the launch of the *Strategic Plan to Foster Immigration to Francophone Minority Communities*.[18] The key objective of the *Strategic Plan* is to increase the percentage of French-speaking immigrants by 2008: In 2001, about 3.1 percent of immigrants were French-speaking people who immigrated to francophone communities outside Quebec. The *Strategic Plan* has a goal of raising this to a minimum of 4.4 percent of overall immigration by 2008. It proposes to increase, in particular, the number of French-speaking economic class immigrants, and students in Francophone minority communities. The *Strategic Plan* also suggests these communities need to work in close partnership with federal, provincial and territorial governments to recruit people that meet their needs, and to help them succeed. It suggests strengthening a number of integration services, including language and skills training, community awareness and local support networks (Winnemore and Biles 2006).

A Canada for All: Canada's Action Plan Against Racism

Finally, in addition to its specific programs, Canadian Heritage is also the lead on the cross-government $56 million *A Canada for All: Canada's Action Plan Against Racism,* a five-year action plan involving Canadian Heritage, Human Resources and Social Development Canada, Justice Canada and Citizenship and Immigration Canada. It focuses on six priority areas:

1. Assisting victims and groups vulnerable to racism and related forms of discrimination;
2. Developing forward-looking approaches to promote diversity and combat racism;
3. Strengthening the role of civil society;
4. Strengthening regional and international co-operation;
5. Educating children and youth on diversity and anti-racism; and
6. Countering hate and bias (GoC 2005c).

To date, a wide range of activities have been funded under this initiative, including additional funding for the LEAD initiative described above. Canadian Heritage has also allocated $2.1 million to a Secretariat on the Inclusive Institutions Initiative. This Secretariat is based at Canadian Heritage within the Multiculturalism Program. It is designed to forge long-lasting collaboration with other federal institutions like Citizenship and Immigration Canada and Human Resources and Social Development Canada (GoC 2006e).

Human Resources and Social Development Canada (HRSDC)

HRSDC is one of the largest departments in the Government of Canada. Its mandate is to provide all Canadians with the tools they need to thrive and prosper in the workplace and community. It supports human capital development and labour market development and is dedicated to establishing a culture of lifelong learning for Canadians.

From the perspective of newcomer integration, almost all programs in HRSDC are important. HRSDC and Industry Canada are the lead departments for the 2002 Government of Canada's *Innovation Strategy*. This strategy is based on two papers that focused on what Canada must do to ensure equality of opportunity and economic innovation in a knowledge-based economy and society. HRSDC took the lead on one of these papers, *Knowledge Matters: Skills and Learning for Canadians* (2002a), while Industry Canada took the lead on the other, *Achieving Excellence: Investing in People, Knowledge and Opportunity* (2002b).

Knowledge Matters devotes an entire section to "Helping Immigrants Achieve Their Full Potential." It focuses on three key areas:

- Developing an integrated and transparent approach to the recognition of foreign credentials;
- Better supporting the integration of immigrants into Canada's labour market; and
- Helping immigrants achieve their full potential over their working lives.

In addition, the Government of Canada committed itself to two primary objectives in labour market policy: by 2010, raising the number of adult immigrants with post-secondary education from 58 percent (in 2000) to 65 percent; and reducing the income gap between immigrants and Canadian-born workers by 50 percent (GoC 2002a, 49–54).

Not surprisingly, then, immigrants have become a targeted population of increasing importance to HRSDC's programs. For example, Service Canada, Canada's one-stop service for all Canadians, has developed a *Newcomers to Canada Client Segment Strategy*, which targets newcomers in several key populations.[19] Service Canada has also recently started a *Multi-language Service Initiative Pilot Project*, which resulted in five different pilot projects on in-person multi-language service delivery in different locations across the country. These projects are currently being evaluated in order to ascertain whether they should be expanded across the Service Canada network (GoC 2007d). In addition, Service Canada provides services to the Foreign

Credentials Referral Office described in the CIC section above (GoC 2007g).

Immigrants are also a significant target population for general HRSDC programming in the Workplace Skills Initiative (WSI), which provides ongoing funding to businesses to promote awareness of workplace skills issues and to mobilize employers and workers to make workplaces more competitive, productive, and highly skilled. The WSI was created in 2005 with a budget of $125 million over three years. Eligible proposals to this initiative must be in one of the following areas: Newcomers to Canada; Older Workers; or Low-Skilled Workers. In the first round of proposals, 15 projects worth $30 million were funded, including two in the Newcomers category, receiving nearly $3 million: one proposed by the University of Ottawa to develop and pilot-test bilingual blended-learning modules to support human resources professionals and immigrants to understand the barriers to integration into Canada's workplaces and to implement strategies to overcome these barriers; and a second by the Hamilton-based Settlement and Integration Services Organization for an Employer Toolkit for hiring and retention of internationally-trained professionals (GoC 2007e).

In addition to its regular programs, HRSDC also has several programs that play a special role in the integration of newcomers: (i) foreign credential recognition, (ii) the labour program, and (iii) the housing and homelessness branch.[20]

Foreign Credential Recognition Program

Foreign credential recognition is perhaps the most commonly cited obstacle to labour market participation of highly skilled immigrants in Canada, and remains one of the most complex.[21] HRSDC chairs the interdepartmental committee on immigrant labour market integration[22] that is responsible for tackling accreditation issues on behalf of the Government of Canada and continues to work with the provinces and territories as well as the professional associations and the sector councils[23] to ensure that this problem receives the attention it deserves.

The Foreign Credential Recognition Program (FCRP) provides the primary support for foreign credential recognition. FCRP has been allocated $68 million over a six-year period (2003–04 to 2008–09). It works with public and private sector partners to "develop coherent, transparent, fair and equitable foreign credential assessment and recognition processes to enhance labour market outcomes of foreign-trained individuals in targeted occupations and sectors" (GoC 2007f). Initially, the program targeted nurses, doctors, and engineers, but it has since expanded to cover a wider cross-section of regulated professions, as well as playing a role in facilitating foreign credential recognition in non-regulated occupations, such as aviation maintenance and tourism (GoC 2006d).

As of October 2006, 66 projects had received funding,[24] and agreements had been reached with seven sector councils (GoC 2007f). These projects include those designed to accelerate the assessment and recognition of credentials; those that implement the enhanced language training initiative described above in the CIC section; and those that provide up-to-date and pertinent labour market information.[25]

One of the most common issues surrounding foreign credential recognition is the difficulty in getting the correct information. In order to ensure that accurate information is available, the Government of Canada has allocated $38.1 million over five years to allow HRSDC and CIC to create the online Going to Canada Portal and thereafter $7.1 million a year to maintain it. This portal is a one-stop Internet resource for prospective immigrants to Canada. A key component of this portal is the Working in Canada Tool, which provides labour market information to prospective immigrants.[26] HRSDC provides targeted information on the labour market, employment, job search, foreign credential recognition,[27] essential skills, and workers' rights, as well as online skills assessments and information regarding learning opportunities that will assist in attaining Canadian credentials (EKOS 2007).

In addition to the foreign credential recognition program that focuses on the immigrants' side of the two-way street of integration, the labour program and the housing and homelessness branch at HRSDC focus on the other side of the street.

Labour Program

The Labour Program is a key partner in *A Canada for All: Canada's Action Plan Against Racism.* Its objective is to promote a fair, safe, healthy, stable, co-operative, and productive work environment, which contributes to the social and economic well-being of all Canadians. It received $13 million of the $56 million available under the *Action Plan.*

Included within this program is responsibility for Employment Equity.[28] An extremely high proportion of visible minorities[29] are newcomers to Canada (84 percent are first generation, 14 percent are second generation, and 2 percent are third-plus generation). As a result, the *Employment Equity Act* and its program have an important impact on the labour market outcomes of newcomers. As the chapter on economic integration pointed out, immigrants are not yet fully integrated into the federal public service or regulated industries covered by the *Employment Equity Act*. For this reason, the labour program continues to work with departments across the federal government and regulated employers to improve this situation.

Housing and Homelessness

Labour market conditions and housing are not unrelated issues. Indeed, a recent survey undertaken by Ipsos Reid for RBC Financial Services Inc. showed that the top two concerns of polled immigrants were having a good job and owning their home (Beauchesne 2007). According to the Longitudinal Survey of Immigrants to Canada, a Statistics Canada and CIC survey, approximately 30 percent of newcomers reported their chief housing problem as cost. This varied across the country, with 37 percent in Ontario reporting problems versus 20 percent in Quebec (GoC 2003b, 18).

In the most severe cases this can lead to homelessness. As early as 1999, homelessness was becoming a crisis in large and small cities across Canada, largely driven by the lack of affordable housing and cuts to social services (Layton 2000). In response to this crisis, the Government of Canada announced the National Homelessness Initiative, a three-year initiative designed to help ensure community access to programs, services, and support for alleviating homelessness in communities located in all provinces and territories. The Government of Canada renewed the National Homelessness Initiative for an additional three years, with an investment of another $405 million. When the program was changed to the Homelessness Partnering Strategy in 2007, it received another $269.6 million over two years. For all three stages of homelessness investments, immigrants and refugees have been one of the identified target client groups.

As Ballay and Bulthuis (2004) note, "historically, new immigrants and refugees have often been housed in precarious situations"; but they observe that this situation has worsened today to the point where "immigrants and refugees are increasingly falling under the category of absolutely homeless" (119–23). This is especially true of refugees and undocumented migrants. While the seriousness of the situation is presently most pronounced in Toronto (home to the largest percentage of recent newcomers to Canada), there is concern that this phenomenon could be replicated in other cities receiving increasing numbers of newcomers. Ballay and Bulthuis observe:

> Co-ordination across the government orders and the various sectors that
> address the needs of newcomers, as well as between the homelessness

assistance system and settlement and integration system is necessary. Funds are often directed through separate streams—including shelter capital costs, settlement and integration staff and employment supports—inherently limiting the dialogue among those involved (2004, 122).

The Homelessness Partnering Strategy continues to explore the intersection between immigration and homelessness through an extensive research program that is presently underway.

Similarly, the Canada Mortgage and Housing Corporation (CMHC), which is now a member of the HRSDC portfolio, also has an interest in the housing experiences of immigrants. In particular, research has suggested that discrimination remains an obstacle for immigrants and minorities (Teixeira 2006) and that immigrants have difficulties finding affordable housing (Mendez, Hiebert and Wyly 2006). To help tackle this problem, CMHC has published "The Newcomer's Guide to Canadian Housing."

While most integration issues pertain to multiple jurisdictions, housing and labour market issues—especially credential recognition—are issues where the federal role is less direct, and the role of other orders of government is more decisive. However, polled service provider organizations have stated that in order to maintain consistency of delivery and ensure a continuing focus on services to newcomers,[30] not to mention tackling issues related to secondary migration (Houle 2007), a continued federal involvement in the settlement and integration of newcomers is vital (GoC 2005d). However, provincial governments have become increasingly active and important to the integration of immigrants.

Provincial Governments

The *Immigration and Refugee Protection Act* (2002) allows the Minister of Citizenship and Immigration Canada to enter into agreements to share responsibility for immigration with Canada's ten provinces and three territories. The *Canada–Quebec Accord* is the most comprehensive of these agreements. Signed in 1991, it gives Quebec selection powers and control over its own settlement services. Canada retains responsibility for defining immigrant categories, setting levels, and enforcement.[31]

The federal government has also negotiated substantive agreements with Manitoba (1996), British Columbia (1998) and Ontario (2005). Manitoba and British Columbia deliver settlement and integration services within their jurisdictions, rather than through CIC;[32] and in Ontario, CIC has agreed to increase expenditures on integration and settlement programs in the province.

All of the other provinces (plus Yukon) have also signed agreements with the Government of Canada, although they are less elaborate than those of Quebec, Manitoba, British Columbia, and Ontario.[33] According to these agreements, settlement and integration programs continue to be delivered by CIC, but the provincial and territorial governments have the authority to select some immigrants through provincial nominee programs to meet specific labour-market needs.

This latest rise in provincial interest in immigration was given a boost in October 2002, when then-Minister for Citizenship and Immigration Canada, Denis Coderre, convened a meeting in Winnipeg of federal, provincial, and territorial ministers responsible for immigration. This meeting was the first meeting of immigration ministers since Confederation in 1867, even though it is one of only two shared areas of jurisdiction according to the *Constitution Act* (GoC 2002c).

At this inaugural national meeting on immigration, participants agreed that the provinces, territories and federal government would work together to:

- break down the barriers to the recognition of foreign credentials;
- attract and select highly skilled workers;
- expedite the entry of foreign students, including transition to permanent status for those who choose to remain;
- enhance settlement services to facilitate newcomers' full participation in Canadian society; and
- share best practices.

The ministers met a second time in January 2004 in British Columbia. They discussed their region's initiatives to attract skilled immigrants and help them better integrate into Canadian society and the labour market. These initiatives included measures to enhance language training, to expand Provincial Nominee Programs, and to attract and retain international students in Canada. The ministers also highlighted the importance of providing better labour market information to immigrants to improve outcomes for newcomers to Canada (GoC 2004).

The third meeting took place in Gatineau, Quebec, in November 2004. The ministers agreed to work together on an immigration framework for attracting, settling, and retaining newcomers in all regions of Canada, as well as approaches to improve the integration of foreign-trained professionals and other workers into the labour market (GoC 2004e). This meeting was followed by a fourth meeting that took place in Ottawa in November 2005. Here, the ministers agreed on strategic directions on immigration. These included improved selection (multi-year levels planning, development of an in-Canada economic class, issues of mix, and a more aggressive and effective international promotion of Canada and all its regions), improved outcomes for immigrants (skills utilization, funding, improved information), increased regionalization, and improved client services (GoC 2005e). Subsequent meetings held in June 2006 and May 2007 further solidified the shared strategic directions agreed upon at the 2005 Ottawa meeting.

Although Quebec, Manitoba, and British Columbia are the only provinces that have assumed responsibility for integration services, the other provinces are still active participants in these issues. To a great extent, provincial participation in integration is due to the fact that many sectors integral to the integration process are the responsibility of provincial governments, such as housing, education, and health. In addition, concerns with population size and labour market growth have encouraged the provinces (especially those that have received fewer immigrants in recent years) to become more actively engaged (Casey 2007; Hurley 2007).

Accordingly, many provincial governments have recently begun to articulate explicit immigration policies and to create dedicated departments or bureaucratic units responsible for immigration. For example, since 2005, Alberta, New Brunswick, Newfoundland and Labrador, Nova Scotia, and Ontario have published immigration plans, and Quebec has continued its practice of publishing a three-year plan.

In 2006–07, there were over 1,200 provincial employees across the country working directly on immigration and immigrant integration. In addition, the provincial governments spent in excess of $260 million dollars on immigration and immigrant integration (see Table 1).

To some extent, the creation of these bureaucratic units as the leads for providing services to immigrants has helped co-ordinate efforts within provincial ministries; however, it is still difficult to ascertain the full range of integration-related policies that exist at the provincial level. For example, integration-related expenses in departments responsible for education, employment, and health remain hidden in most cases: Calculating these costs remains a challenge for provincial governments, just as it is for the other orders of government.

Apart from major expenses such as health care and education (including English and/or French as a second language education), the provincial governments are on the front line of foreign credential recognition, since many professional organizations and regulations are managed at the provincial level (Mata 1999). For example, in 1992 , the Alberta government released *Bridging the Gap: A Report of the Task Force on the Recognition of Foreign Qualifications,* which recommended establishing a central agency to assess foreign education and credentials.

Table 1: Provincial Budgets, Full-Time Equivalents, and Web Addresses for Immigration-Related Programming

Province	Lead Organization	Operating Budget	# FTE	Web Address	Public Policy Document / Plan
British Columbia	Ministry of Attorney General (Settlement and Multiculturalism Division)	$7,156,000 (2006/07)[1]	38	www.ag.gov.bc/immigration	No
Alberta	Employment, Immigration and Industry	$5,993,000[2]	33[3]	www.alberta-canada.com/immigration	"Supporting Immigrants and Immigration to Alberta" (2005)
Saskatchewan	Immigration Branch, Advanced Education, Employment, and Labour	$4,668,000[4]	23[5]	www.immigration.gov.sk.ca	No
Manitoba	Manitoba Labour and Immigration	$18,233,000[6]	48	www.gov.mb.ca/labour	No
Ontario	Ontario Ministry of Citizenship and Immigration	$92,095,000[7]	280[8]	www.citizenship.gov.on.ca	Strategic Plan for Settlement and Language Training
Quebec	Ministère de l'Immigration et des Communautés culturelles	$124,296,500[9]	843[10]	www.micc.gouv.qc.ca	Plan Stratégique 2005–2008
New Brunswick	Population Growth Secretariat	$3,000,000[11]	14[12]	www.gnb.ca/immigration	Be Our Future: New Brunswick's Population Growth Strategy (2008)
Nova Scotia	Office of Immigration	$3,018,000[13]	13.64	www.novascotiaimmigration.com	Nova Scotia Immigration Strategy (January 2005)

Prince Edward Island	Department of Development and Technology (Immigration Services)	>$1,641,540[14]	3	www.gov.pe.ca/immigration	No
Newfoundland and Labrador	Department of Human Resources, Labour and Employment (Office of Immigration and Multiculturalism)	$2,000,000[15]	2+[16]	www.hrle.gov.nl.ca/hrle/immigration	Diversity, Opportunity and Growth: An Immigration Strategy for Newfoundland and Labrador (March 2007)

Notes:

[1] Government of British Columbia. 2007. "Ministry of Attorney General: Law Reform, Justice and Legal Services to Government and Minister Responsible for Multiculturalism 2006/07 Annual Service Plan Report."

[2] Government of Alberta. 2007. "Employment, Immigration and Industry Annual Report 2006–07," p. 135.

[3] Counted from Government of Alberta on-line employee directory.

[4] Government of Saskatchewan. 2007. "Saskatchewan Advanced Education and Employment 2006/07 Annual Report," p. 20.

[5] Counted from Government of Saskatchewan on-line employee directory.

[6] Government of Manitoba. 2007. "'Labour and Immigration Annual Report 2006–2007." Note that the budget and FTE figures listed include both immigration and multiculturalism branches.

[7] Government of Ontario. 2007. "Results-based Briefing Book 2007–08 Ministry of Citizenship and Immigration."

[8] Note that the public FTE figure of 350 covers the entire department including both the women's and seniors' secretariats which combined represent about 1/5 of the budget of the department. A fair estimation of immigration FTEs might, therefore be 4/5, or the 280 listed in the table.

[9] Government of Quebec. 2007. "Rapport Annuel du Ministère de l'Immigration et des Communautés culturelles 2006–2007."

[10] An additional 563 part time workers, primarily teachers on call, were also employed by the Ministry in 2006–07.

[11] Government of New Brunswick. 2007. "Main Estimates 2007–8," p. 38.

[12] Counted from on-line directory of Government of New Brunswick employees.

[13] Government of Nova Scotia. 2007. "Nova Scotia Office of Immigration Annual Accountability Report for the Fiscal Year 2006–07."

[14] Government of PEI. 2006. "Annual Report Department of Development and Technology 2005–06." Note that the Population Secretariat's budget is not split off from general operating expenses of the Ministry so an exact budget figure is hard to uncover.

[15] Government of Newfoundland and Labrador. 2007. "International Students to be Covered Under Province's Medical Care Plan," Press Release, 5 June.

[16] Only two people were found in the Government of Newfoundland and Labrador's on-line government directory.

In Ontario, the Ontario Task Force Report (1989) on the *Access to Professions and Trades* acknowledged the presence of several professional accreditation barriers in the province. Since that time, a province-wide coalition called the Ontario Network for Access to Professions and Trades has been established to advocate for accreditation for foreign trained workers. In 2006, Ontario broke new ground with its *Fair Access to Regulated Professions Act* that requires all 34 regulated professions in Ontario to have licensing processes that are "fair, open and timely assessment" of the credentials of foreign trained professionals. It also created the Office of the Fairness Commissioner to oversee the process (Government of Ontario 2006).

At the same time, provincial governments have also adapted strategies for addressing the other side of the integration two-way street, and most have multiculturalism programs in place to tackle barriers and discrimination. Space does not allow for an exploration of these strategies here; but Garcea (2006) describes the evolution of these policies and their present-day incarnations.

Municipal Governments

Given the overwhelmingly urban nature of immigration flows to Canada, it is hardly surprising that municipalities have become more vocal about demanding a seat at the table when immigration, integration, and diversity issues are discussed. Moreover, due to cutbacks and provincial downloading, municipalities are becoming more central in the delivery of many programs that impact the successful integration of newcomers to Canada. In May 2001, former Prime Minister Jean Chrétien established a Liberal Caucus Task Force on Urban Issues that issued its final report in November 2002 recommending three priority areas: (i) a national affordable housing program, (ii) a national infrastructure program, and (iii) a national transportation program. The Federation of Canadian Municipalities presented these arguments in its *Brief to the Prime Minister's Caucus Task Force on Urban Issues*:

> Despite the fact that municipalities provide services to new immigrants and refugees, immigration policy rarely takes into account municipal perspectives. Municipal governments welcome new Canadians in their communities not only because they contribute to a richer cultural fabric, but also because they fuel economic growth. But while there are benefits, there are also costs. Often municipalities must provide income support,

subsidized housing, emergency shelter, child care, and health care, and often must provide these services in numerous languages. The federal government has failed to recognize these costs, and has not provided adequate financial support for them (Federation of Canadian Municipalities 2002, under "Immigration").

Although the Federation of Canadian Municipalities was disappointed with the outcome of the task force, the federal government continued to demonstrate that urban issues were a priority: the 2003 *Speech from the Throne* underlined this priority by arguing that Canada must strengthen our cities by bringing "municipalities to the national decision-making table" (Martin 2003). The short-lived Martin Government created a Minister of State for Infrastructure and Communities with a special emphasis on cities.

Judy Sgro, who had also been a city councillor for ten years and chair of the Liberal Caucus Task Force on Urban Issues, was appointed as the Minister of Citizenship and Immigration. While holding that position, she began to find ways to bring municipalities to the table. For example, she met with both her Ontario counterpart and seven municipal leaders in February 2004. She observed that the meeting provided "a good first step as cities become engaged in the planning of Canada's immigration program" (GoC 2004f). Ultimately, this led to the inclusion of an annex on partnerships with municipalities in the *Canada-Ontario Immigration Agreement*.

Despite the fact that cities do not possess the political or financial authority over many of the services important to the successful integration of newcomers, many cities have been extremely creative and innovative in their response to integration issues. The following examples are just a few of some of these pioneering municipal projects.

Winnipeg's "Homegrown Economic Development Plan" calls for several strategic priorities, including "Closing the Skills Gap and Enhancing Immigration" (City of Winnipeg 2001). Building on this plan, in 2002, the City of Winnipeg adopted the Winnipeg Private Refugee Sponsorship Assurance Program. This program represents the first time a city government has been recognized as a partner in immigration and population growth strategy. Its objective is to increase the number of immigrants going to Winnipeg. For the pilot program, the City of Winnipeg has set aside $250,000 of municipal funds, which can be accessed to cover refugee support in circumstances including those when a private sponsor is no longer able to meet its commitment. In addition to other elements of the agreement, the three governments acknowledged that "adequate support systems need to be in place for refugees to ensure their settlement and integration in Winnipeg."

Not surprisingly, Toronto, Canada's largest immigrant receiving municipality and one of the most diverse cities in the world, has long embraced diversity—even adopting "Diversity Our Strength" as the city's official motto. As a result of its dedication to diversity issues, the city has a range of diversity-related working groups including one on immigrant and refugee issues. This working group gathers community input from over 40 community coalitions/agencies and addresses the following issues:

- The City of Toronto's Plan of Action for the Elimination of Racism and Discrimination
- Immigrants' access to professions and trades
- Methodologies for measuring progress made by immigrants and refugees in their settlement
- City services and how they can be accessible and beneficial to the immigrants and refugees living in Toronto
- Federal and provincial legislation and programs that affect immigrants and refugees

This solid groundwork bore fruit when the tripartite *Canada-Ontario-Toronto Memorandum of Understanding on Immigration and Settlement* was signed in September 2006. This Memorandum of Understanding establishes a framework for the three orders of government to discuss matters related to immigration and settlement in the City of Toronto, with a particular emphasis on citizenship and civic engagement, access to employment and services, and access to education and training. It pledges to be guided by principles of horizontality and co-operation, with an emphasis on results. Given the complex array of actors in the Toronto area, this agreement may facilitate a new level of co-ordination and avoid overlapping of policies and programs.

A third municipal example is Calgary. In Calgary, citizens approached a city councillor in 1999 with a plan to work together to make Calgary more inclusive. This meeting resulted in the formation of the Calgary Cultural and Racial Diversity Task Force in 2000, which comprised community groups, business leaders, city councillors, city staff, and provincial and federal government representatives. The Task Force led to the development of twelve strategies for dealing with a wide range of issues, including discrimination, stakeholder involvement, employment, diversity training, accreditation, curriculum and teaching resources, and access for minorities to systems and services. The project report, *Diversity Calgary: Moving Forward* (City of Calgary 2002), highlighted some of the best practices and included a detailed implementation plan. Unfortunately, the initiative was disbanded in June 2005 due to "differences in vision, lack of funding, a disconnect between community supporters and decision makers, and unclear infrastructure" (City of Calgary 2006). The City argued that its *Fair Calgary Policy*, along with initiatives of other orders of government, were sufficient to ensure the integration of immigrants.[34] Interestingly, the 2007 *Vital Signs* report of the Calgary Foundation graded the immigrant experience in Calgary as a C– (Fortney 2007). The transient nature of many government initiatives, like *Diversity Calgary*, will be revisited in the considerations section of this chapter.

Like the provincial governments, municipal governments have recognized the need for both centralized leadership and widespread engagement across their organizations to ensure the success of immigrant integration into their communities. Some municipalities, such as Montreal, Toronto, and Vancouver, have long recognized this need. Others, such as Calgary and Edmonton, have moved in this direction relatively recently.

Other cities, such as Ottawa, have only just begun to organize themselves effectively to ensure the successful integration of newcomers. As recently as the municipal amalgamations of 2000, when the new City of Ottawa replaced eleven smaller municipal governments, diversity was so far off the radar screen that when the advisory committee structure was first devised, immigration and diversity were not even on the original list. However, in 2007, Ottawa passed a recommendation to establish the Immigration Ottawa Initiative to facilitate the development of a community-led, city-wide labour market integration strategy for immigrants. While this approach is not as comprehensive as Toronto's, it marks the first time that the City of Ottawa has sought to create a leader organization to ensure that newcomers are effectively integrated into the city (City of Ottawa 2007a).

The integration of newcomers is a responsibility of all aspects of government. In the case of Ottawa, in preparing the business case for the Immigration Ottawa Initiative, municipal officials prepared an inventory of projects funded or undertaken by the city to assist the integration of newcomers. They found that four of the six major departments of the city and twelve of their seventeen branches[35] were already actively working in this area, with over 100 initiatives—information sessions, approximately $1 million for services, projects, cultural endeavours specific to immigrant and minority communities, and investments in programs to reduce barriers to universal services, such as those provided through the community health centres (City of Ottawa 2007b).

Community Partners

Of course, governments are not the only key players in immigrant integration in Canada. One of the principal differences between the Canadian approach and those of many other countries is that all three orders of government often deliver services through third parties. The result is a thriving non-governmental sector that works in partnership with governments. This sector is populated by an extremely complex array of organizations, some of which deliver services on behalf of governments, while others are funders of integration programs. For the purposes of this chapter, I will briefly explore different types of organization: (i) the immigrant service provider organizations (SPOs); (ii) the multicultural or ethnic, racial, religious, and linguistic minority organizations; (iii) the issue-based organizations; (iv) the so-called "universal" organizations; and (v) the private sector.

Service Provider Organizations (SPOs)

The majority of Government of Canada–funded integration and settlement services are delivered through immigrant-serving organizations, or service provider organizations (SPOs). The government's priorities are official language acquisition, access to employment, and intergroup relations. Organizations that can apply for SPO funding include businesses, not-for-profit groups, non-governmental organizations, community groups, educational institutions, and individuals. Moreover, other levels of government, including provincial, territorial or municipal governments, may also apply.

SPOs receive federal dollars and then deliver programs such as orientation and information, official language instruction, interpretation and translation, assistance with applications, assistance to sponsors, counselling, advocacy, referrals and assistance with health and housing, employment searches, legal aid, and refugee claimants. CIC has federal contribution agreements with over 300 SPOs that deliver both private sponsorship and settlement programs and services. Importantly, many of these SPOs also receive funding from other orders of government and other funding sources, such as the United Way.

SPOs are efficient in providing these services because volunteers at many SPOs can serve immigrants in their mother tongues. In addition, many volunteers are themselves recent immigrants, so they understand the displacement of the immigration experience. As the composition of immigrants changes, the organizations can relatively easily adapt their staffing complement to address cultural and linguistic needs of new clients. As a result, the SPO arrangement minimizes expenses. An excellent example of an SPO is the Ottawa Community Immigrant Services Organization, a community-based non-profit agency that provides services to newcomers, including language training, counselling, housing information, and legal referrals. This organization receives funds from all three levels of government, including the federal departments of Citizenship and Immigration Canada and Canadian Heritage, the Ontario Ministry of Health, and the City of Ottawa.

The greatest level of co-ordination within the integration field in Canada has occurred among the SPOs. For example, the Alberta Association of Immigrant Serving Agencies has been active since 1980 as an umbrella organization for immigrant-serving agencies in Alberta. Similar umbrella organizations exist in other parts of the country at both the regional and municipal scales. For example, Ottawa's six local settlement agencies have formed a loose entity entitled Local Agencies Serving Immigrants, which meets quarterly and ensures co-ordination and the avoidance of overlap between the SPOs in Ottawa. On a regional scale, the Atlantic Regional Association for Immigrant Serving Agencies was established in 1994 to bring together the seventeen immigrant-serving agencies in the region (now down to fourteen) (Smith Green & Associates Inc. 2001).

CIC has also moved over the last few years to encourage co-ordination among the SPOs on a national scale. The Government of Canada's Voluntary Sector Initiative (Brock 2006) funded a settlement sector project entitled "Strengthening the Settlement Sector." This project brought together SPOs from across the country at two national conferences (the first held in Kingston, Ontario, in 2001, and the second in Calgary in October 2003). The overall objectives were to provide a national forum for meaningful dialogue around priority policy issues, to assist in enhancing the overall capacity of the sector to develop policy, and to facilitate learning within the sector. This initiative has evolved following the two national conferences. Work has continued, especially that of the smaller community strategy group, which has been developing a small centre tool box to assist smaller communities in attracting and retaining newcomers.[36] This group has also created the Canadian

Immigrant Settlement Sector Alliance,[37] a national umbrella of service provider organizations. This co-ordination effort marks a significant departure for a previously fragmented SPO sector and will act as a national counterpart to the Canadian Council for Refugees, which draws together stakeholders working on refugee issues.

Multicultural Organizations

Multicultural organizations are non-governmental organizations whose mandate is to ensure that all Canadians can express and maintain their cultural identity, take pride in their ancestry, are treated equally, and have a sense of belonging in Canada. These organizations receive funding from all different levels of government and the private sector to carry out a range of projects, including community outreach and capacity building, anti-racism, and the maintenance of cultural heritage. There are two major types of NGOs in this area: ethno-specific organizations that look after the concerns and needs of a specific community, and broader umbrella organizations that address issues that cut across community lines.

Ethno-specific organizations tend to exist at multiple levels, with national umbrella organizations represented on the Canadian Ethnocultural Council's board. The work of the Canadian Cambodian Association of Ontario illustrates how ethno-specific organizations can assist in the integration of newcomers. This group was recently funded by the Multiculturalism Program (Canadian Heritage) for a project entitled "Lao and Cambodian Youth and Academic Initiative." The aim of the project was to get Cambodian and Laotian parents actively engaged in school decision-making.

The Canadian Ethnocultural Council is a non-profit, non-partisan coalition of national ethnocultural umbrella organizations which, in turn, represent a cross-section of ethnocultural groups across Canada. Its objectives are to ensure the preservation, enhancement, and sharing of the cultural heritage of Canadians; the removal of barriers that prevent some Canadians from participating fully and equally in society; the elimination of racism; and the preservation of a united Canada.

Smaller umbrella organizations exist in most provinces and major municipalities. For example, the Multicultural Association of Fredericton has recently been working with the Multiculturalism Program (Canadian Heritage) on three projects: (i) Multicultural Leadership and Diversity Competency; (ii) Responding to Racism; and (iii) Capacity Building in Youth.[38] Similarly, the provincial umbrella organization, the

New Brunswick Multicultural Council, has been funded to bring communities across the province together to address common concerns.

Issue-Based Organizations

Unlike multicultural organizations, the objective of issue-based organizations is to address one or more integration or diversity challenges or issues, such as racism and hate crime, media awareness, health, housing, education, or social justice. For example, the Canadian Race Relations Foundation (CRRF) is an arms-length crown corporation created in 1996. As part of the Japanese-Canadian Redress Agreement, the CRRF received an endowment of $24 million to combat racism across Canada. Every year, it invests roughly $1 million in anti-racism education and training, community-based initiatives countering racism, and research (CRRF 2007).

Universal Organizations

Universal organizations are large, generally not-for-profit organizations that respond to a multitude of issues facing Canadians. For example, the United Way of Canada is a network of locally run organizations that focuses on increasing the organized capacity of people to care for one another. It creates a common ground where labour, business, community leaders, and government come to the table to identify needs and solve problems. It helps build—idea by idea, solution by solution—the communities of tomorrow, delivering health and social services.

Recently, the United Way has taken an increasing interest in immigration. As in the case of municipalities, each United Way has taken a different approach to addressing the needs and concerns of newcomers. Not surprisingly, the United Ways in major immigrant-receiving cities, such as Toronto, are significantly further ahead than those in cities with little recent immigration, or where large-scale immigration is a relatively recent phenomenon. In April 2004, the United Way of Greater Toronto and the Canadian Council on Social Development jointly produced a report entitled "Poverty By Postal Code." The report explored the dense pockets of poverty in certain Toronto-area neighbourhoods, most of which had extremely high concentrations of immigrants. This report led to the announcement of the Neighbourhood Strategy in 2005, which seeks to strengthen 13 under-served inner-city neighbourhoods. In 2006, the United Way spent nearly $14 million in these neighbourhoods, with an additional $400,000 allocated directly to newcomers (United Way of Greater Toronto 2006).

Other United Way organizations in cities with fewer immigrants than Toronto have also begun to develop an immigrant focus. For example, in 2002, United Way Ottawa funded a conference to focus attention on newcomer and diversity issues in Ottawa. "Building the Ottawa Mosaic" garnered attention and encouraged local stakeholders to work together to tackle integration issues. At the same, United Way Ottawa shifted its philosophy away from fund-raising and towards community-building. After research and consultations, it decided to focus on six key impact areas, one of which was new Canadians and immigrants.[39]

As a result, United Way Ottawa created Impact Councils which comprise volunteers who are leaders in their respective fields. These councils are tasked with developing strategies for the Ottawa United Way, including the allocation of nearly $15 million annually to local agencies for community projects. The New Canadians and Immigrants Impact Council has provided funds for community projects ($357,435 in 2006 and $482,472 in 2007) as well as pursuing several strategic objectives: working with the United Way itself to make it more reflective of diversity; working with immigrant communities to facilitate civic engagement; and bringing together employers in the city to reduce employment barriers for new Canadians (United Way Ottawa n.d.).

Private Sector

The underemployment and the underutilization of immigrants in the Canadian workforce (Reitz 2001) is an issue of concern not just for the government and immigrant serving organizations, but for Canadian businesses as well. The private sector, which comprises businesses and individuals, is becoming more aware that the failure to integrate highly skilled immigrants into the workforce has a significant negative impact on their industries. Thus, the private sector is now working in partnership with other sectors of Canadian society to accelerate the integration of immigrants into the workforce by providing innovative ways to obtain Canadian experience, speed up accreditation of foreign training and education, and remove other systematic barriers.

For example, the Halifax Chamber of Commerce published a discussion paper on immigration, recommending that Nova Scotia bring together stakeholders to develop a co-ordinated plan for increasing immigration to Nova Scotia (2004). The report argued that the fact that immigration rates in Nova Scotia were declining at the same time that population growth in the province was decreasing was creating a significant problem for Nova Scotia's labour force. Immigration was seen to be an important factor in economic growth for the province, and the Chamber of Commerce encouraged the province to take on a more active role in this area.

Other examples include projects designed to engage employers. Again, not surprisingly Toronto has been a leader. Following the Toronto City Summit Alliance meetings in 2003, the City established the Toronto Region Immigrant Employment Council (TRIEC). TRIEC is a partnership of employers, labour, occupational regulatory bodies, post-secondary institutions, assessment service providers, community organizations, and three levels of government, which over four years has placed 660 immigrants in bridge-to-work internships with over 250 employers; matched over 2,000 skilled immigrants in mentoring partnerships; and worked with almost 400 employers to raise awareness of immigrant integration (TRIEC 2007).

Other cities, such as Waterloo and Ottawa, have followed suit. The Waterloo Region Immigrant Employment Network (WRIEN) was created in 2006, following a local process that established the necessary partnerships to launch a collaborative enterprise of this nature (McFadden and Janzen 2007). In Ottawa, the Internationally Trained Workers Project created by the Canadian Labour Business Council, the United Way / Centraide Ottawa, and Local Agencies Serving Immigrants has examined the problem of underemployed immigrants and the best ways to rectify this problem. It has recommended encouraging businesses to sponsor work experience programs, such as internships, job shadowing, and mentorship programs, and to develop workplace language programs (Adey and Gagnon 2007).

Considerations and Challenges

The multi-level efforts show that the integration of immigrants is truly a societal endeavour. Widespread engagement with integration clearly gives Canada an immigration advantage and has positioned Canada well relative to most other immigrant-receiving countries (Winnemore and Biles 2006). However, multi-level programming has some concomitant challenges. The biggest challenge is co-ordination—how best to share information and best practices among both immigrants themselves and with others involved in integration. Continuity of programming also remains a significant issue and contributes to challenges in evaluating outcomes. These are not insurmountable challenges, but they are also not insignificant ones.

Co-ordination

The most pressing of the challenges is co-ordination (GoC 2004c; GoC 2005d). In an environment of finite resources (both human and financial), duplication and overlap have to be minimized, and major players must work together. Recent and encouraging movement in this area has included closer relations among at least the federal and provincial governments,[40] and increasing relations with municipal ones too (for example, the tripartite agreement between the City of Toronto, Ontario, and Canada). Similarly, better co-ordination can be seen in the community partners sphere, where the arrival of the Canadian Immigrant Settlement Sector Alliance signals a new level of national collaboration among service provider organizations.

However, there remains a great deal of latitude for organizations to work in silos. For example, there is no obligation for the provincial governments of Quebec, Manitoba, British Columbia, and now Ontario to share their evaluation results with their federal colleagues.[41] The result is a fragmented system where expenditures and outcomes are very difficult to track, even within an order of government. Collaborative shared information would be useful to all levels of government. For example, the federal government could create an annual inventory of federally-funded activities and expenditures, like the annual reports on multiculturalism, employment equity, official languages, and human rights, which are already tabled in Parliament. A similar endeavour covering provincial and potentially municipal programming would also be extremely useful, but would obviously complicate the matter considerably. This volume, in a way, establishes a precedent and subsequent iterations could tackle this kind of multi-sectoral reporting.

Information

Related to co-ordination is the flow of information. If co-ordination and the sharing of information and best practices remains a major challenge for those providing services to immigrants, imagine the challenge immigrants face in gathering the relevant information they need to ensure integration success.

This challenge has been recognized, and work has begun to help resolve it. Unfortunately, much of it has also been undertaken in silos and poses a new co-ordination challenge. For example, the Government of Canada has attempted to create one-stop shopping with Service Canada and the Going to Canada Portal, while cities have attempted to provide similar services with their 311 telephone number, and NGOs have begun to do the same with 211 numbers (Morris 2007). The Foreign Credentials Referral Office is another example of a federal information site for prospective and recent immigrants to find the relevant information on credential recognition. Unfortunately, it is one more website among many, and evaluations of integration programs suggest that newcomers may not be actively searching these materials out (GoC 2005d).

There are, of course, other promising information initiatives, including the Going to Canada immigration portal and the newcomer information centres. As well, an Ontario pilot project promotes CIC's immigrant settlement and adaptation program in ethnic newspapers and in areas where immigrants gather, such as ethnic restaurants and cultural venues. But there is no agreed-upon systemic approach to trying to reach immigrants.

Equally important is the lack of spaces where those who provide integration services and support can share past practices (both the good practices to emulate and the terrible practices to avoid). The national venues where this kind of exchange can be done are *ad hoc* or one-off events, like the two settlement sector conferences described above.

One notable exception is the Metropolis Project, now in its third five-year funding phase. The Metropolis Project is an international network for comparative research and public policy development on migration, diversity, and immigrant integration in cities in Canada and around the world. It brings together local organizations through five university-based Centres of Excellence and brings together national organizations at its annual national conference. The Metropolis national conferences are the largest regularly scheduled events to bring policy-makers, community organizations, and researchers together. Annually, these conferences attract between 750 and 1000 participants to discuss research results, past practices, and potential solutions to policy challenges. Since the conferences are held in different locations each year, over time, even those organizations with fewer resources are able to participate.

Given the undoubted success of the Metropolis Project, as noted by Deputy Ministers and heads of think tanks in a recent review (Clippingdale 2006), it seems remarkable that more is not made of such venues. Many evaluations of major integration programs managed by CIC (where the Metropolis Secretariat is based), as well as an evaluation of Canadian Heritage's multiculturalism program, all mentioned Metropolis as a useful venue to exploit; yet all of the evaluations suggested a venue was desperately needed (GoC 2004b; 2004c; 2005d; 2006c). This would be an easy oversight to correct.

Continuity

One of the largest challenges facing individuals and organizations working with immigrants is the continuity—or more aptly, the lack of continuity—in government-funded initiatives. An over-reliance on one-offs and pilot projects makes planning extremely difficult and evaluation extremely challenging. How does one measure the impact of small-scale one-off projects of short duration? Even gathering information for this chapter was extremely difficult, since initiatives morph and change over time or are repackaged to allow an additional political announcement of the same resources. Other initiatives simply fade away from a lack of funding. For example, since the start of the preliminary research for this chapter, both the LEAD network described in the section on Canadian Heritage and the Diversity Calgary Initiative in the municipal government section have had their funding cut. This instability is clearly an inefficient and frustrating state of affairs, but perhaps an unavoidable one given our political realities. Nevertheless, a few changes could have a significant impact. For example, taking more advantage of long-term, predictable opportunities, such as the annual National Metropolis Conferences, would allow regular connections among key players, regardless of the vagaries of funding. Similarly, the inventory or annual report on integration activities mentioned above would inject some much needed transparency into this field.

Evaluation

Finally, there is a significant challenge with evaluating whether or not the polices, programs, and practices we have in place are, in fact, facilitating the integration of immigrants into the social, cultural, economic, and political fabric of Canada. Evaluation challenges are exacerbated by the fact that integration is a long process, even an inter-generational process; so it is exceptionally difficult to gauge the efficacy of individual programs. However, the challenges of evaluation does not make it any less important. This volume is an attempt to ensure that both sides of the two-way street of integration are explored at a societal level.

Following an evaluation of the immigrant settlement and adaptation program, CIC committed to "explore the possibility of developing and piloting a national survey for immigrants to complete during their citizenship process. This survey would capture which settlement services immigrants accessed and which were found to be the most beneficial in the settlement process" (GoC 2005d). Such a survey would be invaluable to explore the societal engagement of immigrants in Canada. But it would be useful only if it were a broad-based survey that asked about the full gamut of services available, not just those provided by one federal department, and only if it also asked Canadians about their role and how they learned to perform it more successfully. An added advantage of such a survey would be to reduce the administrative burden of accountability felt by most service provider organizations. According to one recent study, almost 22 percent of budgets in the non-governmental sector are expended on meeting disparate accountability requirements by various funders (Eakin 2008). Clearly anything that directs more of these funds to integration services, the better.

The challenges of co-ordination, information, continuity, and evaluation are, in the grand scheme of things, fortunate challenges to have. There is clearly interest across Canadian society in ensuring the successful integration of immigrants. Individuals, organizations, and all three levels of government are increasingly putting their money where their mouths are. Let's help them spend wisely!

Notes

The opinions expressed in this chapter are those of the author and do not necessarily reflect the views of the Metropolis Project, Citizenship and Immigration Canada, or the Government of Canada. The author would like to thank both Mary-Lee Mulholland and Lara Winnemore, who co-authored earlier pieces on related themes, for spurring his thinking along.

1. Annex F of the *Canada-Ontario Agreement* (2005) "lays the foundation for the two levels of government to work collaboratively with Ontario municipalities to improve the social and economic integration of immigrants" (GoC 2006a, 11).
2. Community organizations, particularly religious organizations, have a long history of assisting immigrants and refugees arriving in Canada (Biles and Ibrahim 2005). Settlement assistance for Canadians was only introduced by the federal government in 1949, primarily to help the families of Canadian soldiers and war refugees adjust to Canadian life. Prior to this, the Government of Canada had not taken any responsibility for immigrants. The government's position was that immigrants should assume responsibility for their own integration along with the agents who brought them to the country (e.g., the Canadian National Railway and the Hudson Bay Company). By 1966, the Settlement Assistance Program was phased out and the federal government had reverted to its previous position wherein it assumed no responsibility or involvement in the settlement and integration of immigrants. The prevailing philosophy was that immigrants

should access mainstream services that all Canadians drew upon (e.g., schools, health, social services) to help them integrate. However, with the influx of Indochinese refugees in the early 1970s, the federal government began to provide financial assistance to NGOs through the new Immigrant Settlement and Adaptation Program, which continues today.

3. In 2001, there were over 400 federal contribution agreements in place with over 300 service delivery organizations across Canada to help immigrants integrate into Canadian society (GoC 2001).

4. At least 14 departments and agencies of the Government of Canada have a direct connection to the integration of immigrants. In many cases immigrants are but one of the target populations of interest. A good measure of this interest are the funding partners of the Metropolis Project (an international network for comparative research and public policy development on migration, diversity, and immigrant integration in cities in Canada and around the world).

   Funders in addition to the Social Science and Humanities Research Council include Citizenship and Immigration Canada, Canadian Heritage, Canada Mortgage and Housing Corporation, Human Resources and Social Development Canada, Public Health Agency of Canada, Public Safety Canada, Atlantic Canada Opportunities Agency, Justice Canada, Royal Canadian Mounted Police, Canada Border Services Agency, Canada Economic Development for Quebec Regions, FedNor, and the Rural and Co-operative Secretariats of Agriculture and Agri-Food Canada. Since Metropolis has just entered its third five-year funding period this interest is clearly long-term. For more information visit www.metropolis.net.

5. Settlement refers to the short-term transitional issues faced by newcomers, while integration is an on-going process of mutual accommodation between newcomers and Canadian society as a whole.

6. It should be noted that these numbers indicate a massive increase in expenditures over previous years, in part due to a recognition that newcomers were not faring as well in the integration process, and that expenditures had not increased on integration programs since their inception (see table).

Planned Expenditures	2003–2004	2007–2008
Quebec	$164 million	$224.4 million
Other Provinces	$45 million	$97.5 million*
LINC	$100 million	$174.7 million
ISAP	$30 million	$173.6 million
RAP	$47 million	$49.5 million
Host	$2.8 million	$10 million
Total	**$388.8 million**	**$729.7 million**

*On December 17, 2007, Citizenship and Immigration Minister Diane Finley announced an additional $121.6 million over the next three fiscal years to support integration programs in the provinces and territories outside of Quebec and Ontario (GoC 2007).

7. Eligibility is restricted to those with legal status under the *Immigration and Refugee Protection Act* and who are at least 18 years of age. Refugee claimants are not eligible for settlement programs.
8. About 20 percent of newcomers participate in the LINC Program (GoC 2004b).
9. Integration-net engages non-governmental organizations from across the country to share best practices aimed at assisting newcomers in their settlement and integration. See http://integration-net.cic.gc.ca/english/index.cfm.
10. Recent studies suggest they ultimately repay the investment Canadians make in their initial settlement (Tolley 2004).
11. Of course, CIC does also work through citizenship promotion activities to ensure receptivity on the part of Canadians and their institutions, and Canadian Heritage does also work with newcomers and their communities to build capacity.
12. A good description of the importance of this area of Canadian Heritage's work can be found in Tolley (2004).
13. While the Multiculturalism Program used to primarily fund identity-based activities (i.e., festivals and cultural expression) this aspect of the program has long been eclipsed by foci on race relations and institutional change.
14. While these priorities tend to be reworded to meet political exigencies, in content they are remarkably stable over time. They focus on both encouraging minorities to participate actively, and on removing barriers and obstacles that impede this participation.

Annual Report	2001–02	2002–03	2003–04	2004–05	2005–06
Minister	Jean Augustine (Liberal)	Jean Augustine (Liberal)	Raymond Chan (Liberal)	Bev Oda (Conservative)	Jason Kenney (Conservative)
Priority 1	Combating racism and discrimination	Combating racism and discrimination	Fostering cross-cultural understanding	Fostering cross-cultural understanding	Building the capacity of ethnocultural/racial minorities to participate in public decision-making
Priority 2	Making Canadian institutions more reflective of Canadian diversity	Promoting cross-cultural understanding and a shared sense of citizenship	Combating racism and discrimination	Combating racism and discrimination	Helping public institutions to break down systemic barriers to diverse populations
Priority 3	Promoting shared citizenship	Helping to make Canadian institutions more representative of Canadian society	Promoting shared citizenship	Civic participation	Helping federal institutions to integrate diversity consideration into policies, programs, and services
Priority 4	Cross-cultural understanding	N.A.	Making Canadian institutions more reflective of Canadian diversity	Making Canadian institutions more reflective of Canadian diversity	Encouraging communities and the broad public to engage in informed dialogue and sustained action to combat racism

15. It is interesting to note that the June 22, 2006 apology by Stephen Harper to Chinese Canadians for the Chinese Head Tax is very similar to the Japanese Canadian Redress Agreement, reached in 1988 by former (and also Conservative) Prime Minister Brian Mulroney, which also led to the creation of the Canadian Race Relations Foundation. In both cases, a specific historical wrong was recognized and a longer-term, more broad-based element (the CRRF or the Community Historical Recognition Program) was created. It is, however, also important to recognize that the previous Liberal Government under then-Prime Minister Paul Martin had announced an "Acknowledgement, Commemoration and Education (ACE) Program" a year earlier that was replaced by the Community Historical Recognition Program after the government had changed. As some commentators argue elections can really impact multiculturalism-related initiatives (Schiffer-Graham 1989)!

16. The result of these discussions and the strategies proposed by the participants can be found in the report of the Forum (http://www.pch.gc.ca/progs/multi/pubs/police/index_e.cfm).

17. This Canadian Association of Chiefs of Police initiative was a response to recommendations made during the conferences "Policing in a Multicultural Society" (2002–2003) and "Respect in Service—Aboriginal and Cultural Diversity Policing" (2003–2004). Facilitated by a partnership between the Multiculturalism Program and the Royal Canadian Mounted Police, LEAD has enabled people in law enforcement at all levels to learn about and share successful approaches to serving Canada's Aboriginal and ethnocultural and ethnoracial communities (GoC 2005b).

18. The plan is available at http://www.cic.gc.ca/english/pub/plan-minorities.html.

19. For example fact sheets on Service Canada itself, social insurance numbers, the Universal Child Care Benefit, Employment Insurance, the Canada Pension Plan, the Guaranteed Income Supplement, Old Age Security and labour standards in Canada are now all available in 12 languages (Mandarin, Punjabi, Urdu, Arabic, Spanish, Russian, Korean, Tagalog, Cantonese, Persian, Gujarati, and Tamil), in addition to English and French and eight Aboriginal languages (GoC 2007d).

20. There is also the temporary foreign worker program, but its focus is temporary workers, so there are few immediate ramifications for integration policy.

21. According to a recent evaluation of the Foreign Credential Recognition Program (GoC 2007f), there are 51 regulated occupations, more than 200 apprenticeable trades, over 400 regulatory bodies, 15 federal departments and agencies with direct interests in foreign-educated immigrants, and at

least 3 ministries (education/advanced education, labour, health) involved with immigrant integration in each province in Canada.

22. The interdepartmental working group on immigrant labour market integration meets very irregularly, but has included Citizenship and Immigration Canada, Human Resources and Social Development Canada, Canadian Heritage, Health Canada, Industry Canada, Atlantic Canada Opportunities Agency, Western Economic Diversification, Treasury Board Secretariat, Privy Council Office, Finance Canada, Canada Economic Development for Quebec Regions, Foreign Affairs Canada, Public Service Human Resources Agency, Infrastructure Canada and Public Safety Canada.

23. HRSDC created and funds 29 national sector councils that bring together business, labour, and education stakeholders in key industries to identify and address common human resources and skills issues, and to find solutions that benefit that sector. They are designed to be instrumental in ensuring that workers already employed and those seeking employment are well prepared for the challenges of the rapidly evolving labour market.

24. Descriptions of many of these projects can be found in *Canadian Issues/ Thèmes canadiens* (Association for Canadian Studies 2007).

25. A good example of one of these funded projects is an initiative called Career Bridge in Toronto, a paid internship program, that has managed more than 130 paid internships since 2003. Another managed by the Edmonton Mennonite Centre for Newcomers has over an 80 percent success rate of assisting foreign trained engineering technologists find work in their field after assessment, training and work placement opportunities (Prince St-Amand 2005).

26. It is interesting to note that in a recent evaluation of the "Working in Canada" tool (EKOS 2007), only half of focus group participants had sought labour market information *before* immigrating. For those who had, the most prevalent and reliable source was deemed to be the internet; although none indicated using the Going to Canada Portal.

27. The majority of information developed on foreign credential recognition processes is now handled by the Foreign Credentials Referral Office, based at CIC, which was created in 2007.

28. Employment Equity is the term developed by Judge Rosalie Silberman Abella, Commissioner of the Royal Commission on Equality in Employment (1984), to describe a distinct Canadian process for achieving equality in all aspects of employment. This term was meant to distinguish the process from the primarily American "Affirmative Action" model as well as to move beyond the "Equal Opportunity" measures available in Canada at that time. Recognizing that "systemic discrimination" was responsible

for most of the inequality found in employment, the Commission outlined a systemic response and chose the term "Employment Equity" to
describe the process.

29. Visible minority is a term designated by the *Employment Equity Act* (1995)
to mean "persons, other than aboriginal peoples, who are non-Caucasian
in race or non-white in colour."

30. In recent years both Quebec (Boivin 2007; Presse canadienne 2007) and
British Columbia's (BC 2002; Chouhan 2006) provincial governments have
been accused of diverting settlement dollars into general revenues. Critics
argue that the funding allocated by the Government of Canada should be
equivalent to the resources spent by the lead ministry working on the integration of immigrants; whereas the provincial governments argue that
other ministries are also involved in the integration of newcomers, and
should be resourced accordingly.

31. For more information, visit either www.micc.gouv.qc.ca or www.
conseilinterculturel.gouv.qc.ca.

32. CIC continues to provide settlement services directly to government-
assisted refugees.

33. CIC has "co-management agreements" with both Alberta and Ontario,
essentially meaning that the two provincial governments and CIC have
agreed to ensure that their programming is complementary.

34. Interestingly, while Aboriginals, children and the disabled are all singled
out as important populations under this policy, immigrants are never specifically identified as a group of citizens needing fairness from the City of
Calgary.

35. The four major departments that listed immigrant-specific activities were:
Corporate Services Branch; Community and Protective Services; Ottawa
Police; and Ottawa Public Library. The two departments that did not report any immigration-specific activities were Public Works and Services
as well as Planning, Transit and the Environment. These are significant
omissions given the requirement that municipal planners take a
multicultural approach according to Ontario legislation. Further, as research has demonstrated, newcomers are more likely to use public transit
than the Canadian-born; so when considering changes to transit, this seems
an important community to consult (Heisz and Schellenberg 2004).

The twelve branches that listed immigrant-specific activities included:
City Clerk's Branch; Chief Corporate Services Officer; Cultural Services
and Community Funding; Client Services and Public Information; Employment and Financial Assistance; Employee Services; Financial Services;
Housing; Police Services; Parks and Recreation; Ottawa Public Health;
Ottawa Public Library. The five branches that did not report any
immigration-specific activities were the By-Law Service; Information

Technology Services; Legal Services; Ottawa Paramedic Service; and Real Property Asset Management. At least two of these are extremely surprising. In the first instance, the pool of highly qualified immigrants who work in the IT sector in Ottawa makes it seem odd that this branch does not appear to have sought to capitalize on this pool of talent. In the second case, given the concerns with healthcare provision to all citizens regardless of language ability, it seems odd that the Ottawa Paramedic Service has not reported any activities where they seek to provide service in languages other than English or French. One would expect that this must be worked out on the fly where circumstances warrant.

36. The Tool Box can be found at http://integration-net.ca/inet/english/prof/tbo/.
37. http://www.cissa-acsei.ca/index.asp.
38. Note that when multicultural organizations address needs of newcomers, they often do so in conjunction with the immigrant serving agencies or their umbrella organizations. For example, the Multicultural Association of Fredericton was funded to assist in the annual Atlantic Regional Immigrant Serving Agencies' Conference. This kind of cooperation is essential if newcomers themselves are to be seamlessly integrated despite the three year settlement cut-off that applies to funding from Citizenship and Immigration Canada.
39. The other impact areas are children and youth, seniors, people with disabilities, individuals and families in need and crisis, and agency, neighbourhood, and community capacity.
40. A settlement and integration working group has been established as part of the Federal-Provincial-Territorial process.
41. There are loose accountability provisions in the Federal-Provincial Agreements, but they are primarily of a voluntary nature.

References

Adey, G., and C. Gagnon. 2007. "Engaging Employers: Strategies for the Integration of Internationally Trained Workers in Ottawa," *Our Diverse Cities* 4: 54–58.

Allport, G.W. 1954. *The Nature of Prejudice*. Cambridge: Addison-Wesley Publishing Company.

Anisef, P., M. Poteet, D. Anisef, G. Farr, C. Poirier, and H. Wang. 2005. "Issues Confronting Newcomer Youth in Canada: Alternative Models for a National Youth Host Program," CERIS Working Paper no. 39. At www.ceris.metropolis.net.

Association for Canadian Studies. 2007. *Canadian Issues/Thèmes canadiens,* Special edition on foreign credential recognition. Spring.

Ballay, P., and M. Bulthuis. 2004. "The Changing Portrait of Homelessness," *Our Diverse Cities,* Spring: 119–23.

Beauchesne, E. 2007. "Good Job, Own Home Are Top Priority for Immigrants," *Vancouver Sun,* 25 September: C5.

Beiser, M. 1999. *Strangers at the Gate: The "Boat People's" First Ten Years in Canada.* Toronto: University of Toronto Press.

Biles, J., and M. Burstein. 2003. "Immigration: Economics and More," *Canadian Issues/Thèmes canadiens: Immigration Opportunities and Challenges* April: 13–15.

Biles, J., and H. Ibrahim. 2002. "Testing the 'Canadian Model': Hate, Bias and Fear after September 11th," *Canadian Issues/Thèmes canadiens: 9/11: Canada and the World, One Year Later* September: 54–58.

——— 2005. "Religion and Public Policy: Immigration, Citizenship and Multiculturalism—Guess Who's Coming to Dinner?" in *Religion and Ethnicity in Canada,* ed. P. Bramadat and D. Seljak. Toronto: Pearson Education Canada Inc., pp. 154–77.

Boivin, M. 2007. "L'argent d'Ottawa détourné," *Le journal de Montréal,* 19 September: 4.

British Columbia Coalition for Immigrant Integration. 2002. "Inter-Provincial Report Card on Immigrant Settlement & Labour Market Integration Services." At http://www.ocasi.org/downloads/Report%20Card%20(8.5X14).doc.

Brock, K. 2006. "The Devil's in the Detail: The Chrétien Legacy for the Third Sector," in *The Chrétien Legacy: Politics and Public Policy in Canada,* ed. L. Harder and S. Patten. Montreal and Kingston: McGill-Queen's University Press, pp. 255–75.

Buhel, O., and R. Janzen. 2007. "A National Review of Immigrant Access to Professions and Trades Initiatives," *Canadian Issues/Thèmes canadiens,* Spring: 59–62.

Canadian Race Relations Foundation (CRRF). 2007. "CRRF Annual Report 2006–2007."

Casey, Q. 2007. "Province Reverses Population Trend," *New Brunswick Telegraph Journal,* 28 September: A1.

Chouhan, R. 2006. "B.C. Liberals Need to Get Serious About Immigration Issues." At http://www.voiceonline.com/voice/060211/headline5.php.

City of Calgary. 2002. "Diversity Calgary: Moving Forward." Calgary: Springboard Consulting Inc.

——— 2006. "Coalition of Municipalities Against Racism Consultation," 16 May.

City of Ottawa. 2007a. "Faces of Ottawa: A Snapshot of Immigrant Labour Market Integration." March.

——— 2007b. "Immigration Services Mapping Survey Amalgamation of City of Ottawa Branches and Departments." 28 March.

City of Winnipeg. 2001. "A Homegrown Economic Development Strategy for Winnipeg." At http://www.winnipeg.ca/interhom/pdfs/mayors_office/economic_dev_strategy.pdf.

Clippingdale, R. 2006. "Strategic Interviews on the Metropolis Project and on Transferring Knowledge to Policy Makers." At http://canada.metropolis.net/pdfs/strategic_interviews_reportMayro_06_e.pdf.

Eakin, L. 2008. "The Administrative Burden NGOs Acquire When Dealing with Funder Accountability and Compliance Practices." Speech to the Calgary United Way, Calgary, AB: 8 January.

EKOS Research Associates Inc. 2007. "Qualitative Research on the 'Working in Canada' Tool of the Going to Canada Immigration Portal." March.

Federation of Canadian Municipalities. 2002. "Brief to Prime Minister's Urban Task Force." At www.fcm.ca/english/documents/taskforce.html.

Fortney, V. 2007. "Immigrants Struggle to Find Equal Footing in City," *Calgary Herald,* 12 October: A1.

Garcea, J. 1994. "Federal-Provincial Relations in Immigration 1971–1991: A Case Study of Asymmetrical Federalism." Dissertation. Ottawa: Carleton University.

——— 2006. "Provincial Multiculturalism Policies in Canada, 1974–2004: A Content Analysis," *Canadian Ethnic Studies* 38(3): 1–20.

Goss Gilroy Inc. 2007. "Enhanced Language Training Initiative: Formative Evaluation (Final Draft Report)." 8 October.

Government of Alberta. 1992. "Bridging the Gap: A Report of the Task Force on the Recognition of Foreign Qualifications." Edmonton: Professions and Occupations Bureau.

Government of Canada (GoC). 2001. "Immigrant Integration in Canada: Policy Objectives, Program Delivery and Challenges." Ottawa: Integration Branch of Citizenship and Immigration Canada.

——— 2002a. "Knowledge Matters: Skills and Learning for Canadians." Ottawa: Human Resources Development Canada.

——— 2002b. "Achieving Excellence: Investing in People, Knowledge and Opportunity." Ottawa: Industry Canada.

——— 2002c. "Ministers Agree to Work Together to Share the Benefits of Immigration." Ottawa: Citizenship and Immigration Canada News Release, 16 October.

——— 2003a. "2002–03 Annual Report on the Operation of the *Canadian Multiculturalism Act.*" Ottawa: Canadian Heritage.

——— 2003b. "Longitudinal Survey of Immigrants to Canada: Process, Progress and Prospects." Catalogue no. 89-611-XIE. Ottawa: Statistics Canada.

——— 2004. "Federal-Provincial-Territorial Meeting of Ministers Responsible for Immigration." Ottawa: Canadian Intergovernmental Conference Secretariat News Release, 22 January.

——— 2004a. "Speech from the Throne to Open the First Session of the 38th Parliament of Canada." 2 February.

——— 2004b. "Evaluation of the Language Instruction for Newcomers to Canada (LINC) Program." September.

———— 2004c. "Evaluation of HOST." November. At www.cic.gc.ca/English/resources/evaluation/host/exec-summary.asp.

———— 2004d. "Citizenship and Immigration Canada: Report on Plans and Priorities, 2004–2005 Estimates." Citizenship and Immigration Canada.

———— 2004e. Citizenship and Immigration Canada Transcript of 15 November 2004 press conference at Holiday Inn, Gatineau.

———— 2004f. "Immigration Ministers Meet with Ontario Municipalities." Ottawa: Citizenship and Immigration Canada News Release, 9 February.

———— 2005a. "Report on the Evaluation of the Delivery of the Canadian Orientation Abroad Initiative." June.

———— 2005b. "2003–04 Annual Report on the Operation of the Canadian *Multiculturalism Act."* Ottawa: Canadian Heritage.

———— 2005c. *A Canada for All: Canada's Action Plan Against Racism.* At http://www.pch.gc.ca/multi/plan_action_plan/index_e.cfm.

———— 2005d. "Evaluation of the Immigration Settlement and Adaptation Program (ISAP)." January.

———— 2005e. "Ministers Agree on Strategic Direction on Immigration." News Release, 4 November.

———— 2006a. "Backgrounder: Enhanced Language Training." News Release, 25 April.

———— 2006b. "Frequently Asked Questions." At http://www.pch.gc.ca/progs/multi/redress-redressement/faq_e.cfm.

———— 2006c. "Summative Evaluation of the Multiculturalism Program." 28 June.

———— 2006d. "Overview: Foreign Credential Recognition." At www.hrsdc.gc.ca/en/ws/programs/fcr/overview.shtml.

———— 2006e. "2004–2005 Annual Report on the Operation of the *Canadian Multiculturalism Act.* Ottawa: Canadian Heritage.

———— 2007. "Minister Finley Announces New Federal Commitments to Help Newcomers Settle in Canada." News Release, 17 December.

———— 2007a. "Summative Evaluation of the Private Sponsorship of Refugees Program," April.

———— 2007b. "2005–06 Annual Report on the Operation of the *Canadian Multiculturalism Act."* Ottawa: Canadian Heritage.

———— 2007c. "Official Languages Annual Report 2005–06, Volume 1: Official Languages Support Programs." At www.pch.gc.ca/progs/lo-ol/pubs/2005-2—6/ra-ar/05-06v1_3.pdf.

———— 2007d. "Multi-language Service Initiative." Paper presented at IPCA Conference, Winnipeg, 28 August.

———— 2007e. "Workplace Skills Initiative First Call for Proposals Project Details." August.

———— 2007f. "Formative Evaluation of the Foreign Credential Recognition Program." February.

———— 2007g. "Backgrounder: Foreign Credentials Referral Office." 24 May.

Government of Ontario. 1989. "Access to Professions and Trades." Toronto: Ontario Task Force Report.

———— 2006. "Unprecedented Legislation Breaks Down Barriers for Newcomers: Bill 124, Fair Access to Regulated Professions Act, 2006, Passes." Press Release, 13 December.

Halifax Chamber of Commerce. 2004. "Immigration in Nova Scotia." Halifax.

Heisz, A., and G. Schellenberg. 2004. **"**Public Transit Use Among Immigrants," *Canadian Journal of Urban Research* 13(1), June: 170–90.

Houle, R. 2007. "Secondary Migration of New Immigrants to Canada," *Our Diverse Cities* 3: 16–24.

Hurley, M. 2007. "Immigrants Choose Manitoba," *Winnipeg Free Press,* 28 September: A1.

Layton, J. 2000. *Homelessness: The Making and Unmaking of a Crisis.* Toronto: Penguin.

Li, P.S., and J.L. Kunz. 2004. "Introduction," *Journal of International Migration and Integration* 5(2): 165–71.

Martin, P. 2003. "Making History: The Politics of Achievement." Speech given at the Liberal Leadership Convention.

Mata, F. 1999. "The Non-Accreditation of Immigrant Professionals in Canada: Societal Dimensions of the Problem." Ottawa: Multiculturalism Program, Department of Canadian Heritage.

McFadden, P., and R. Janzen. 2007. "The Importance of Immigrants to Waterloo Region's Prosperity: A Dynamic Collaborative Community Response," *Our Diverse Cities* 4: 104–07.

Mendez, P., D. Hiebert, and E. Wyly. 2006. "Landing at Home: Insights on Immigration and Metropolitan Housing Markets from the Longitudinal Survey of Immigrants," *Canadian Journal of Urban Research,* Special Issue: Our Diverse Cities: Challenges and Opportunities, 15(2) : Supplement.

Morris, B. 2007. "211: Social Innovation Confronts Nagging Problems," *Our Diverse Cities* 4: 152–55.

Nugent, A. 2006. "Demography, National Myths and Political Origins: Perceiving Official Multiculturalism in Quebec," *Canadian Ethnic Studies* 38(3): 21–36.

Presse canadienne. 2007. "Le Ministère de l'immigration ne touche pas tout l'argent fédéral reçu," 18 September.

Prince St-Amand, C. 2005. "Foreign Credential Recognition and Bridge to Work," Presentation to Pan-Canadian Sector Council and Immigrant Dialogue 9, Ottawa, 9 September.

Quirke, L. 2007. "More Than Books: Examining the Settlement Services of the Toronto and Windsor Public Libraries," *Our Diverse Cities* 4: 156–60.

Reitz, J.G. 2001. "Immigrant Skill Utilization in the Canadian Labour Market: Implications of Human Capital Research," *Journal of International Migration and Integration* 2: 347–78.

Schiffer-Graham, B. 1989. The Federal Policy of Multiculturalism in Canada (1971–1988). M.A. thesis, University of Manitoba, Winnipeg.

Smith Green & Associates. 2001. "Final Report: ARAISA Positioning, 2001." Charlottetown, PEI.

Teixeira, C. 2006. "Housing Experiences of Black Africans in Toronto's Rental Market: A Case Study of Angolan and Mozambican Immigrants," *Canadian Ethnic Studies* 38(3): 58–86.

Tolley, E. 2004. "National Identity and the 'Canadian Way': Values, Connections and Culture," *Canadian Diversity/Diversité canadienne: National Identity and Diversity* 3:11–15.

Toronto City Summit Alliance. 2003. *Enough Talk: An Action Plan for the Toronto Region.* At http://www.unitedwaytoronto.com/who_we_help/pdfs/TCSA_report.pdf.

Toronto Region Immigrant Employment Council (TRIEC). 2007. "Overview." At http://www.hireimmigrants.ca/triec.ca.

United Way/Centraide Ottawa. No Date. "Breaking New Ground."

United Way of Greater Toronto. 2006. "2006 Report to the Community."

Winnemore, L., and J. Biles. 2006. "Canada's Two-Way Street Integration Model: Not Without Its Stains, Strains, and Growing Pains," *Canadian Diversity/Diversité canadienne* 5(1), Winter: 23–30.

Chapter 6

Integration Policies in Quebec:
A Need to Expand the Structures?[1]

PATRICIA RIMOK AND RALPH ROUZIER
CONSEIL DES RELATIONS INTERCULTURELLES (QC)

Introduction

In 2001, immigrants accounted for 9.9 percent of Quebec's total population (Statistics Canada 2001a). Among Quebec residents born in Quebec or elsewhere in Canada, more than 8.8 percent had at least one immigrant parent (Statistics Canada 2001b; Institut de la statistique du Québec 2001; Duchesne and Goulet 2000).[2] Visible minorities[3] made up 6.9 percent of the population (Statistics Canada 2001c), and 46.5 percent of immigrants were members of visible minorities (MRCI 2004). Visible minority immigrants were 4.6 percent of the population; native-born visible minorities, 2.3 percent (MRCI 2004a). The black community is the largest visible minority group in Quebec (Statistics Canada 2001d); 54 percent of Quebec blacks are immigrants (MICC 2005). According to projections, visible minorities will account for 19 to 23 percent of Canada's population by 2017 (Bélanger and Malenfant 2005).

In response to the question on ethnic origin in the 2001 Census of Canada (Statistics Canada 2001e), 73 percent of Quebecers reported only one origin. Close to 15 percent of the population declared a single origin other than Canadian, French, English or Quebecer. The rationale for excluding the "English" category here is that while Quebecers of English-Canadian origin are a minority, they do not necessarily experience the same problems as other ethnocultural minorities. It should also be noted that approximately 26 percent of Quebecers declared more than one ethnic origin in 2001.

These statistics confirm that integration policies must be tailored to the changing face of immigration. The number of immigrants admitted

Immigration and Integration in Canada in the Twenty-first Century, eds. J. Biles, M. Burstein, and J. Frideres.
Montreal and Kingston: McGill-Queen's University Press, Queen's Policy Studies Series.
© 2008 The School of Policy Studies, Queen's University at Kingston. All rights reserved.

to Quebec increased from 35,500 in 2000 to more than 48,000 in 2007, according to the immigration levels plan of the ministère de l'Immigration et des Communautés culturelles (MICC), formerly the ministère des Relations avec les citoyens et de l'Immigration (MRCI) (MRCI 2003). Moreover, newcomers' countries of origin have become more diverse than they were during the 1960s and 1970s. While Europe remains the leading continent of birth of immigrants, its proportion of the total decreased from 50 percent in 1991 to 40.3 percent in 2001. The relative weight of the other continents in 2001 was 26.9 percent for Asia (50 percent of whom were recent immigrants), 21.1 percent for the Americas, and 11.5 percent for Africa (the majority of whom were recent immigrants) (MRCI 2004a).

As ethnocultural diversity increases and Quebec society becomes more mixed, the question arises as to whether existing tools and policies for managing ethnocultural diversity and promoting immigrant integration are still suitable. To answer this question, we will consider the role of schools, municipalities, regions, and provincial and federal governments in integrating immigrants. We are including the education system because it has adopted a newcomer integration policy and action plan; we examine municipalities and regions because they have signed agreements with the MICC to improve immigrant integration; and we consider the provincial and federal governments in terms of (among other things) their visions and actions related to immigration. We conclude with some points that the actors should take into account to more effectively promote the integration of immigrants.

The Education System

Policies

In 1998, the Quebec department of education released a policy statement entitled "A School for the Future: Educational Integration and Intercultural Education" (Ministère de l'Éducation 1998). Aside from the MICC, the ministère de l'Éducation is the only department that has a policy on immigrant integration and an action plan, as shall be seen, although other departments may have developed programs or initiatives in this area. As the policy title indicates, its purpose was to facilitate the integration of immigrant students into the school system, while educating all students at the youth, adult, and junior college levels in intercultural relations. At the same time, the policy advocated that students participate "in social interaction in a democratic, francophone, pluralistic Quebec" (Ministère de l'Éducation 1998, iv). This policy state-ment was therefore informed by the 1990 statement on immigration in the broad sense, entitled "Let's Build Québec Together: A Policy State-ment on Immigration and Integration" (MCCI 1991), which continues to influence policy-making on immigration to this day. Since 1998, then, the integration of immigrant students has been the business of Quebec society as a whole, and all Quebecers have been urged to become aware of Quebec's increasing ethnocultural diversity while "sharing the same social values." The schools were therefore given responsibility for sup-porting this openness to diversity and preparing students to live in a pluralistic society.

The first section of the education department's policy[4]—educational integration—includes three guidelines. The first guideline indicates that integrating students who are new to Quebec is the joint responsibility of all school staff, regardless of whether the school has transition classes (which exist notably to help students learn French) and corresponding organizational structures. Staff awareness and training in issues related to ethnocultural diversity are therefore seen as vitally important. The second guideline calls for timely intervention with immigrant students experiencing difficulty with educational integration. In addition to help-ing students develop their French-language skills, transition classes can also help students in difficulty catch up in other subjects. The third guideline calls for involving the family and the community—for exam-ple, local organizations such as local community service centres, com-munity organizations and the police—to enable educational institutions to accomplish their mission more effectively. Naturally, the department of education and the school boards were also expected to adopt a simi-lar approach, particularly in terms of partnerships. They were to link with organizations that address problems affecting immigrant youths attending school (immigration, social services, etc.) in order to "improve and coordinate services and to produce and distribute a resource bank on the theme of integration" (Ministère de l'Éducation 1998, 21).

The second section of the policy—intercultural education—includes five guidelines. The first emphasizes the learning of French as an ongo-ing process and hence the need to adapt this process to individual needs. The second guideline relates to the common language of public life, understood as a vehicle of culture. This does not mean that other lan-guages are to be rejected but that French should be valued by the edu-cational community. The third guideline holds that openness to ethnocultural, linguistic, and religious diversity is part of the heritage and shared values of Quebec, to which all should subscribe. This should therefore be reflected in both the curriculum and school life. Conse-quently, the fourth guideline calls for all school staff to receive training in issues related to ethnocultural diversity so they can meet educational challenges. This applies to all schools, including those with little ethnocultural diversity, since these issues should concern the entire population. The fifth guideline states that ethnocultural diversity should be reflected in all categories of school staff, as a matter of equity and also to encourage student identification with a diverse society.

Action Plans

The policy statement was accompanied by a "Plan of Action for Educational Integration and Intercultural Education" (Ministère de l'Éducation 1998a), which covered the 1998 to 2002 period and was renewed until 2008, when it was to be evaluated (MELS 2005). The long wait for enlightenment on the impact of the policy and the action plan, and for the recommendations that are to accompany the evaluation, certainly appears regrettable. A dozen years, if not more, will likely have elapsed before the department knows whether the tools it is applying have yielded positive results.

The objectives of the action plan were the following:

1. to implement the policy in the schools (pre-school, elementary school, high school, junior college)
2. to integrate newly arrived students
3. to learn how to live together in a francophone, democratic, pluralistic society
4. to ensure that school staff receive training and to set up an exchange network
5. to follow up and evaluate the action plan

We will have to wait for the evaluation of the action plan to ascertain its full impact. It is noteworthy, however, that since the introduction of the action plan, school boards and educational institutions have developed intercultural policies.[5] The department of education, leisure and sport (MELS) and school boards have developed teaching materials adapted to growing ethnocultural diversity and intercultural training has been provided (Ministère de la Culture et des communications et al., 2005). An evaluation is therefore necessary; it should describe best practices, given that various actors in the education system will have developed approaches adapted to their specific circumstances. It would in fact be desirable to immediately identify such best practices so that institutions experiencing difficulty managing ethnocultural diversity can look to them for guidance so as to prevent the problems from becoming still more serious.

Agreements with Municipalities and Regions

Local communities that receive immigrants need support from public authorities in order to facilitate the integration of newcomers into Quebec society, particularly through employment. It is probably desirable that local solutions come from a variety of stakeholders. For example, in a given city, partnerships could be beneficial for achieving the economic integration of newcomers through joint efforts by employers, unions, the educational system, professional corporations, and immigrant-serving community organizations. While these actors can set priorities at the local level, they need to develop partnerships with other levels of government, notably the federal and provincial governments or other jurisdictions (multilateral agreements). This is one of the favourable conditions that could enable a town to attract and retain immigrants (McIsaac 2003).

The regional conferences of elected officials (CRÉ)[6] and some Quebec municipalities have therefore signed three-year immigration agreements with the MICC. The purpose of these agreements is not only to attract and retain immigrants but also to promote the social, economic, and cultural integration of immigrants, notably to fill labour shortages and offset demographic decline. These agreements are accompanied by action plans and sometimes bring together a variety of partners.

The first agreement was signed in 1999 by the MRCI (now the MICC) and the City of Montreal. A subsequent agreement was signed at the end of 2007. The accompanying 2007–10 action plan for ethnocultural diversity consists of six components: (i) economic development, (ii) job entry and equal opportunity, (iii) housing, (iv) services to citizens, (v) programming to combat discrimination, exclusion and xenophobia, and (vi) leadership with governments and partners. Various projects related to these components will be carried out, as before, in participating boroughs or throughout the city: meetings between resident and newcomer families, sporting activities, awareness-raising events, internships with social insertion companies, training, accelerated implementation of the city's equal opportunity program, etc. (Ville de Montréal and MRCI 2004).

Other agreements are in effect across the province. For example, an agreement in Laval that involves the CRÉ and the municipality runs until 2009. Some agreements were renewed in 2007, notably in Quebec

City (three years) and Gatineau (one year); and in 2006, notably in Saguenay-Lac-Saint-Jean (three years) and the Lower Saint Lawrence (three years). Several agreements are under evaluation or pending renewal, such as Abitibi-Témiscamingue's agreement. Specific agreements may also be signed for specific projects, such as promoting the integration of women or of young immigrants.

In municipalities, the culture, sport, leisure and social development department is often responsible for implementing agreements at the local level—that is, at the level of a city or borough. Agreements with regions often have many more signatory parties than do those with cities. However, various partners may be involved in implementing agreements, as in the case of the City of Montreal. The City's department of human services and other services, the departments of culture, sport, leisure and social development of various boroughs, and community organizations that were not signatories to the agreement between the MICC and the City were all involved in the development of the City's action plan in 2004–05 and likely as well with the 2007–10 plan.

Questions have been raised about the funding of the agreements. Between 2002 and 2005, Montreal, which was home to close to 70 percent of immigrants living in Quebec, received 53 percent of the $3.66 million granted by the MICC for the various agreements signed in 2002 and 2003. By comparison, Abitibi-Témiscamingue, which had 0.2 percent of Quebec's immigrants, received 8 percent of the total between 2003 and 2006. While the regionalization of immigration has been an important issue for decades, and significant resources are needed to make it possible, the Montreal area should probably receive more resources. However, the impact of the funded initiatives would have to be evaluated. In addition to counting the number of individuals taking part in an event or program, one would need to be able to concretely assess the impact in terms of integration. Based on these observations, in 2007, the MICC raised the grants to Montreal to $4.5 million over three years.

These agreements probably help the MICC more effectively plan its own activities. Governments are responsible for admitting immigrants, but it is local communities that receive them, in the sense that local communities are where immigrants settle. Since the MICC's activities are targeted at recent immigrants (in Canada less than five years), communities are responsible for promoting short- and long-term integration of immigrants, given that this is a process that can extend over several years. And the responsibility often falls to the municipalities

(Germain 2000), although it may also be assumed at the regional level. In 2001, close to 88 percent of all immigrants settled in Quebec were living in the Montreal census metropolitan area (Statistics Canada 2001f); in 2006, 87 percent of all immigrants were living in the Montreal census metropolitan area (Statistics Canada 2006).

Provincial Government

First Steps

The Act creating the Quebec department of immigration received assent in 1968. Section 3 of the Act stipulates that "the functions of the Minister shall be to promote the settling in the province of Quebec of immigrants capable of contributing to its development and of participating in its progress, and also to facilitate the adaptation of immigrants to the Quebec environment" (Quebec 1970). These principles would subsequently guide immigration policy, although how they were applied changed over the course of time. Over the years, other initiatives in support of the proposition that the host society must help integrate immigrants were added:

- the three-volume Gendron Report, of which one volume dealt with ethnic rights (1972)
- the Quebec Charter of Human Rights and Freedoms (1975)
- the Charter of the French Language (1977)
- the "Couture/Cullen" federal-provincial agreement on immigrant selection (1978)
- the white paper on cultural development (1978), which called for Quebec to be developed with the help of all Quebecers, whatever their ethnic or cultural origins may be (Quebec 1980)
- the "Autant de façons d'être Québécois" action plan (1981), intended to be a policy of cultural convergence, bringing ethnic cultures together under the aegis of the francophone majority, which would maintain priority (Bilan du siècle 1981). It therefore presented Quebec as a nation within which French-language culture was to play a catalyzing role. Nevertheless, the plan recognized the specific features of the "cultural communities," which could be maintained and developed.
- the Act respecting the Conseil des communautés culturelles et de l'immigration,[7] passed in 1984. Section 13 stipulates that the

Conseil is responsible for "advising the Minister on any matter related to intercultural relations or immigrant integration, particularly with regard to closer intercultural relations and openness to pluralism."

- the resolution recognizing Aboriginal nations (1985)
- the policy statement on immigration and integration entitled "Let's Build Québec Together" (1990), which introduced the concept of a moral contract binding newcomers and Quebec society within a common public culture. Once again, the goal was to bring individuals and social groups together behind a common or unifying goal.
- the Canada-Québec Accord (1991), which recognizes Quebec's distinct character in relation to immigrant integration. The federal government remains responsible for (among other things) "national standards and objectives relating to immigration, the admission of all immigrants and the admission and control of visitors." The Accord provides that the Quebec government "is responsible for the selection, reception and integration of immigrants to Quebec" (Young 2004).

Recent Initiatives

In 1996, the government created the MRCI. Its mission was to foster intercultural contacts and to ensure that Quebecers as a whole would be open to pluralism (MRCI 1996). In 2000, the MRCI organized a national forum on citizenship and integration, in connection with which a discussion paper was published. As in the early 1990s, the paper mentioned contracts; but these were "civic" contracts, which consisted of abandoning approaches based on ethnic classification for one which considers newcomers as citizens in their relations with the state. The paper also underscored the importance of defining guidelines to ensure respect for diversity and differences.

In 2000, the MRCI submitted a three-year immigration plan (2001–03) for public consultation. The plan outlined policies to promote the regionalization of immigration. The main focuses were (i) the fostering of an increased volume of immigration, adjusted for Quebec's receiving capacity, (ii) the selection of candidates with a knowledge of French, and (iii) the choice of candidates with professional qualifications with a view to fast-track integration into the labour market (MRCI 2000). Shortly thereafter, in the strategic plan accompanying the three-year plan, the MRCI stressed better representation of diversity at all levels in order to promote citizen participation and foster a sense of belonging to Quebec society (MRCI 2001).

In 2004, the MRCI—the name of which would be changed to MICC in 2005—released a new action plan to secure participation by "cultural communities" in Quebec's development (MRCI 2004). It should be noted that the MICC produces immigration-level planning documents, action plans, and strategic plans. The former deal with the number of immigrants to be admitted and the reasons for their admission, and the latter deal with the quality of immigrant integration into Quebec society. Public consultations are held on immigration-level planning. Theoretically, the government must take consultation into account in preparing its immigration action plans and strategic plans, although these plans do not have their own consultation process.

In its 2004–07 action plan on immigration, integration and intercultural relations, the MICC reflected the government's 1990 policy statement aimed to promote immigrant integration while taking advantage of the participation of newcomers in economic development and the building of a French-speaking society (MRCI 2004). At the time, the department of cultural communities and immigration (MCCI) held that:

- immigration was a force for development and an asset for Quebec's future;
- this force was related to the integration and full participation of immigrants and their descendants in Quebec society; and
- this integration was to be based on respect by all for the social choices governing Quebec.

Immigrants therefore had to be selected on the basis of these orientations. At the same time, family reunification, based on criteria derived from the principles of international solidarity (refugees), also remained a priority. In this policy, the term *integration* implies the following:

- learning and using the French language in public life (Charter of the French Language);
- full participation by immigrants and by all "cultural communities" in economic, social, cultural and institutional life (Quebec Charter of Human Rights and Freedoms, Quebec government statement on interethnic and interracial relations); and
- the development of harmonious intercommunity relations rooted in respect for basic democratic values (MCCI 1991).

Immigration was a major issue, since it was part of the process of building a distinct society (MCCI 1991). For integration to succeed, newcomers and all citizens had to be active participants; hence the idea of a "moral contract" between newcomers and the host society. The action plan called for efforts to integrate immigrants, particularly in the health and social services field and the municipal sector, as well as education, public security, and communications, through the development of adapted services. "Reasonable accommodation" of religious practices was also mentioned, which meant that minorities should be able to practice their religion, and that organizations were urged to be flexible about religion, but without undermining efficiency and productivity.[8] Finally, the government's integration policies included training caseworkers to respond to immigrants' specific problems, developing partnerships with community organizations concerned with these issues, and promoting participation in decision-making and advisory bodies by Quebecers from "cultural communities."

It should be noted that a clause about integration was added to the Act respecting immigration to Quebec in 1991. It stipulated: "The Minister shall establish and maintain, for those persons who settle in Quebec, an integration program for the purpose of favouring their introduction to Quebec life" (par. 3.2.2). Linguistic integration was to be an important part of the process.

In 2004, the Government of Quebec reiterated some of these principles. Its 2004–07 action plan listed five pillars of immigration and integration:

1. "An immigration policy true to Quebec's needs and values";
2. "Reception and lasting job integration," meaning economic integration of newcomers and also of Quebecers from "cultural communities," which requires programs and initiatives targeted at employers (private companies and public organizations) and recognition of qualifications, such as diplomas;
3. "Learning French: as a gauge of success," which aims to develop a sense of belonging by encouraging certain groups of immigrants to use francization services;
4. "A Quebec proud of its diversity" consists in developing a variety of initiatives to promote recognition of the contribution made by "cultural communities" to Quebec's development through intercultural dialogue, openness to diversity, and fighting racism and xenophobia. These initiatives are considered important by

the government to promote the development of links between "cultural communities" and their representative community organizations;

5. "The Capitale-Nationale, metropolitan Montréal and the regions committed to action" consists in developing initiatives to encourage more even distribution of immigrants across Quebec and to achieve an acceptable retention rate (MRCI 2004b).

In 2005, the MICC set targets for its immigration strategic plan for the years 2005–08, taking into account immigration-level planning for 2005–07. Public consultations were held on the immigration levels, and 85 briefs dealing with a variety of subjects, including diversity, regionalization and municipal policies, were submitted. The discussion paper (MRCI 2004b) circulated to elicit briefs, forecast labour shortages, note the importance of recruiting immigrants with a knowledge of French, and discuss the desirability of encouraging immigrants to settle in all parts of Quebec, since areas outside the major centres were expected to experience significant demographic deficits. The 2005–08 immigration strategic plan therefore identified two issues: the strategic contribution of immigration and of "cultural communities" to Quebec's development and prosperity, and improving the quality of client services and modernizing the state. The first issue involves four points:

- encouraging a suitable inflow of immigrants and selecting candidates who meet Quebec's needs;
- supporting the integration of newcomers and promoting long-term employment;
- fostering better understanding of diversity on the part of citizens and supporting acceptance of diversity; and
- securing the involvement of local and regional bodies in immigration, integration and intercultural relations.

The second issue consists in just one point: modernizing service delivery and providing a rewarding work environment (MICC 2005a).

The statements, action plans and strategic plans released in recent years point to at least two sets of problems:

- difficulty aligning the actions launched under previous policies with those undertaken under the new policies; and
- few prescriptions in the plans on how to implement the policies at the national, regional and local levels, or within spheres of activity.

However, this does not mean that major initiatives were not undertaken. On the contrary, there are more than 150 community organizations offering services for immigrants (MICC 2008a). Their goal is to promote immigrant integration through programs such as the Support Program for the Integration of New Arrivals (PANA), which funds 68 organizations (MICC 2006) that offer services for immigrants. Other programs include the following:

- the Employment Integration Program for Immigrants and Visible Minorities (PRIIME), which provides wage subsidies to help target groups acquire work experience;
- the Regional Integration Program (PRI), which encourages local and regional partnerships to ensure that immigration contributes to Quebec's demographic, social and economic development;
- the Support Program for Civic and Intercultural Relations (PARCI), which provides financial assistance to organizations that help develop and maintain harmonious relations between groups and individuals of diverse origins; and
- the Financial Aid Program for the Linguistic Integration of Immigrants (PAFILI), which provides immigrants with financial assistance while taking French classes (MICC 2006a).

Twinning of immigrants and non-immigrants and events organized to promote better understanding of intercultural relations and fight racism are also worthy of note. The MICC has also produced a guide to promote immigrant integration (MICC 2005b). As well, the MICC currently has six liaison officers serving more than 130 ethnocultural minority communities and performing the following roles:

- reporting on the experiences of cultural communities, in conjunction with the communities in question;
- supporting cultural communities in the search for solutions tailored to their needs;
- building and maintaining bridges between cultural communities and government departments and agencies;
- facilitating access to the services offered by departments, public agencies, and community organizations;
- promoting co-operation among these actors;
- supporting the fight against racism and exclusion by promoting intercultural understanding; and
- representing the MICC at activities organized by cultural communities (MICC 2008b).

Need for Evaluation

A specific model therefore seems to have been predominant for several years. In general, the MICC is responsible for the selection, settlement, and integration of immigrants. The Conseil des relations interculturelles plays an advisory role; the MICC may ask it to provide information on various matters related to the above-mentioned responsibilities. Other departments and agencies may also deal with one or another of these responsibilities. For example, the department of employment and social solidarity (MESS) supports the integration of immigrants. Thus, Québec pluriel, launched by the MESS in 2004, works to reduce the socioeconomic inequalities experienced by youths belonging to "cultural communities" and visible minorities, whether immigrant or not. However, Québec pluriel is only one program among others at the MESS, and its long-term survival is not guaranteed. Meanwhile, though the MICC works with numerous partners on specific problems, the resulting projects, albeit highly commendable, tend to produce short-term rather than long-term outcomes, since they are not interconnected and are carried out in an ad hoc manner.

In other words, while significant human and material resources are devoted to supporting immigrant integration, there are difficulties co-ordinating the activities conducted under each initiative with the various action plans and with each other. For example, how have the four priorities in the MICC's 2004–07 action plan—creating an immigrant/visible minority integration support program, addressing the issues of job entry, francizing newcomers, and reaching out to ethnocultural minority women living in isolation—been linked? Could the fourth priority be integrated into the other three? Action plans and strategic plans that reflect the government's commitment to managing ethnocultural diversity should support this type of co-ordination.

This co-ordination issue raises at least two questions. First, since these plans stem from immigration plans on which public consultations have been held, should they not be developed in concert with the various social and economic stakeholders concerned with or involved in these issues, and in conjunction with all government departments and agencies? Second, would it not be important for these same stakeholders to meet and jointly evaluate the impacts, social and economic costs and benefits, etc., of the concrete actions carried out for the purpose of achieving the objectives in the strategic plans?

Federal Government

Towards an Institutionalized Policy

In the nineteenth century, when the first Chinese, German, Icelandic, Ukrainian and Russian immigrants were settling in Canada, the "racist assimilation" approach to immigrant reception was predominant. Subsequently, until the 1960s, the "functional assimilation" model prevailed. At that time, policy-makers considered it necessary for newcomers to assimilate into the national culture in order to make an effective contribution to the perpetuation of society. This approach was criticized by ethnocultural minorities, who saw little difference between it and the first approach. In both cases, it appeared to them that the goal was to eradicate minority cultures (Bérubé 2004). At the same time, ethnic groups were concerned about the report of the Royal Commission on Bilingualism and Biculturalism, established in 1963, which led to the adoption of the Official Languages Act in 1969 (Esses and Gardner 1996). They asked what place they would have in Canadian society in relation to citizens of French or British origin. Partly as a result, in 1971 Canada introduced a multiculturalism policy, the aim of which was not to assimilate newcomers but to integrate them while allowing them to preserve elements of their own culture. Multiculturalism was also supposed to help forge a new Canadian identity (Centre for Canadian Studies 2004).

The multiculturalism policy also prompted criticism. Francophone Quebecers, anglo-conformist Canadians, and other groups feared it would lead to the creation of ghettos and marginalize Canadians in ethnic enclaves (Troper and Weinfeld 1999). Policy-makers therefore needed to place the policy on a firmer footing. They buttressed it by adopting the Canadian Human Rights Act (1977), the Citizenship Act (1977), the Canadian Charter of Rights and Freedoms (1982), and the Employment Equity Act (1986), all of which were guided by principles of non-discrimination (Department of Canadian Heritage 2004). Therefore, while it was not clearly defined as a system, multiculturalism came to be supported by numerous texts that would favour its institutionalization. Canada's move was followed by Sweden, which introduced a multiculturalism policy in 1975, and Australia, which announced similar measures in 1978 (Férréol and Jucquois 2003).

Multiculturalism

In 1988, Canada passed the *Canadian Multiculturalism Act*, becoming the first country to adopt a law of this type at the national level (Leman

2006). Since that time, federal agencies have sought to apply it through various programs and initiatives designed, notably, to manage ethnocultural diversity. It all remains a question of interpretation. The preamble to the Act states that all Canadian citizens are equal and have the same rights and duties. Nevertheless, multiculturalism reflects the cultural and racial diversity of Canadian society, and the government "acknowledges the freedom of all members of Canadian society to preserve, enhance and share their cultural heritage" (Canada 1988, par. 3(1)(*a*)). The Multiculturalism Act recognizes and promotes the proposition that all should recognize and accept Canada's ethnocultural diversity, which constitutes "a national asset, and...a basis for leadership in an increasingly complex world of economic globalization" (Department of Canadian Heritage 2004, vi).

In 1991, the federal government created the Department of Multiculturalism and Citizenship. This department defended the principles of multiculturalism while encouraging the various communities to participate inclusively in collective life, stressing intercultural understanding. The department was replaced in 1993 by the Department of Canadian Heritage, which created a Secretary of State for Multiculturalism, whose objectives include developing a Canadian identity through cultural diversity (Leman 1999).

In 2001, the Canadian government passed the *Immigration and Refugee Protection Act*, which is administered by Citizenship and Immigration Canada, a department created in 1994 "to link immigration services with citizenship registration to promote the unique ideals all Canadians share and to help build a stronger Canada" (CIC 2001, 1). The purpose of the Act is, among other things, "to enrich and strengthen the social and cultural fabric of Canadian society, while respecting the federal, bilingual and multicultural character of Canada" (ss 3(b)) and to "support and assist the development of minority official languages communities in Canada" (ss 3(b.1)).

In 2004, Canadian Heritage organized an event designed to raise awareness of ethnocultural diversity among public servants. The participants discussed the idea of partnering with civil society, employers, and police to evaluate the government's anti-racism policies and programs. Canadian Heritage's *Action Plan Against Racism* followed in 2005. In the same year, Canadian Heritage hosted a policy forum called "Canada 2017—Serving Canada's Multicultural Population for the Future"; 150 participants gathered to discuss cities, labour markets, health and social services, and public institutions. The forum decided to form an interdepartmental committee to identify policy options in the wake of the forum, which had underscored the positive impact of diversity on productivity by, for example, introducing new ideas that help organizations innovate. The forum also pointed out that immigrants go where there is work. While this is not surprising, the importance of developing initiatives to attract and retain immigrants in both urban and rural communities was raised.

In short, these initiatives show that the government of Canada is constantly reassessing its position in order to manage growing ethnocultural diversity.[9] These assessments also address new concerns. For example, during the 1990s Canadian Heritage focused on forging a Canadian identity; in 2004, it also underscored the need to employ members of ethnocultural minorities.

Promoting diversity while encouraging the integration of minorities into collective life can be problematic, which is why this effort generally targets immigrants but not necessarily their descendants. In this view, problems of integration are generally greater for newcomers than for their Canadian-born descendants. Bear in mind that while Canada promotes diversity, it also needs to foster social cohesion. Assimilation or integration will occur in an environment in which individuals are recognized as equal to the "old-stock" population while keeping certain cultural traits (Doomernik 1998). When this occurs, the process of "Canadianization," which can proceed through attraction or coercion, will have contributed to diluting immigrant cultures and identities. This does not mean, however, that they will have disappeared and that Canada will not itself have been transformed by the contact with immigrant cultures (Troper and Weinfeld 1999).

While the culture of the host society contributes to immigrant acculturation to a certain degree, it will not have the same effect on the second generation, which, having been born in the country, will be imbued with the host culture. First-generation immigrants will often try to integrate by forging links through an ethnic community (McAndrew and Weinfeld 1997); but their children will not necessarily do the same, or, if they do, it will probably be for different reasons. However, this view ignores the existence of specific problems that can affect the descendants of immigrants. While they do not necessarily experience the same integration problems as their parents, they can also experience many difficulties in social and economic integration due to their origins. This concern applies to visible minorities as well, even when they no longer have any immigrant connection, as in the case of blacks whose ancestors came to Canada at the same time or prior to the ancestors of whites (e.g., descendants of British or French settlers).

While the multiculturalism policy aims to be inclusive, it cannot conceal the existence of tensions in inter-group relations related to issues such as the living conditions of Aboriginal peoples, relations between people of English- and French-Canadian origin (and not only in Quebec), and prejudices against visible minorities (Esses and Gardner 1996). Tensions of this type are even more likely to develop when ethnocultural minorities are encouraged to identify with a group that has practices rooted in a country other than Canada, which raises questions about individual and collective identity. These identities are multiple, since individuals are not wholly "ethnic" or Canadian.

Quebec/Canada

The government of Quebec has not adopted the approach advocated by multiculturalism. However, at both levels of government, immigrant integration policies aim to elicit participation by all while respecting diverse identities (Bérubé 2004). In this sense, Quebec and federal policies have points in common, particularly regarding respect for pluralism, commitment to social justice, and civic participation by citizens of all origins (Labelle 2005). In both cases, integration policies are intended to support political inclusion, socio-economic equality and cultural and religious equity (Penninx 2005). However, federal and Quebec policies diverge on the question of language, since Quebec stresses the learning of French whereas Canadian multiculturalism policy is vague on learning the official languages (Ouellet 2005). More specifically, it has been argued, Quebec is trying to "combine identification with a common mainstay of identity (language and shared liberal values) and respect for particularism (identity-pluralism)" (Gagnon and Jézéquel 2004, translation). While Quebec has embraced the discourse of diversity and inclusion, it has been suggested that the scope of this appropriation has not been clearly defined (Juteau 2000).

Thus, though Quebec has some responsibilities in the field of immigration, it is dependent on decisions made at the federal level. Most importantly, federal authorities grant Canadian citizenship or permanent resident status and decide the number of immigrants to be admitted for the entire country.[10] Integration policies developed at the federal level can influence immigrants' perceptions of the policies developed by the government of Quebec. While they may not necessarily be contradictory, they can give rise to some confusion about identity. There may therefore be a certain confusion between the tools used by the federal government and those used by Quebec, and this confusion is manifested in the discourse. And it is at the level of discourse that identities are articulated or resist articulation. For example, can a person consider himself Québécois, Canadian, Beninese, and Bariba, all with equal intensity?

Conclusion

There are many Quebec initiatives geared towards promoting immigrant integration, notably in the field of education and at the municipal, regional, provincial and federal levels. However, while all of these initiatives are entirely legitimate and necessary, there seem to be shortcomings in at least two areas. First, there do not really appear to be any evaluations that measure the practical impact of the various initiatives on immigrant integration. Neither are there any systemic evaluations of the impact, notably in terms of fostering harmonious social relations and helping people live together. In both cases, research would be necessary in order to establish relevant indicators for measuring impacts. Secondly, the actors seem to be working in isolation; some partnerships do exist, but these are formed and dissolved according to the nature and scope of the projects.

It is therefore necessary to develop conducive conditions for bringing together all the actors concerned with immigrant integration, as well as all ethnocultural minorities, and indeed the population of Quebec as a whole, to co-ordinate their efforts in this area. The individuals targeted by the various measures, programs, and actions must be empowered, rather than passive, objects of the initiatives aimed at them. Moreover, civil society, market, and state players involved in integration should co-ordinate their efforts to make sure the activities of stakeholders are complementary within each sphere and between different spheres. This means establishing co-ordinating mechanisms so that integration policies, which are currently unfocused, can have a long-term fundamental impact on society as a whole. The social exclusion that may result from unsuccessful integration clearly has negative impacts on the individuals involved. But these impacts also ripple through the entire society, where they can spawn violence or illness or leave people dependent on social programs for their survival.

Actors in the education system, the municipalities, the regions, and the provincial and federal governments should therefore meet and discuss with their partners in community organizations, the social economy, and the business community to produce a strategy and action plan for the best possible integration of all newcomers, regardless of age. This effort could serve as a pilot project and demonstrate the appropriateness of developing a dynamic of this type if it is accompanied by ongoing evaluation mechanisms. To this end, researchers should also be involved in the project.

Notes

1. This text is based in large part on an opinion that has been released by the Conseil des relations interculturelles in December of 2007 (Rouzier et al. 2007).
2. The figure is an estimate.
3. "The concept of visible minority applies to persons who are identified according to the Employment Equity Act as being non-Caucasian in race or non-white in colour. Under the Act, Aboriginal persons are not considered to be members of visible minority groups." (www.statcan.ca/english/concepts/definitions/vis-minorit.htm). Statistics Canada uses the following categories: Chinese, South Asian (e.g., East Indian, Pakistani, Punjabi, Sri Lankan), Black (e.g., African, Haitian, Jamaican), Arab/West Asian (e.g., Armenian, Egyptian, Iranian, Lebanese, Moroccan), Filipino, South East Asian (e.g., Cambodian, Indonesian, Laotian, Vietnamese), Latin American, Japanese, Korean (www.statcan.ca/english/concepts/definitions/vis-minorit01.htm).
4. Now the Ministère de l'éducation, du loisir et du sport.
5. For example, the Commission scolaire Marguerite-Bourgeoys, with its "Politique d'intégration scolaire des élèves non francophones, d'éducation interculturelle et d'éducation à la citoyenneté" in 1999; the Cégep du Vieux Montréal, with its "Politique d'intégration scolaire et d'éducation interculturelle" in 2001; and the Commission scolaire Marie-Victorin, with its "Politique d'intégration scolaire des élèves immigrants et d'éducation interculturelle" in 2004.
6. The CRÉ support consultation and planning of regional economic development. They are the government's main contact at the regional level and may sign specific agreements with ministers.
7. Known since 1996 as the Conseil des relations interculturelles.
8. It should be noted that while the concept of reasonable accommodation is aimed at preventing social exclusion or harmoniously integrating individuals into a society (Ross 1993), it has also had a legal status since the mid-1980s, when the Supreme Court of Canada recognized that an apparently neutral standard (in the case at hand, a work schedule) can have a discriminatory effect on an employee if it is incompatible with the employee's religious practices; hence the requirement to take the necessary measures to protect equality rights. Therefore, to apply the principles of equality in practice, the employer was legally required to make a reasonable

accommodation—in this case, to change the employee's work schedule. (Bosset 2005, 2).

9. See www.pch.gc.ca/progs/multi/index_e.cfm.

10. Under the Canada-Quebec Accord, Quebec can receive a percentage of immigrants equal to or up to five percentage points greater than its percentage of Canada's population (Young 2004, 2).

References

Bélanger, A., and É. Malenfant. 2005. "Projections de la population des groupes de minorités visibles, Canada, provinces et régions: 2001–2017." Ottawa: Statistique Canada (Ministère de l'Industrie).

Bérubé, L. 2004. *Parents d'ailleurs, enfants d'ici. Dynamique d'adaptation du rôle parental chez les immigrants.* Sainte-Foy: Presses de l'Université du Québec.

Bilan du siècle. 1981. "Publication du plan d'action du gouvernment du Québec concernant les communautés culturelles." At bilan.usherbrooke.ca/bilan/pages/evenements/20244.html.

Bosset, P. 2005. "Réflexion sur la portée et les limites de l'obligation de l'accommodement raisonnable en matière religieuse." Quebec: Commission des droits de la personne et des droits de la jeunesse.

Canada. 1988. *Canadian Multiculturalism Act.* R.S., 1985, c. 24 (4th Supp.).

Centre for Canadian Studies. 2004. "Le multiculturalisme au Canada." Série *Réalités canadiennes*. Sackville, NB: Mount Allison University.

Citizenship and Immigration Canada (CIC). 2001. "Serving Canada and the World." Ottawa: Minister of Public Works and Government Services Canada.

Department of Canadian Heritage. 2004. "Annual Report on the Operation of the *Canadian Multiculturalism Act* 2002–2003: Canada's Diversity: Respecting our Differences." Ottawa: Department of Public Works and Government Services Canada.

Doomernik, J. 1998. "The Effectiveness of Integration Policies towards Immigrants and their Descendants in France, Germany and the Netherlands." Geneva: International Labour Organization.

Duchesne, L., and S. Goulet. 2000. "Un enfant sur cinq a un parent né à l'étranger," *Données sociodémographiques en bref* 4(3): 3–4.

Esses, V.M., and R.C. Gardner. 1996. "Le multiculturalisme au Canada: Contexte et état actuel." *Revue canadienne des sciences du comportement*. Ottawa: Société canadienne de psychologie.

Férréol, G., and G. Jucquois (eds.). 2003. *Dictionnaire de l'altérité et des relations interculturelles*. Paris: Armand Collin.

Gagnon, A-G., and M. Jézéquel. 2004. "Le modèle québécois d"intégration culturelle est à préserver." *Le Devoir*, 17 May. At www.ledevoir.com/2004/05/17/54731.html.

Germain, A. 2000. "Les défis de la gestion de la diversité ethnoculturelle dans la région montréalaise." At http://canada.metropolis.net/events/urban-forum/Montreal_F.html.

Institut de la statistique du Québec. 2001. *Population selon le groupe d'âge, régions administratives du Québec.* At www.stat.gouv.qc.ca/regions/lequebec/population_que/poptot20.htm.

Juteau, D. 2000. "What True Pluralism Requires." *Options politiques*, Institut de recherche en politiques publiques (January/February): 70–72.

Labelle, M. 2005. "Le défi de la diversité au Canada et au Québec." *Options politiques*, Institut de recherche en politiques publiques (March/April): 92–97.

Leman, M. "Le multiculturalisme canadien." Ottawa: Division des affaires politiques et sociales, Gouvernement du Canada.

McAndrew, M., and M. Weinfeld. 1997. "L'intégration sociale des immigrants et la réaction des institutions." Metropolis: Première Conférence Milan, 13–15 novembre 1996. Essais réunis par Marco Lombardi Quaderni I.S.MU.

McIsaac, E. 2003. "Immigrants in Canadian Cities: Census 2001–What Do the Data Tell Us?" *Policy Options* (May): 58–63.

Ministère de la Culture et des communications, Ministère de l'Éducation, du loisir et du sport, Ministère de la Famille, des aînés et de la condition féminine, et Ministère de l'Immigration et des communautés culturelles. 2005. "Rapprochement interculturel chez les jeunes d'âge scolaire (2005–2007): Projet." Montréal: Ministère de l'Éducation, du loisir et du sport (Direction des services aux communautés culturelles).

Ministère des Communautés culturelles et de l'Immigration (MCCI). 1991. "Au Québec pour bâtir ensemble: Énoncé de politique en matière d'immigration et d'intégration." Québec: Gouvernement du Québec.

Ministère de l'Éducation. 1998. "Une école d'avenir: Politique d'intégration scolaire et d'éducation interculturelle." Québec: Gouvernement du Québec.

——— 1998a. "Plan d'action en matière d'intégration scolaire et d'éducation interculturelle, 1998–2002." Québec: Gouvernement du Québec.

Ministère de l'Éducation, du loisir et du sport (MELS). 2005. "Plan stratégique du ministère de l'Éducation, du loisir et du sport, 2005–2008." Québec: Gouvernement du Québec.

Ministère de l'Immigration et des communautés culturelles (MICC). 2005. "Des valeurs partagées, des intérêts communs. La pleine participation à la société québécoise des communautés noires." Québec: Gouvernement du Québec.

——— 2005a. "Plan stratégique 2005–2008." Québec: Gouvernement du Québec.

——— 2005b. "Apprendre le Québec. Guide pour réussir mon intégration." Québec: Gouvernement du Québec.

——— 2006. "Répertoire des organismes partenaires du MICC 2005–2006." Québec: Gouvernement du Québec.

——— 2006a. "Programmes." At www.micc.gouv.qc.ca/fr/programmes.html.

———— 2008a. "Partenaires du ministère." At www.immigration-quebec.gouv.
qc.ca/fr/partenaires/index.html.

———— 2008b. "Bureaux de liaison avec les communautés culturelles." At http://
/www.quebecinterculturel.gouv.qc.ca/fr/informations/nousjoindre/
bureau-liaison.html#augustin.

Ministère des Relations avec les citoyens et de l'Immigration (MRCI). 1996.
"Rapport annuel, 1996–1997." Québec: Gouvernement du Québec.

———— 2000. "L'immigration au Québec. Un choix de développement, 2001–
2003." Québec: Gouvernement du Québec.

———— 2001. "Plan stratégique, 2001–2004." Québec: Gouvernement du Québec.

———— 2003. "La planification des niveaux d'immigration, 2005–2007." Québec:
Gouvernement du Québec.

———— 2004. "Des valeurs partagées, des intérêts communs : Pour assurer la
pleine participation des Québécois des communautés culturelles au
développement du Québec—Plan d'action 2004–2007." Québec: Gouvernement du Québec.

———— 2004a. "Population immigrée recensée au Québec et dans les régions
en 2001: Caractéristiques générales, Recensement de 2001—Données
ethnoculturelles." Québec: Gouvernement du Québec.

———— 2004b. "Summary Document—Shared Values, Common Interests: To
Ensure the Full Participation of Quebecers from Cultural Communities in
the Development of Québec—Action Plan 2004–2007." Quebec: Government
of Quebec.

Ouellet, F. 2005. "L'éducation interculturelle au Québec: L'émergence d'une
approche distincte," in *Les institutions face aux défis du pluralisme ethnoculturel,*
ed. F. Ouellet. Québec: Institut québécois de recherche sur la culture, pp. 21–45.

Penninx, R. 2005. "Integration Policies for Europe's Immigrants: Performance,
Condition and Evaluation." An expert paper for the Sachverstängenrat für
Zuwanderung und Integration. At www2.fmg.uva.nl/imes/publications/
documents/penninx-integrationpol.pdf.

Quebec. 1980. "Rapport du groupe de travail interministériel formé par le
CIPDC." At www.cslf.gouv.qc.ca/Publications/PubC116/C116-I.html.

Quebec. 1970. *Immigration Department Act.* R.S.Q. 1970 C. 68.

Ross, V. 1993. "Gérer la diversité dans un Québec francophone, démocratique
et pluraliste. Principes de fond et de procédure pour guider la recherche
d'accommodements raisonnables." Montréal: Conseil des communautés
culturelles et de l'immigration.

Rouzier, R., et al. 2007. "Avis sur la prise en compte et la gestion de la diversité
ethnoculturelle." Montréal: Conseil des relations interculturelles.

Statistics Canada. 2001a. "Table 97F0010XCB2001003."At http://www12
.statcan.ca/francais/census01/products/standard/themes/
RetrieveProductTable.cfm?Temporal=2001&PID=62913&APATH=3&GID=
431515&METH=1&PTYPE=55440&THEME=44&FOCUS=0&AID=
0&PLACENAME=0&PROVINCE=0&SEARCH=0&GC=0&GK=0&VID=
0&VNAMEE=&VNAMEF=&FL=0&RL=0&FREE=0.

Statistics Canada. 2001b. "Table 97F0009XCB2001006." At http://www12
.statcan.ca/francais/census01/products/standard/themes/
RetrieveProductTable.cfm?Temporal=2001&PID=64717&APATH=3&GID=
355313&METH=1&PTYPE=55440&THEME=43&FOCUS=0&AID=
0&PLACENAME=0&PROVINCE=0&SEARCH=0&GC=0&GK=0&VID=
0&VNAMEE=&VNAMEF=&FL=0&RL=0&FREE=0.

Statistics Canada. 2001c. "Profile: Quebec." At www12.statcan.ca/english/
census01/products/standard/prprofile/prprofile.cfm?G=24.

Statistics Canada. 2001d. "Provinces and Territories. " At www12.statcan.ca/
english/census01/products/analytic/companion/etoimm/provs.cfm.

Statistics Canada. 2001e. "Population by Selected Ethnic Origins, by Province
and Territory (2001 Census): Quebec." At http://www40.statcan.ca/l01/
cst01/demo26a.htm.

Statistics Canada. 2001f. "Community Profiles." At http://www12.statcan.ca/
english/Profil01/CP01/Details/Page.cfm?Lang=F&Geo1=CMA&Code1=
462__&Geo2=PR&Code2=24&Data=Count&SearchText=montréal&SearchType=
Begins&SearchPR=01&B1=All&Custom=.

——— 2006. "Community Profiles." At http://www12.statcan.ca/english/
census06/data/profiles/community/Details/Page.cfm?Lang=F&Geo1=
CMA&Code1=462__&Geo2=PR&Code2=24&Data= Count&SearchText=
montréal&SearchType=Begins&SearchPR=01&B1=All&Custom=.

Troper, H., and M. Weinfeld. 1999. "Diversity in Canada," in *Ethnicity, Politics,
and Public Policy*, ed. H. Troper and M. Weinfeld. Toronto: University of Toronto Press, pp. 3–25.

Ville de Montréal and Ministère des relations avec les citoyens et l'immigration.
2004. "Entente entre la ville de Montréal et le MRCI. Plan d'action 2004–
2005." Montréal: Ville de Montréal and Ministère des Relations avec les
citoyens et l'Immigration.

Young, M. 2004. "L"immigration: L'Accord Canada–Québec." Ottawa: Law
and Government Division, Government of Canada.

Chapter 7

Receiving and Giving: How Does the Canadian Public Feel about Immigration and Integration?

Jack Jedwab

Introduction

Measuring public opinion on social issues can be a powerfully important tool, not only in analyzing people's views on various matters, but also in potentially modifying their perceptions. This is because survey results are frequently a central part of public education or social marketing campaigns and often provide justification for existing public policies or changes in policy direction. Immigration is by no means an exception to this pattern. As Canada receives a relatively significant number of new arrivals each year, there is ongoing monitoring of public opinion not only to track support for levels of immigration but also to understand views around the process of immigrant settlement and adjustment. Public opinion surveys revealing that most Canadians are satisfied with the numbers of immigrants the country receives may help counter criticism that we are letting too many newcomers into the country. Such favourable survey results also allow government officials to declare that Canada is a welcoming place for immigrants in recruitment programs. As a result of the continued public support for the actual number of newcomers entering the country, those who are concerned about the numbers of immigrants that Canada receives seem to focus more in public debates on the capacity to integrate immigrants than they do on the volume of immigration.

Analysis of public opinion in Canada often leaves the impression that integration of immigrants is a matter viewed quite separately from levels of immigration. In part, the disconnecting of "immigration from integration" is attributable to the way in which the issues are packaged

Immigration and Integration in Canada in the Twenty-first Century, eds. J. Biles, M. Burstein, and J. Frideres.
Montreal and Kingston: McGill-Queen's University Press, Queen's Policy Studies Series.

by Canadian policy-makers and media alike. As we shall observe, over the past decade, public opinion surveys in Canada suggest that the population can be favourable toward receiving significant numbers of newcomers while simultaneously expressing serious concerns about their integration. Paradoxically, in many immigrant-receiving countries, the perceived breakdown in the immigrant adjustment or integration process directly contributes to the questioning of the numbers of immigrants. The link between the two, however, does not appear to have been made successfully in Canada by those who express concerns over the numbers of new arrivals, if we are to judge by the continued support on the part of most Canadians for current levels of immigration. While they may grudgingly acknowledge that Canadians are less concerned with the numbers entering the country, they insist that preoccupations with the process of immigrant integration remain quite widely held.

Moreover, this separation of the two issues has given rise to what some regard as a set of contradictory attitudes amongst Canadians towards immigration. An important section of the population agree on the one hand that immigrants enrich Canadian culture; but at the same time, many of the same people also appear to want the new arrivals to abandon their cultures and become more like other Canadians.

This chapter examines public opinion around the relationship between immigration and integration in Canada. Are attitudes around this relationship indeed contradictory, or are there several segments of public opinion that hold divergent opinions? To address this question, the chapter examines a series of public opinion polls about levels of immigration in Canada. This examination identifies three groups or clusters: those who think Canada receives "too many" immigrants, those who feel we receive "too few," and those who feel that the numbers are "about right." The chapter then analyzes their respective views on several facets of immigrant integration. It offers insights about those areas where there appears to be convergence or divergence of opinion across the groups. In other words, how far apart are those in each of the three clusters on issues of integration? Is there sufficient agreement among them to speak about a consensus on certain matters? As is often the case regarding public opinion, views on immigration issues are often in a state of flux; hence we must compare responses over time. Furthermore, to situate Canadian views in some context, this chapter compares Canada with various other countries.

Without assessing public opinion over time, policy-makers often have no reference through which to determine whether a profound change in opinion has occurred. They often assume that openness to immigration implies generally positive attitudes across the spectrum of diversity issues. While this may seem apparent to many observers, attitudes amongst the population do not always follow such patterns.

When evaluating the results of public opinion surveys on immigration and integration, it is critical to look at the manner in which the questions are formulated. This is especially true for matters of social integration that attempt to measure belonging to and/or identification with Canada. Assumptions are often built into questions on immigration and integration, and these embedded assumptions risk generating conclusions about public opinion that support a particular hypothesis. The definitions and/or concepts that underlie the question can be critical—because for matters addressing immigrant integration, it is important to know what is meant by "integration." Often the manner in which the question is formulated implies some definition of integration.

Levels of Immigration in Canada: Historic Patterns of Support on Levels of Immigration

When testing public opinion on immigration, pollsters usually ask questions about the numbers or levels of newcomers entering the country. Such questions usually offer three possible answers to respondents: there are too many, too few, or just enough immigrants. The options provided can have an important impact on the results and thereafter the way they are "spun" by those interpreting them. If little or no concern is expressed about such levels, the poll may reinforce the view that the current policy direction is satisfactory. On the other hand, if the conclusion is that "too many" Canadians are concerned with immigration levels, the poll may result in policy-makers providing additional resources for immigrant integration, rather than reducing the numbers of immigrants.

In the December 2006 wave of Citizenship and Immigration Canada's (CIC's) immigration tracking polls, nearly half of respondents said that Canada was receiving the right number of immigrants, while just over one-quarter felt that there are too many immigrants coming to the country, and just under one-fifth said there were too few (see Table 1).

As mentioned at the beginning, public opinion on immigration should ideally be put in some historic context so that it does not appear to be presented in a vacuum. The time at which the survey is conducted may influence the state of mind of the population. For example, changes in public opinion around levels of immigration are believed to be particularly affected by the prevailing economic conditions.

Table 1: Attitudes Toward Immigration Levels

Question: In your opinion, do you feel that there are too many, too few, or about the right number of immigrants coming to Canada?

| | Percentage declaring "Too many" | | |
Poll Date	Percent	Poll Date	Percent
Jan 1996	46	July 2004	31
Jan 1998	41	Dec 2004	29
Jan 1999	38	July 2005	31
Jan 2000	37	Nov 2005	30
Mar 2001	33	Mar 2006	26
Jun 2001	34	Nov 2006	28
Oct 2001	36	May 2007	27

Source: Environics Research Group 1998–2001; CIC 2005, 2006 and 2007.

More recently, international opinion on immigration levels is believed to have been influenced by security concerns. The terrorist attacks on the World Trade Centre on September 11, 2001, were broadly expected to cause a shift in attitudes about immigration. In measuring the impact of this event, pollsters and policy-makers must determine whether the effect is short- or long-term. According to an October 2001 Environics survey, the number of Canadians who said Canada allows in the right number of immigrants stood at 50 percent, up three percentage points from the weeks immediately following the September 11 attacks, but similar to levels recorded previously. However, those saying Canada let in too many immigrants (36 percent) is only slightly higher than in the previous survey but remained down significantly (–10 percentage points) from levels recorded in January 1996 (Environics Research Group 1998–2001).

When the questions and/or the responses are worded differently, the surveys can yield a different result. A February 2002 Leger Marketing poll found that more than half of Canadians felt the country admits too many immigrants (Leger Marketing 2002). However, this result can be largely explained by the response choices: responses were confined to "too many" (54 percent), "not enough" (26 percent), or "I don't know" (20 percent). By dropping the opportunity to say the number of immigrants is "about right," the poll produced a more pessimistic result.

Immigration to Canada: How Many is Too Many?

Underlying divergent assessments of public opinion on immigration levels are questions about the population's knowledge of the actual numbers of immigrants arriving in the country. Traditionally, questions about immigration levels pay less attention to knowledge of the numbers and are more preoccupied with the perception or feeling people have about the presence of immigrants. After all, knowing the numbers without some context within which to situate them may not generate meaningful conclusions.

What happens to public opinion when questions on immigration levels are preceded with actual numbers? In this regard, in a January 2006 Ipsos poll (CIC 2006), Ipsos first informed participants that Canada was accepting about 225,000 immigrants annually. When questioned about immigration levels after learning this information, 44 percent of participants declared the number too high, 34 percent said it was about right, 10 percent said it was too low, and 12 percent did not express an opinion. Thus, the revelation of the number nearly inverts the "too high" and "about right" results. In other words, opinion shifted, with a certain percentage changing from "about right" to "too high."

Polls commissioned by the federal government have attempted to test awareness about the numbers of immigrants coming to Canada annually before asking questions about the levels. When asked about their knowledge, about 95 percent of Canadians say they do have an idea of the approximate percentage of people in their neighborhood that are immigrants. Surveys done by Ipsos in October 2005 and November 2006 (CIC 2005, 2006) reveal that about one in five Canadians (22 percent) believe that Canada allows entry of fewer than 150,000 immigrants annually. Two in five (39 percent) believe the government allows in between 150,000 and 249,000 immigrants annually, while one in four (24 percent) believe the government allows in between 250,000 and 499,000 annually. Fewer than one in ten (6 percent) believe Canada allows more than 500,000 immigrants to enter Canada annually. Those who are most likely to say there are between 150,000 and 249,000 immigrants coming to Canada annually are those who choose the "about right" answer (44 percent), compared to those who say there are too many (34 percent) (see Table 2).

In the same survey, when respondents heard the actual numbers—between 240 000 and 265 000—they were slightly more likely to change their answer to "too many." But while those feeling there were "too many" rose from some 29 percent to 36 percent, the percentage saying the numbers of new arrivals were about right remained virtually unchanged at 48 percent (CIC 2006). When they were made aware of the numbers, the "don't know / refused" respondents changed their answer and raised the "too many" responses. Thus, changes in opinion based on knowledge of the actual annual immigration levels is also conditioned, at least in part, by the way in which the figure is presented to respondents. For this reason, the value of including the numbers of immigrants in the question when gauging public opinion remains uncertain.

Table 2: Estimates of Immigration Levels

In total, approximately how many new immigrants do you think that Canada allows into the country each year? In your opinion, do you feel there are too many, too few, or about the right number of immigrants coming to Canada?

Number estimated	Too many %	Too few %	About right %	Total %
Less than 150,000	20.5	27.4	21.7	21.8
150,000 to 249,000	33.2	40.0	42.5	38.1
250,000 to 499,000	24.6	20.0	24.9	23.4
500,000 or more	9.2	5.3	4.9	6.3
Don't know/Refused	12.4	7.4	6.0	10.4

Source: CIC 2006.

In addition to examining Canadian opinion on immigration over time, it is useful to compare Canadian poll results with those of other countries. Comparison allows analysts to put opinions into context and determine the comparative degree to which Canadians are open to immigration. Unlike people in the United States and many European countries, Canadians do not rank immigration issues among their government's top priorities. This suggests that, for the time being, the numbers of immigrants does not appear to be viewed as a major problem by the population.

As already observed, the percentage of Canadians calling for reductions in the number of immigrants is not significant when compared to most other immigrant-receiving countries. Indeed as revealed in a March–April 2004 survey, when contrasted with several other countries, Canadians and Australians were most inclined to support increases in immigration levels (see Table 3).

A Gallup International Poll conducted in 2005 and 2006 also reveals that in Canada, more people actually preferred increases to decreases in immigration (Newport 2006). This outcome contrasts with Gallup results in Great Britain and the United States, where far more people prefer decreases than increases. Six in ten Americans and Brits favoured decreases in their national levels of immigration, compared to some 20 percent of Canadians.

Table 3: Opinions on Levels of Immigration by Selected Countries, 2003–04

Countries	Decrease %	Remain the same %	Increase %
Canada	32.2	38.7	29.1
Australia	39.0	37.6	23.4
Switzerland	44.6	49.7	5.7
Portugal	56.2	40.7	3.1
United States	56.3	32.4	11.3
New Zealand	56.6	27.7	15.7
Sweden	57.8	30.3	11.9
Ireland	58.7	32.1	9.2
Austria	61.0	32.2	6.8
France	66.1	26.2	7.7
Germany (West)	70.3	24.3	5.4
Norway	71.3	21.6	7.1
Great Britain	77.8	16.4	5.8
Total (35 countries)	56.0	32.9	11.1

Source: Carleton University Survey Centre 2004.

Integration

Is the Canadian tendency to be less likely to support decreases to immigration a function of a better selection and integration process, as some European observers contend (Bernard-Meunier 2007)? The answer is likely not reflected in Canadian opinion on integration. As noted at the beginning, cracks appear in the mosaic of public opinion when Canadians are asked questions about immigrant integration and adaptation. There is a far greater consensus on levels of immigration than there is on integration, particularly around social and cultural integration. On such matters, the manner in which the question is framed is critical. Supporters and detractors of Canada's immigration policies make extensive use of survey questions to bolster their respective cases; consequently, analysts (including this author) must always scrutinize their interpretation of polling numbers on such issues.

Analysts also must pay attention to the assumptions that are often built into questions on immigration. They must also ensure that the terms and/or concepts that find their way into questions are understood by respondents. Sometimes the wording of a question may implicitly suggest a "proper" response to the respondent. When drafting survey questions, government departments often commission studies into what causes the public to make generalizations about immigration; but this process may obscure a wider range of opinion held by the population on such matters. Defining the terms of immigrant integration is complex, and analysts are better served by allowing the diversity of opinions to emerge from a survey, rather than leading that opinion in a pre-determined direction.

When it comes to the integration of newcomers, those who feel that there are too many or too few immigrants do not disagree on all matters. Some 88 percent of those who feel there are too many immigrants agree that they feel comfortable in social situations with people of different races (53 percent strongly agree, and 35 percent somewhat agree). By comparison, some 96 percent of those who feel there are either the right number or too few immigrants agree they are comfortable in social situations with people of different races (76 percent strongly agree, and 20 percent somewhat agree) (CIC 2007). Independent of what they think of the numbers, seven in ten Canadians agree that immigrants need to make efforts to integrate into Canadian society. Eighty percent of Canadians also think that their neighborhood is a welcoming place for immigrants; ironically, 70 percent of Canadians that think that there are too many immigrants also hold this view (they likely think that Canadians are too welcoming) (CIC 2007). It might be assumed that Canadians that are most concerned about the numbers of immigrants coming to Canada would think that integration efforts are insufficient. About 60 percent of respondents who believe that the country admits too many immigrants agree that Canadians have a responsibility to help immigrants integrate into society. However, over 25 percent who agree that there are too many immigrants do not think that they have any responsibility to integrate into Canadian society (CIC 2007).

In addition, 80 percent of respondents who believe immigrants have a responsibility to integrate into Canadian society also believe that Canadians have a responsibility to help them do so. However, six in ten who feel that Canadians do not have any responsibility to assist immigrants to integrate nonetheless feel that immigrants have a responsibility to integrate (CIC 2007).

Correlating responses on immigration levels with the perceived impact of immigrants on one's community reveals that respondents most uncomfortable with higher levels of immigration are also more inclined to feel newcomers have a negative effect on the community. Of those most likely to agree that there are too many immigrants, about seven in ten contend that immigration has a negative effect on their community, compared to just over 10 percent feeling it has a positive effect (see Table 4). On the other hand, those who are most likely to feel there are about the right number of immigrants include those who say that immigration has a positive effect on their community (57 percent), compared to those who feel it has a negative effect (20 percent) (CIC 2006).

Table 4: Opinions on Effects of Immigration on the Community

In general, what effect does immigration to this country have on your community?	In your opinion, do you feel there are too many, too few, or about the right number of immigrants coming to Canada?			
	Too many	Too few	About the right number	Total
	%	%	%	%
Very positive	4.3	40.5	12.3	14.3
Somewhat positive	18.2	41.6	47.8	37.0
Neither positive nor negative	28.0	13.7	30.7	27.8
Somewhat negative	30.9	2.6	6.3	13.1
Very negative	14.2	1.6	1.6	5.3
Don't know/Refused	4.3	–	1.2	2.5

Source: CIC 2006.

These results suggest that Canadians are divided on the best approach to immigrant/minority adaptation. As academics and policy-makers continue to debate the meaning of immigrant integration, public opinion will continue to reflect such confusion. A majority of Canadians (57 percent) agree that the presence of immigrants from several different cultures in Canada strengthens Canadian culture. Of those feeling Canada accepts too many immigrants, about one in five agree that racial and cultural groups enrich the cultural life of Canada. By contrast, nearly half of those that feel Canada is accepting the right number of immigrants and two-thirds who feel that Canada has too few immigrants agree that people from different racial and cultural groups enrich the cultural life of Canada (CIC 2007).

One key question in debates about immigrant integration focuses on integration priorities. Is it better to encourage Canadians as a whole to try to accept minority groups and their customs and languages or to encourage minority groups to try to change to be more like most Canadians? Certainly, immigrants can be fit into the dominant Canadian culture while maintaining their customs and languages. Still, this question or variations of it are so frequently asked in one form or another that it is regarded as a standard index for measuring immigrant integration. In 1998, Angus Reid reported that 52 percent of Canadians felt that minority groups should be encouraged to try to change to be more like most Canadians. Two years later, in 2000, 43 percent of Canadians felt that Canada should encourage Canadians to try to accept members of minority groups and their customs and languages, while 45 percent felt that minority groups should try to change to be more like most Canadians (7 percent felt that neither option was valid, and 5 percent could not say or did not know) (Angus Reid Group 2000).

In a March–April 2004 Environics survey, about 45 percent of Canadians said that Canada's priority should be "to encourage minority groups to try to change to be more like most Canadians," while 43 percent preferred that Canadians as a whole be encouraged to accept minority groups and their customs and languages (Environics Canada 2004). However, in a variation of the same question asked by Environics in the fall of 2006, 49 percent of respondents said that immigrants should be free to maintain their cultural and religious practices, while 41 percent thought they should blend into Canadian society. As observed below, those who believe that there is too much immigration to Canada prefer immigrants to blend in, while those who don't believe there is too much immigration prefer immigrants to maintain their religious and cultural practices, or both blend in and retain traditional practices equally (see Table 5) (Environics Canada 2006).

Table 5: Blending In *vs.* Retaining Religion and Culture

Question: Which of these points of view is closest to your own? Immigrants should blend into Canadian society or be free to maintain their religious/cultural practices or both equally?

Do you strongly/somewhat agree/disagree that: Overall, there is too much immigration to Canada?	Blend into Canadian society n=849 %	Be free to maintain their religious/ cultural practices n=938 %	Both equally n=181 %
Strongly agree	33.6	12.1	18.2
Somewhat agree	25.0	17.5	17.1
Somewhat disagree	20.9	28.1	33.1
Strongly disagree	16.3	39.5	25.4

Source: Environics Canada 2006.

In June 2007, another Ipsos poll revealed that some 58 percent of Canadians agreed that it was a higher priority for Canada to encourage minority groups to try to change to be more like most Canadians, while 38 percent thought Canadians should be encouraged to try to accept minority groups and their customs and languages. The rest of the survey respondents expressed no opinion. Quebecers surveyed were much more likely to want immigrants to become more like other Canadians, with over three-quarters endorsing this view. Elsewhere in Canada respondents were somewhat more divided on the issue, with 52 percent endorsing the view that immigrants should become more like other Canadians (CIC 2007). In the same survey, 61 percent of respondents who felt that there were too many immigrants preferred that minority groups become more like other Canadians, while only 31 percent preferred to accept the customs and languages of minorities. In contrast, the respondents who preferred acceptance were mainly those who regarded the number of immigrants in Canada as "too few" (56 percent versus 32 percent) or "about right" (50 percent versus 37 percent) (CIC 2007).

Age is another important factor in these surveys. One-third (34 percent) of respondents between 18 and 29 years of age want minority groups to change to be more like Canadians. This preference increases with age—to 43 percent of those between 30 and 44 years, 49 percent of those between 45 and 59 years, and more than half (54 percent) of those 60 years old or older. Meanwhile, three in five young adult Canadians (59 percent) feel that acceptance should be a higher priority. Predictably, this preference decreases with age—to 45 percent of those between 30 and 44 years, 37 percent of those between 45 and 59 years, and only 30 percent of those in the oldest age group (60 years and older) (CIC 2007).

Compared to the rest of the world, Canada ranks amongst the countries most inclined to value the cultural contribution of newcomers. Canadians are more likely to agree that immigrants have a positive influence on their country than are citizens of most other immigrant-receiving countries. A May 2004 Ipsos International Affairs Poll reveals that about 73 percent of Canadians believe that immigrants have a good influence on their country, compared with 42 percent of Americans and 37 percent of Europeans (Gross 2004). As Table 6 shows, Canadians rank second in an international survey in a question on whether immigrants improve their society by bringing in new ideas and cultures.

Table 6: Attitudes Toward Immigration, by Country

Do immigrants improve [Country Nationality] society by bringing in new ideas and cultures?

Country	Agree	Neither agree nor disagree	Disagree
	%	%	%
Switzerland	76.8	13.5	9.7
Canada	67.2	20.4	12.4
New Zealand	60.4	23.0	16.6
Sweden	58.5	27.0	14.5
Australia	57.8	17.2	8.0
United States	57.2	24.7	18.1
Ireland	57.1	15.4	27.5
Germany (West)	56.5	24.9	18.6
Portugal	53.2	24.4	22.4
Austria	46.6	24.0	29.4
Norway	42.4	30.6	27.0
France	41.3	24.7	34.0
Great Britain	33.6	35.6	30.8
Total	47.3	26.2	26.5

Source: Carleton University Survey Centre 2004.

Barriers to Integration

Canadians have shown an awareness of barriers to integration in recent polls. When asked what is the most important barrier to integration, about two-thirds of Canadians mention language and/or cultural barriers, just under one-quarter mention employment or related economic concerns, and a similar percentage mention social concerns (i.e., housing, daycare, racism) (CIC 2007). The respondents' opinions about immigration levels made very little difference to their answers, though respondents who felt there were "too few" immigrants somewhat more frequently mentioned economic and social concerns than did those who felt there were too many immigrants. Similarly, when asked for suggestions about what immigrants should do to integrate (see Table 7), respondents mentioned learning one of the national languages first. However, for the relative importance of learning about Canada and its history or mixing with others, there is little divergence in opinion. Respondents who felt that the number of immigrants is "about right" or "too few" were somewhat more likely to encourage involvement in broader social and community life, while those who felt that there are "too many" immigrants were slightly more inclined to mention accepting the Canadian way of life and respecting the law (CIC 2006). Interestingly, the adoption of Canadian values and norms is generally not frequently mentioned in open-ended questions about immigrant integration. This does not mean that if a direct question were put to them that respondents would not identify values and norms as important; rather, it suggests that when it comes to matters of integration, Canadians do not immediately frame integration in terms of values and norms.

Table 7: Suggestions for Integration of Immigrants Relative to Attitudes toward Immigration Levels

What should individual immigrants do to integrate into Canadian society? (First mention)	In your opinion, do you feel there are too many, too few, or about the right number of immigrants coming to Canada?			
	Too many %	Too few %	About the right number %	Total %
Accept/learn the language/learn English	20.5	25.3	18.7	20.1
Learn Canadian history/culture/ learn about Canada	13.8	15.1	13.0	13.6
Mix in with the community/ integrate/get out more	8.5	7.2	7.1	7.6
Accept the Canadian way of life (unspecified)	7.2	1.8	5.3	5.2
Learn/ follow/abide by Canadian laws	5.9	2.4	3.1	3.9
Become active/involved in the community	2.7	8.4	8.7	6.7
Join social clubs/activities	2.4	6.6	6.4	5.2
Get to know people/neighbors	2.7	5.4	6.1	4.7
Accept Canadian beliefs/values (unspecified)	1.9	2.4	3.0	2.4
Accept/learn the social norms of Canadian society	0.8	1.2	0.5	0.7

Source: CIC 2006.

Furthermore, when asked what they could do to help immigrants integrate into Canadian society, respondents gave a wide range of answers. Being more welcoming was the single most common response. Indeed, the most popular responses were simply variations of this idea. Around 30 percent of those who believe there are too many immigrants mentioned being welcoming, helpful, friendly, supportive, and patient. These same suggestions came to mind for about 40 percent of respondents that felt that we have either the right number or too few immigrants.

Although Canadians do not mention economic concerns as the principal barrier facing immigrants in their integration, the preoccupation with language acquisition may actually be a concern about economic adjustment. In general, according to a 2003–2004 poll, Canadians think that immigration is good for the economy, with nearly two-thirds in agreement with this view, putting us just behind the Australians (Carleton University Survey Centre 2004). Still there are differences in opinion around the impact of immigration on employment in Canada. Respondents feeling that there are too many immigrants express strong concerns: about two-thirds say that immigrants either increase unemployment a lot (34.7 percent) or a little (31.7 percent). About one-fourth of those who believe that we have the right number share that view, with 4.4 percent believing immigration increases unemployment a lot; and 15 percent of those who feel that Canada has too few immigrants also believe immigrants increase unemployment, with 4.3 percent feeling they do so a lot.

Economic concerns tend to focus on jobs. A 2006 Ipsos survey reveals that 46 percent feel that immigrants coming to Canada today mostly "take jobs that Canadians don't want" and a further 19 percent feel they "create new jobs for themselves." Only one in five (22 percent) think immigrants "take away jobs from Canadians," and 13 percent say they don't know (CIC 2006). Paradoxically, according to the ISSP survey, more than one in four respondents internationally agreeing that immigrants are good for the economy also agree that they take jobs away from the domestic born (Carleton University Survey Centre 2004).

Many of the same Canadians who believe that immigrants weaken "our" culture also feel that immigration increases unemployment. As Table 8 shows, those least inclined to think immigrants weaken our culture are most likely to think that immigration generally increases employment opportunities. In effect, those who have concerns about immigration tend to connect these to other concerns.

Table 8: Opinions on Immigration and Culture

Overall, what would you say is the effect of immigration on unemployment among people already living here?	*Does the fact that we accept immigrants from many different cultures make our culture stronger or weaker?*					
	Much weaker	*Weaker*	*Neither weaker nor stronger*	*Stronger*	*Much stronger*	*Total*
	%	%	%	%	%	%
Increase unemployment a lot	44.2	21.1	13.5	6.3	4.9	13.3
Increase unemployment a little	22.1	27.9	22.7	26.8	10.4	23.3
Neither	15.1	23.7	39.0	33.7	38.7	31.7
Increase employment opportunities a little	14.0	19.5	19.9	22.4	28.2	21.7
Increase employment opportunities a lot	3.5	4.7	2.8	7.6	15.3	7.2
Don't know/Refused	1.2	3.2	2.1	3.2	2.5	2.8

Source: CIC 2006.

Role of the State

Another area that interests government is how its performance is rated by the public. As noted earlier, most Canadians agree that they themselves have an important role to play in assisting in the immigrant integration process. Not surprisingly, they agree that the state does as well: about 87 percent of Canadians feel that the government of Canada has an important part to play in helping immigrants integrate into Canadian society (CIC 2006). However, those who feel that Canada accepts either the right number or too few immigrants are more likely to express strong agreement that the government of Canada has an important part to play in assisting immigrant integration.

Similarly, nine in ten Canadians agree that the federal government has an important part to play in helping Canadians accept and welcome immigrants into their communities. However, one-third of respondents who feel there are too many immigrants strongly agree that the government should help Canadians welcome immigrants, compared with half of respondents who feel that Canada receives the right number, and two-thirds who feel there are too few immigrants (CIC 2006).

Table 9: Opinions on Government Roles in Integration of Immigrants Relative to Attitudes toward Immigration

The Government of Canada has an important part to play in helping immigrants integrate into Canadian society.	*In your opinion, do you feel there are too many, too few, or about the right number of immigrants coming to Canada?*			
	Too many	*Too few*	*About the right number*	*Total*
	%	%	%	%
Strongly agree	39.7	67.3	58.7	54.3
Somewhat agree	34.3	23.5	35.6	33.1
Neither agree nor disagree	5.0	3.1	1.1	2.8
Somewhat disagree	7.7	3.7	3.4	4.7
Strongly disagree	13.0	2.5	1.1	4.9

Source: CIC 2006.

Canadians give the government a positive evaluation on how it manages the process of immigrant integration. In a 2006 Ispos poll for CIC, seven in ten agree that Canada does a good job helping immigrants settle into their new communities (see Table 10). Respondents gave the highest ratings to Canada's ability to assist newcomers in adapting to their new country, with about half agreeing that the program is doing a very good or good job. However, when it comes to rating the government's performance in promoting a sense of belonging and pride among new Canadians just under half find it either very good or good.

Paradoxically, data from the 2002 Ethnic Diversity Survey of Statistics Canada reveal that on average, immigrants possess a stronger sense of belonging to Canada than non-immigrants (Statistics Canada 2002). Yet there are many Canadians who feel that at the root of the challenge of integration is the need to strengthen the newcomers' sense of belonging to Canada (Jedwab 2007; Reitz and Banerjee 2007).

Conclusion

Can it be said that there is a consensus on immigration levels in Canada? The answer depends upon the percentage that is used to define consensus. Most Canadians are satisfied with levels of immigration as reflected in the important percentage that think the numbers of immigrants are "about right." Beyond that finding, however, there remain more Canadians who feel there are too many immigrants than Canadians who think that there are too few. Hence, they are distinct or definable segments of opinion that cannot be dismissed in any analysis of public opinion. Awareness of the actual numbers of immigrants settling in the country increases somewhat the percentage of respondents who feel that there are too many immigrants; but it is uncertain that the respondents' knowledge gives a clearer indication of how Canadians feel about the levels. As revealed above, independent of the actual numbers, Canadians feel that they have a good idea of how many immigrants the country takes in.

On matters of immigrant integration, clear differences of opinion result from different opinions about levels of immigrants. It is worth noting, however, that there is an important degree of convergence in opinion around some matters, notably that immigrants have a responsibility to integrate, that the population has a responsibility to assist them, that the government has an important role to play in this regard, that language and culture are the principal barriers to integration in Canada, and that local communities must be welcoming places for immigrants.

Table 10: Ratings of Government Performance on Immigration Issues Relative to Attitudes toward Immigration

Rating the performance of our immigration program on the following: Promoting a sense of belonging and pride among new Canadians	In your opinion, do you feel there are too many, too few, or about the right number of immigrants coming to Canada?			
	Too many	Too few	About the right number	Total
	%	%	%	%
Very good	10.1	11.6	10.6	10.8
Good	28.6	40.0	38.1	35.1
Fair	28.0	26.8	30.5	28.6
Poor	18.2	15.8	13.1	14.9
Very poor	10.4	5.3	3.9	6.2
Don't know/Refused	4.6	0.5	3.9	4.4

Source: CIC 2006.

The principal divergences in opinion are as follows. Respondents who feel that Canada admits too many immigrants feel that the country is far too welcoming. Hence, these respondents are far more likely than others to want immigrants to abandon their cultures than are those who are either satisfied with the numbers of immigrants or believe there are too few. Those who favour reductions in the numbers of immigrants are also more likely to think that immigrants have a negative impact on the local communities, weaken "our" culture, and potentially increase unemployment. Moreover, for respondents who feel that immigration levels are too high, these concerns seem intertwined. In contrast, those who feel the numbers of immigrants are about right are more likely to share the views of those who feel that there are too few. As regards policies in the area of immigration and integration, respondents feeling the numbers are too few or about right share similar views about the government's performance.

In addition, compared to citizens of most other countries, Canadians are far less likely to favour reducing immigration levels and somewhat more likely to value the cultural and economic contribution of immigrants. That said, it would be a mistake to assume that supporters of current immigration levels are not seriously concerned about integration. Opinion about integration depends on how immigrant integration gets defined; and if the definition changes, so too may public opinion, thereby creating important challenges for policy-makers.

One might be tempted to assume that openness to immigration implies generally positive attitudes about diversity. But attitudes do not always follow such tidy patterns. Our analysis suggests that opinions about integration can conflict with opinions about immigration levels. Respondents who are satisfied with current levels of immigration—by far the largest of the three groups—are more inclined to have the same views about diversity as those who feel that the numbers of immigrants are too few. Both groups tend to treat the issues of integration separate from opinion about levels of immigration. Consequently, respondents who feel there are too many immigrants may indeed find many others who share their concerns but may have not made significant inroads in persuading others that reducing the numbers of immigrants will ease preoccupations over integration. Until this group is able to make a stronger link between integration concerns and immigration levels, policy-makers in Canada are very likely to maintain current immigration levels.

References

Angus Reid Group. 2000. Paper on immigration and integration in Canada and the United States. Presented at Pioneers 2000, a forum organized by the Business Council of Manitoba and the Council for Canadian Unity: Winnipeg, 4 May.

Bernard-Meunier, M. 2007. "Le défi de la diversité." *La Presse*, 5 mars. At www.cyberpresse.ca.

Carleton University Survey Centre. 2004. "Survey on Immigration and National Identity" for the International Social Survey Program, 2003–2004. At http://www.carleton.ca/sjc/cusc/.

Citizenship and Immigration Canada (CIC). 2005. "Annual Tracking Survey." Conducted by Ipsos, June. At http://epe.lac-bac.gc.ca/100/200/301/pwgsc-tpsgc/por-ef/citizenship_immigration/.

—— 2006. "Annual Tracking Survey." Conducted by Ipsos, December. At http://epe.lac-bac.gc.ca/100/200/301/pwgsc-tpsgc/por-ef/citizenship_immigration/.

—— 2007. "Annual Tracking Survey." Conducted by Ipsos, November. At http://epe.lac-bac.gc.ca/100/200/301/pwgsc-tpsgc/por-ef/citizenship_immigration/.

Environics Canada. 2004. "Survey on Immigration." March–April. At www.environics.ca.

—— 2006. "Survey on Muslims." For the Trudeau Foundation. October. At www.foundationtrudeau.ca.

Environics Research Group. 1998–2001. Selected polls on immigration levels.

Gross, M. 2004. "Reactions To Migration In Leading Nations," Ipsos International Poll. 27 May.

Jedwab, J. 2007. "The Young and the Rootless: Measuring Ethnicity and Belonging to Canada." Presented at the Association for Canadian Studies, 26 June. At www.acs-aec.ca/.

Leger Marketing. 2002. "Les Canadiens et l'immigration." 28 March. At www.legermarketing.com/.

Newport, F. 2006. "Canadians More Positive About Immigration Than Americans or Britons: Majority in United States and Britain Want Immigration Levels Decreased," in Gallup International Polls for 20 November–20 December. Published 22–31 August and 26 August–8 September. At www.gallup.com.

Reitz, J.G., and R. Banerjee. 2007. "Racial Inequality, Social Cohesion and Policy Issues in Canada," in *Belonging? Diversity, Recognition and Shared Citizenship in Canada,* ed. K. Banting, T.J. Courchene, and F.L. Seidle. Montreal: Institute for Research on Public Policy, pp. 489–545.

Statistics Canada. 2002. *Ethnic Diversity Survey: Portrait of a Multicultural Society*. At http://www.statcan.ca/bsolc/english/bsolc?catno=89-593-X.

Chapter 8

How are Immigrants Seen—and What do they Want to See? Contemporary Research on the Representation of Immigrants in the Canadian English-Language Media

MINELLE MAHTANI

Introduction

This chapter provides a brief overview of the literature on media and immigration over the last decade.[1] While there have been significant advancements in the field, with contributions from scholars in a variety of disciplines, there are ongoing patterns of misrepresentation and underrepresentation of immigrants more broadly that reinforce their ongoing exclusion in the national body politic. The chapter points to key areas that remain unexplored in this field, paying particular attention to the value of developing a multidimensional approach in critical media scholarship—a scholarship that, up until this point, has not yet looked at the potential links between media production and consumption. The chapter suggests that a multidimensional approach may be helpful in developing more accurate depictions of immigrants in the Canadian English-language media.

Media and Immigrants: Why Representation Matters

It is almost commonplace now to state that the media play a significant role in communicating messages about various Canadian social identities (Henry and Tator 2002; Fleras and Kunz 2001; Mahtani 2001). Media scholars have thoroughly documented how the Canadian media have the power to create social agendas, construct ideologies, and frame

Immigration and Integration in Canada in the Twenty-first Century, eds. J. Biles, M. Burstein, and J. Frideres.
Montreal and Kingston: McGill-Queen's University Press, Queen's Policy Studies Series.
© 2008 The School of Policy Studies, Queen's University at Kingston. All rights reserved.

social issues, providing the lens through which Canadians view themselves and their fellow citizens. This is a particularly important issue to consider when examining the topic of immigration in Canada because *what Canadians read and hear about immigrants largely influences their perspective on immigration in this country.* In other words, news helps people learn about the world around them. For example, rural Canadians who do not have face-to-face communication with newly arrived immigrants rely on what they see and hear in the popular media to decipher and understand changes in Canada's demographic reality.

Journalists wield immense power through their framing and perspective of immigration issues. In her analysis of media and diversity, Lehrman (2005) found that journalists have the most influence when audiences live in places or work in jobs that are not very diverse. This is when they most rely on the news media for information about other groups. When certain types of people don't show up in the news, "long-standing cultural stereotypes and misunderstandings ... readily fill in the blanks" (Entman and Rojecki 2000, 15). Thus, the impact of media representations of immigrants cannot be underestimated.

In the next section, I examine the conflation that occurs between competing ethnocultural terms regarding the construction of the immigrant (Karim 1993) and its impact on research in this field.

The Epistemological Conflation

Up until the early 1990s, the majority of research on immigrants and media tended to conflate the category of "immigrant" with "visible minority" and/or "people of colour" or "racialized group." While it is true that many immigrants do fall into the categories of "visible minority" (itself a hotly contested term) and/or "person of colour," it does not necessarily follow that all immigrants imagine themselves within these categories and/or are seen as "visible minorities" or as members of a racialized group. However, a review of the research on immigrants in the media reveals these terms have often been used interchangeably. Canadian scholars from a variety of disciplines who were interested in the links between "race" and media did not necessarily clarify the differences between these loaded categories. This has a significant impact on the epistemological development of research in this field. Much scholarship has analyzed the representation—or more appropriately, the misrepresentation and underrepresentation—of racialized individuals which can include, but is not necessarily limited to, immigrants. Much less work has been dedicated to looking at representations of immigrants specifically.

In this review, I initially attempted to limit the analysis to studies that explored the representation of immigrants specifically. However, scholars have pointed out that "immigrant" within the Canadian press is a fundamentally racialized term (Henry et al. 1995). Jiwani discusses the conflation of race and immigration status through a provocative analysis of the ways immigrants are represented in the Canadian media:

> The category of immigrant is…packed with loaded signifiers that connote difference and inferiority. Further, because this catch-all term dissolves and homogenizes difference, those labeled immigrants are viewed as recent arrivals into the nation—not quite a part of it and yet contained within it. They are never real Canadians, an observation typically leveled at them through daily questions, such as where are you from? (Jiwani 2006, 52)

She explains that a key signifier embedded in the use of the term "immigrant" is the understanding of "the immigrant" as a racialized minority. Thus, it is important to note that this review draws from both the literature on immigration representation and the literature that examines the representation of racialized individuals in the media to ensure that as many pertinent sources are included as possible.

Analyzing Media Portrayal of Immigrants: Production and Consumption

In a critical review of literature on media and minority representation in Canada (Mahtani 2001), I suggested that the majority of research up until that point tended to focus on tabulating the underrepresentation and misrepresentation of minorities through content analyses. I further noted that newer research moved beyond this approach to explore the newer domains of media ownership, audience reception, ethnic media, and media workers. Five years later, a focus on the production of images, favouring content analysis, still makes up the majority of research. However, a growing body of research is concerned with analyzing the media consumption patterns of immigrant audiences in Canada. This interest in audience reception poses some exciting new questions: What are immigrants watching in Canada, and why? What is the role of both the ethnic media and mainstream media in integrating newly arrived immigrants? This research represents a shift in the epistemological and ontological developments in the field, from a focus on the production side to the consumption side. It also effectively attributes greater agency to immigrants in the process of creating images that are more democratic, equitable, and realistic.

I begin by analyzing the research that has examined the production of portrayals of immigrants in the Canadian media before exploring the newer research on audience reception.

The Production Angle: What Representations Are Produced?

Before the new millenium, much of the literature on media production critically analyzed the Canadian media's tendency to either underrepresent or misrepresent racialized minorities, with a focus on the demonization of racialized immigrants who are often imagined as "problem people" or potential troublemakers likely to steal occupations and opportunities from "real" Canadians, and engage in illegal activities, such as drug trafficking and abuse of the welfare system (Henry and Tator 2002; Fleras and Kunz 2001). This type of research has continued, but researchers are now providing more refined analyses that probe the predominant patterns of misrepresentation. These works have emphasized how immigrants continue to be criminalized in the media as deviant, different, and dangerous (Hier and Greenberg 2002; Fleras and Kunz 2001) and how they are envisioned as a threat to the Canadian way of life, potentially abusing and draining Canadian financial resources (Jiwani 2006; Henry and Tator 2002; Mahtani 2001). What is exciting and different about these new content analyses is the way they link pervasive patterns of misrepresentation with new theoretical developments in critical "race" theory, feminist theory, postcolonial studies, poststructuralism, and citizenship studies.

For example, Yasmin Jiwani (2006) provides a cogent analysis linking postcolonial studies, feminist theory and media and immigrant representation in her provocative book, *Discourses of Denial* (Jiwani 2006). Arguing that the media exert a particular form of social control over racialized individuals by portraying them in ways that effectively "Other" them through criminalization, exoticization, and inferiorization, she insists that colonial stereotypes dominate the media landscape. Jiwani emphasizes that the main message is one of assimilation, where immigrants are seen as being outside of real "Canadianness" and are encouraged to "fit in" to Canadian society.

Similarly, in a fascinating auto-ethnographic analysis, Thobani (2003) draws on materialist, anti-racist, and postcolonial feminist theories to examine the way she was demonized in the mainstream English-language press after giving a speech criticizing America's war on terrorism. Thobani shows how the overwhelming media response was one of a personal attack, positioning her as a hostile and irresponsible immigrant woman. She argues that by repeatedly anchoring her status as a non-white, immigrant woman, the media reproduced a racialized discourse about who belongs within the Canadian nation-state and who does not. Deemed an "outsider-within—a challenge which was turned into a 'national' public spectacle" (409), Thobani illustrates through reports in Canadian newspapers how she was deemed to be an "immigrant-outsider-to-the-nation and thus allied with the 'enemy'" (408). Peter Li (2003) has also explored the complex undercurrent of racialized discourse apparent in representation of immigrants in both policy documents and media representations.

I suggest that the current research that examines the complicit and complex relationship between racialization, issues of citizenship, and critiques of meanings of integration in the media were inspired by the groundbreaking work of Frances Henry and Carol Tator (2002), key leaders in the field of media and minority studies. Their work continues to illustrate how the media do not objectively cover reality and instead provide severely distorted views of Canadian immigrants. For example, their analysis of the *National Post*'s discourse on immigration, refugees, and the Tamils shows how Canada's Tamil community has been negatively associated with an alleged "terrorist" organization: "An entire group has been tainted by the actions of a few...nothing positive is ever written about this community." (Henry and Tator 2002, 123).

Another highly productive pair of Canadian media researchers, Sean Hier and Joshua Greenberg, has produced several different analyses of media representations of immigrants (see Greenberg and Hier 2001; Hier and Greenberg 2002). Hier and Greenberg (2002) illustrate Canadians' "collective anxieties" about immigrants through an analysis of news discourse about the 600 illegal migrants on the coast of British Columbia in 1999. Using the concept of moral panic, they explain how the migrant arrival was problematized and transformed into a discursive "crisis" which focused on issues of national security. Their 2001 study analyzed the structures of news access that governed the general organization of coverage of the arrival of the Chinese migrants (who were pejoratively termed "the boat people"), coupled with a discussion of the themes of the coverage. Greenberg and Hier offer an analysis of not only structure and content but also form and style. Insisting that "effective news analysis requires a dual-analytic perspective" (2001, 565), the authors provide an exciting new template for potential future work on news discourse through their dual-site analysis approach.

The incident of the Fujianese Chinese landings in 1999 provided a fruitful case study for other media researchers as well. The fear-mongering in the news coverage of this event typically demonized the claimants, as Vukov (2003) shows, providing a catalyst for more restrictive controls:

> The media framing of the Chinese migrants as "human cargo" signaled the inauguration of a Canadian public discourse on migrant trafficking that is now being governmentalized in highly repressive ways....Media myths such as the trope of "human cargo" act as culturally resonant sites of conflicting values and social tensions...Through media spectacles, affective myths around immigration, such as "porous borders" or "floods" become discursive events that serve to frame specific strategies of policy intervention, giving momentum to particular policy agendas and forms of government regulation (Vukov 2003, 346).

Mahtani and Mountz (2002) also draw upon the Fujianese migrant story to emphasize the role the color line plays in who is considered an acceptable immigrant. They indicate through an analysis of media coverage of immigration issues in the Vancouver and Prince George papers that refugees from Kosovo were represented in a different way from those who arrived from China. Whereas immigrants from Kosovo were seen as positively contributing to Canadian society, and that subsequently "Canadians felt good about themselves through that immigration event" (Mahtani and Mountz 2002, 29), migrants from China were portrayed as problematic and unwelcome. This echoes the work of Fleras and Kunz (2001), who insist that the Canadian media tend to miniaturize immigrants as minorities, refusing to reflect them in a more full and complex manner. As Ismael and Measor state in their discourse analysis of two national newspapers between September 11 2001 and September 11 2002, the 9/11 attacks served as a catalyst for increasingly troubling representations of immigrants: "The Canadian media [reveal an] irrational suspicion of immigrants...[coverage was] sensational, emotional and repetitive" (Ismael and Measor 2003, 123–124). Immigration policies in particular were scrutinized negatively, "ignor[ing] the historical, political, cultural and institutional contexts within which racism has existed in Canada" (124).

Abu-Laban and Garber (2005) provide a useful comparative analysis of the ways that the meaning of immigration settlement patterns is socially constructed through a textual study of newspaper coverage of census findings in both Canada and the United States. They ask: "[I]f the current pattern of immigration settlement is constructed as a problem in the United States or Canada, how and for whom is it interpreted as problematic?" (Abu-Laban and Garber 2005, 521). Drawing from a textual analysis of four Canadian newspapers (the *Toronto Star, The Globe and Mail,* the *National Post* and the *Winnipeg Free Press*), Abu-Laban and Garber specifically follow the coverage following former Citizenship and Immigration Minister Denis Coderre's proposal to "regionalize" immigration. Their analysis found that immigrant settlement is predominantly represented as an outcome that involves the federal government, where national and local media coverage reflected the belief that the federal state can—and should—direct immigration policy.

"In Canada, the geography of immigration has been constructed in a manner that assumes the propriety of national state intervention into where immigrants settle…[reflecting] the continued power of national mythologies in shaping ideas about governance, immigration and social inclusion" (Abu-Laban and Garber 2005, 523). They point out the lack of discussion on racism in the papers, showing that only one article among all the articles examined made specific reference to the term "racial discrimination." "The lack of discussion of contemporary racism is in itself a stunning finding," they note, "given the history of Canada as a settler colony and the ongoing reality of racism in the everyday lived experience of minorities in the country" (Abu-Laban and Garber 2005, 537). Particularly useful is the authors' analysis of the journalistic focus on anecdotal, individual "success stories"—immigrants who experience and acknowledge racism but somehow rise above it either by learning to cope or by migrating to more hospitable places. Abu-Laban and Garber wryly point out the paradox with this coverage: on one hand, these stories may be interpreted as more "positive" representations of immigrants; on the other hand, they demand a downplaying of institutional or structural disadvantage faced by racialized immigrants. Abu-Laban and Garber conclude by stating that the geography of immigration settlement demands more nuanced, critical framings than current media analyses provide.

The Consumption Angle: What Representations Are Consumed?

As the above studies amply illustrate, research analyzing the production of images related to immigration has become more nuanced over the past ten years. The analysis of predominant patterns of misrepresentation of immigrants in the Canadian English-language media has become more detailed, providing us with a greater understanding of the particular paradigms that shape the representation of the immigrant. However, a new arena of research has emerged that shifts from merely analyzing the production of images towards the actual consumption of these images. Simply put, there is growing interest in understanding not only how immigrants are portrayed, but also how they consume these images. What are immigrants watching? And what is the impact of both positive and negative representations on their sense of belonging to the nation-state?

Unfortunately, much of our research on consumption patterns—or audience research—among immigrant groups in Canada remains relatively sophomoric, lagging behind research from the United Kingdom and the Netherlands, where researchers have developed a significant body of literature on immigrant perceptions of television news especially since 9/11 (see Gillespie 2006). The following section looks at studies that are beginning to examine the notion of the immigrant "ethnic audience" in Canada, paying particular attention to the methodological approach employed and the findings and implications of these studies for future research.

The Allure of the "Immigrant/Ethnic Audience"

Research on immigrant/ethnic audiences may well be traced to early studies that analyzed how people changed their consumption of products due to cultural contacts. Lee and Tse (1994) investigated the consumption patterns of Hong Kong immigrants in Canada, finding that new immigrants adjusted their consumption habits by prioritizing and acquiring products they deemed necessary for their life in Canada. While their study focused less on media patterns of consumption (what shows they watched, what newspapers they read, etc.) and more on actual commercial products they purchased (car wax, microwave ovens), the findings were important because they revealed that when the environment of the immigrants changed, their consumption practices changed. "They were found to acquire products essential to Canadian life most readily and abandon consumption habits that were characteristic of Hong Kong" (Lee and Tse 1994, 75). The authors emphasized the need for more conceptualization in acculturation research to more fully understand the immigrant audience.

Through interviews with senior media managers in Canada, Mahtani (2008) has examined the desire in mainstream media organizations to tap into a greater share of what is known as the "ethnic audience." They are recognizing the need to cover stories that are of interest to the ever-growing multicultural population in Canada in order to improve their market share. Through efforts to reach out to the "ethnic audience"—increasingly seen as an untapped source of profit—Canadian media organizations have emphasized the importance of covering "diverse" stories, where diversity is not just seen as making good moral sense, but also good business "cents." Such an approach has been framed under the rubric of "diversity"—a key buzz word in media circles, remaining ill-defined as a concept but imagined as a way to tap into greater profitability. This profit-seeking logic speaks to media organizations' desire to seduce as many readers as possible (Fleras and Kunz 2001). While it can be argued that a commercial, rather than moral, imperative is the motivating factor here, the bottom line is that media organizations are trying to find new ways of covering stories about immigration, multiculturalism, and "race" that are also of interest *to* immigrants and ethnic minorities, with the hopeful result of a larger profit margin. However, confusion still abounds as to what is considered a "diverse" story. Which reports are, in fact, of interest to this seemingly elusive "ethnic audience"? What kinds of stories does this population want to see? To answer this question, many mainstream networks have commissioned focus groups with particular immigrant populations. However, it is difficult to gain access to these studies, given that media outlets want the results to remain confidential in order to stay competitive. Mahtani has further discovered that mainstream media organizations face challenges when actually trying to commission this research. In her study, she interviewed media managers who are in charge of the diversity portfolio for their network. One executive told her:

> We know already that Nielsen's [a media ratings agency] does not have Chinese-speaking recruiters, among other languages; so if they don't have recruiters they obviously don't have Chinese-speaking families or Punjabi-speaking families in their sample. Therefore, they are not being measured, so they can't tell when a story is actually connecting with these audiences" (Mahtani 2008).

This lack of information on immigrant audiences—both privately funded by networks and conducted among academic researchers—has inspired Canadian media scholars to conduct their own research on audience reception. Mahtani (2008) conducted focus groups with newly arrived immigrants from Iran and China, asking them about their media consumption patterns upon arrival. Her research found that members in both focus groups were surprisingly skeptical of ethnic news media in Canada, pointing out discrepancies and the ways it stereotypes other ethnic groups. They also demonstrated a level of distrust in American media. The majority of research participants regularly compared and contrasted Canadian and American programming, displaying a rich and varied "media diet" of sources for information. Zhou, Chen and Cai (2006) offer a similar analysis of Chinese-language media and immigrant life in Canada. Insisting that the upsurge of Chinese-language media mirrors the cultural, socioeconomic, and linguistic diversity of the Chinese diaspora community, they examined the impact of Chinese-language media on Chinese immigrants in North America. This study was groundbreaking, because it was one of the first to ask how Chinese-language media influences the adaptation and integration of international immigrants into their new country. The authors suggest that Chinese-language media connects immigrants to their places of origin, but also serves to provide a roadmap for the first generation to integrate into their new home by promoting home-ownership, entrepreneurship, and second-generation education: "The Chinese-language media…provid[e] an important tool in helping new immigrants adapt to life in a foreign land" (Zhou et al. 2006, 49).

Cheng (2005) also draws upon interviews with ethnic consumers of media in her paper "Constructing a Transnational, Multilocal Sense of Belonging." Cheng complicates conceptions of "home" and the "local" through her suggestion that the "local" in journalism is a fuzzy concept: "It has two dimensions," she argues, "the place and people" (Cheng 2005, 156). Explaining that immigrants develop transnational, multilocal senses of belonging, Cheng believes that the immigrant media constructs and narrates a new relationship between people and multiple locations and thus serves as an ideal site to study how the media help immigrants relate themselves to their place of origin and their new place of residence. Using the *Ming Pao* newspaper as a case study, Cheng suggests that the immigrant press narrates a place-oriented locality for the place of residence (Vancouver) and a people-oriented locality for the place of origin (Hong Kong). Her work provides a window through which we can better understand the relationship between transnational linkages and media use. Cheng also provides a multi-site analysis that media scholars would do well to emulate. Although we have very little research analyzing the effects of media coverage on Canadians' perceptions of immigration, Duck, Lalonde and Weiss (2003) provide an important glimpse of the effect of negative portrayals of immigration on Canadian students. They state that negative representations promoted less favourable views over time (Duck, Lalonde and Weiss 2003). But again, literature in this arena remains limited.

Production and Consumption: Marrying the Two Spheres

New research is beginning to merge these traditionally distinct fields by marrying the production and consumption spheres. Asking new questions about the complex *relationship* that emerges between the production of representations, the consumption of representations, and the impact of those consumptions on understandings, beliefs, and perceptions of immigration among *both* producers and consumers of media, some new studies provide a nuanced analysis hinting at the potential of media and immigration research, with an eye towards the development of more balanced portrayals. At the forefront of this research has been a recent study commissioned by Citizenship and Immigration Canada–Ontario Region, where varied teams of interdisciplinary researchers made up of journalists, not-for-profit workers, public relations specialists and academics have been examining not only what kinds of representations of immigration are in the media, but also asking more detailed questions about who is watching, listening and reading those accounts of immigration at the same time. These studies marry content analysis with critical evaluations of focus groups conducted with immigrants and are complemented by interviews with media workers in both ethnic media and mainstream media; as a result, they reflect a greater diversity in methodological design and composition of the research team, bringing together individuals with a variety of skills and differing access to networks. The research has been primarily concerned with examining the role of ethnic and mainstream media in facilitating integration for newly-arrived immigrants.

In examining the settlement-related content that presently appears in both mainstream and ethnic media in Ontario, Karim et al. (2007) conducted focus groups with ten different ethnic groups and asked them about their needs for settlement information. They found that participants wanted different kinds of settlement information in the media and noted that there was very little local settlement information available in the ethnic media outside of the Greater Toronto Area (GTA). Participants explained that they watch a mix of Canadian, mainstream, and ethnic and satellite TV programming and expressed concerns with the coverage of immigration in some mainstream newspapers (the *Toronto Sun*). In addition, many ethnic communities have strong stigmas attached to mental illness, and therefore they noted that their media and other information sources were reluctant to address it. Karim et al. also interviewed editors of print media and producers of broadcast and web-based media and asked them questions about their general policies related to the inclusion of settlement-related information in their media, target audiences, and future plans for including settlement content. Karim et al. found that most ethnic media lack solid data on audiences and readership and that they wanted clearer information on settlement issues. They also reported that they were often contacted after shows aired and articles were published by viewers/consumers asking how to get in touch with experts and guests in particular stories. Not surprisingly, mainstream media editors and producers recognized the diversity of the population in their cities; but they were not necessarily open to carrying settlement information, as they have seen themselves as primarily offering news and information shows and have been concerned that settlement information is not necessarily "newsworthy." DiversiPro (2007) embarked upon a similar study, interviewing editors and producers, conducting focus groups and analyzing media coverage of settlement-related issues. DiversiPro found in interviews that the mainstream media producers could not cite any examples of settlement information for newcomers. As one producer noted, "Not a lot of our audience is immigrants...we don't want to alienate mainstream readers" (DiversiPro 2007, 15), thus pointing out the discrepancies between media managers' desire to diversify their audience compared to on-the-ground producers' beliefs about who their audience is (Mahtani 2008).

Future Directions

In this final section, I point out some of the omissions in current research related to media and immigration and suggest key arenas for future work in this area. In particular, I emphasize the importance of linking the two arenas of production and consumption through multi-method approaches. I also suggest some of these potential projects.

The Influence of the Neoliberal Turn on Representations of Immigrants

Canadian critical media scholars like Lorimer and Gasher (2004) and Miljan and Cooper (2003) have studied media convergence and deregulation of media markets in Canada. This research has been valuable in analyzing the context of neoliberal deregulation in various Canadian newsrooms and its impact on the media's capacity to contribute to a democratic public sphere (Macdonald 2006). As Lorimer and Gasher point out,

> neoliberal deregulation has sparked a trend in media convergence, resulting in an economic strategy…where media conglomerates take advantage of the digitization of content and government deregulation to reduce operating costs and expand market share (Lorimer and Gasher 2004, 211).

Similarly, Nesbitt-Larking has shown that the increase in corporate convergence of media ownership has resulted in a reshaping of industrial relations in the media workforce across Canada: large numbers of moderately paid workers with stable jobs and long-term employment have been replaced with smaller numbers of highly paid workers in managerial and professional positions and "a floating pool of poorly paid workers who carry out routine tasks" (Nesbitt-Larking 2007, 45). Media critics have emphasized that convergence has had significant impacts on journalists' working conditions, where a drastically cut staff are expected to produce more and varied content. Furthermore, scholars have argued that, through "mergers, takeovers, buyouts, and closures, fewer and fewer companies control the production of the news" (Lorimer and Gasher 2004, 238), resulting in a growing dependence upon institutionalized sources, trivial and superficial coverage, the homogenization of media products and the undermining of journalistic values (Macdonald 2006).

While valuable in pointing out trends in media deregulation in Canada, these studies only document neoliberal deregulation shifts, rather than examining their precise effects on programming. In other words, they state that the neoliberal turn has had an impact, without showing the specific influence of this turn on the representation of marginalized groups (women, the disabled, immigrants) in the media. I suggest that a content analysis conducted immediately after a neoliberal shift, paying particular attention to the ways immigration is covered for a period of time after the event, may well provide a more precise analysis of the impact of the neoliberal turn on the representation of immigration in Canadian English-language media.

Furthermore, research may benefit from explicitly connecting processes of neoliberal job restructuring in the Canadian media sphere with a detailed ethnographic analysis of Canadian newsrooms through participant observation, and in-depth, open-ended qualitative interviews with journalists at the same time. Linking an analysis of the economic restructuring with an "on-the-ground" study of its impact on journalists' day-to-day lives would allow for a greater understanding of the ways structure, governance, and corporate values in newsrooms influence the ways stories are covered. Such scholarship would allow for a more complete picture of the neoliberal forces at play and, in particular, their impact on coverage and mindsets of journalists.

Journalism Education: Beyond the University and Mid-Career Possibilities

It has been said that journalists report on stories the way they do because of the way they are trained at journalism schools (Fisk 2003). It follows, then, that problematic representations of immigration may be traced back to the training journalists receive. Unfortunately, there is a limited research critically assessing the curriculum at journalism schools in Canada. Macdonald (2006), however, provides an important intervention through her critical assessment of current debates on the future of American and Canadian journalism education. She states the need for what she calls a "critical journalism pedagogy" to challenge the "liberal assumptions embedded in much current North American journalism education" (Macdonald 2006, 760). While a thorough analysis of curriculum at the journalism schools in Canada has not yet been conducted, an informal survey demonstrates that only two journalism schools currently offer courses dedicated to a critical analysis of immigrant representation. It has been argued that courses which offer journalism students alternative ways to represent immigrants beyond both the demonization of immigrants and the stereotypical "success story" model offer a mode of intervention for journalists wishing to counteract problematic representations of immigrants (Fisk 2003). An analysis of the current courses offered at journalism schools, paying particular attention to the ways students are taught to cover controversial topics like immigration, may be valuable in developing more equitable representations of immigrants.

While it is important to reach up-and-coming journalists, it is equally important to reach established journalists who cover stories on immigration. Centres like the Poynter Institute in the United States offer courses for mid-career journalists who wish to develop different approaches to storytelling about diverse groups (Poynter Institute 2007). A critical examination of the efficacy of such courses (What did mid-career journalists get out of the course? Did their participation in the course influence their storytelling approaches? What was the incentive for them to participate?) would offer us insight on this side of the border as to whether it would be useful for us to set up a similar course for mid-career journalists in Canada.

Detailed Ethnographic Analysis of Minority Journalists in Canada

Without dismissing the contributions of Miljan and Cooper (2003) and Barber and Rauhala (2005), who have offered accounts of the experiences of journalists, it is still an open question as to how journalists in Canada understand, consider, produce, and/or challenge the portrayal of immigration in the media. While some researchers insist that change is possible through anti-racist training programs that individually address the entrenched beliefs of journalists (Mahtani 2001), others insist that such practices will never fully derail the deeply saturated forms of hegemony that exist in media organizations or make a dent in ongoing neoliberal shifts in media structures. Regardless, we would benefit from benchmark analyses to gauge what power journalists think they have (or do not have!) in regards to producing equitable images, and what structures they believe they are up against when they do try to produce portrayals that challenge the status quo.

Moving Beyond a Focus on Journalistic Representations

The majority of research related to immigrants and media has focused on journalistic representations, as is abundantly clear from this literature review. However, an increasing number of radio dramas, television shows, and Canadian films offer alternative portrayals of the experiences of immigrants. The recent success of the television sitcom *Little Mosque on the Prairie* and its subsequent syndication in several countries offers one example of the way a particular program can challenge stereotypical representations of immigration in Canada. However, we have yet to fully examine how these programs influence the self-esteem of immigrants. Do these shows provide new immigrants with a sense of belonging in Canada because they can see themselves reflected in programming? Are they in fact watching these shows? And how do non-racialized individuals experience this kind of programming? Does it work to alter their perceptions of immigrants? Again, we require new audience research on the perceptions and consumption patterns of programs that explore the experiences of immigration.

Geographies of Immigration and Media

While some scholars have begun to explore the linkages between globalization, transnational practices, the "local," and representations of immigrants in various forms of media, research relating these topics to theoretical developments in cultural geography remains scarce. Researchers have alluded to the potential contribution of cultural geography to analyses of media and immigration, pointing out that a precise analysis of the relationship between the local, the global, and the ways media is consumed on the ground by immigrants in both places may provide a fertile examination which effectively challenges the literature in transnationalism studies, where some critics have suggested that researchers in this area have focused their analyses on elites. An example of research which effectively contributes a new take on transnationalism and media is provided by Tinic (2006), who offers a multi-layered analysis of the relationship between cultural identity and televisual representations of global and local community formations through a case study of TV production in Vancouver. Exploring the ways Vancouver has been positioned as a "global city" by attracting U.S. film producers to use the city as a site for production, Tinic illustrates the contradictions in global media practices.[2] Research like this holds much promise in providing a valuable counterpoint to studies on transnational identities and local practices in Canada.

Biases in Ethnic Media Programming

While some researchers (see Karim 2003) have focused on the transnational elements of covering stories from "home" in ethnic media produced in Canada, the ethnic media, like the mainstream media, is not exempt from the practice of misrepresenting and underrepresenting the immigrant voice. As Zhou et al. (2006) point out in their study of ethnic media, "while it is easier for ethnic media outlets to appear neutral in news coverage, the content in thematic sections often reflects, to varying degrees, editorial biases" (Zhou et al. 2006, 45). Mahtani (2008) also had similar findings in her analysis of focus groups with immigrants in Vancouver. It has been suggested that some ethnic papers can make denigrating comments about ethnic groups other than their own, thereby sending out racist messages. This kind of programming has significant implications for issues of belonging and identity in Canada, and for perceptions of newcomers. As Frideres (2006) has illustrated, the three projected sources for immigrants to Canada in the next decade are Latin America, Asia, and Africa. Consequently, the face of the country will continue to change from one that is dominated by a "white/other" divide to that of an "other/other" divide, thus making it vital to understand the tensions between racialized groups as well as the tensions between whites and racialized groups. Examining the ways that particular racialized groups understand, perceive, and "make sense" of other racialized groups will be imperative. Thus, research on the particular stereotypes and beliefs racialized groups hold about others and how they are communicated in both the mainstream and the ethnic press will prove valuable. Analyzing the actual forms of stereotyping and exclusion that exists in ethnic media will also serve to challenge the dominant "white/other" paradigm so prominent in critical media studies of the immigrant in Canada. Fleras (2007) offers an important intervention here by asking how ethnic and aboriginal media contribute to or detract from the challenges of living together in a multiracial nation.

Conclusion: Focusing on the Paradoxes and Contradictions

This chapter has provided a brief review of contemporary studies related to media and immigration in Canada, paying particular attention to key themes. I have argued that much of the work in this field continues to examine the misrepresentation or underrepresentation of the immigrant in the media, where studies have offered more precise examples of stereotyping and exclusion. While providing more specific data on the forms of representation, much of this work still suffers from the same critique that was leveled ten years ago: namely, that their results can be over-emphasized and become generalized, divorced from context without a full examination of the actual sites of production where the representation is produced or how the product is consumed (Mahtani 2001).

In 1994, Augie Fleras, one of Canada's most prominent media and minority scholars, stated that "studies to date have emphasized descriptive accounts that rarely delve into causes, impacts and solutions" (Fleras 1994, 340). Perhaps inadvertently attending to this call, and inspired by recent research in the U.K., the Netherlands, and Australia, research has developed that explores the consumption of media images, especially among immigrant groups. This new body of knowledge has usefully acknowledged the importance of understanding the consumption patterns of immigrants. However, the impact and potential of this work on the development of more equitable portrayals has yet to be fully developed.

Research that marries the production and consumption spheres seems to share a recognition that their multi-mode research on immigration and the media is complicated and complex, serving to ask more questions than providing clear-cut answers. When coupled with content analyses and qualitative interviews, it can be even more puzzling and contradictory than expected. I recommend that researchers focus on tabulating those contradictions in more detail. For example, the research of Karim et al. (2007), DiversiPro (2007) and Mahtani (2008) all indicate that immigrants develop a varied "media diet" of mainstream media, ethnic media, and news via the Internet. We might then ask: When do they turn to mainstream media? To ethnic media? Do they watch certain kinds of ethnic media for six months? Eight months? Is there a drop-off at a certain point? More longitudinal data would be of benefit here. The next stage of research must more fully integrate the media production and consumption spheres and continue to explore the paradoxes in the literature in order to develop more accurate portrayals of immigration in the Canadian media.

Notes

1. I do not include French language media in this review. While I recognize that there is a body of literature that focuses on representations of immigrants found within the French-language press in Canada (see Belkhodja and Richard 2006 for an example of this scholarship), the French-language press has its own distinct history and context and is beyond the scope of this review.
2. The links to Vancouver's ethnic diversity are not, however, explicitly made until late into the paper, where Tinic insists that alternative media provide an opportunity for groups and individuals to effectively negotiate the cultural contestations related to the sociocultural specificities of the globalizing city. While I am encouraged by the thoughtful analysis Tinic provides in regards to the negotiation of place and identity in Vancouver television, I am concerned that she overemphasizes the impact of

community media by insisting that it provides new immigrants with a space of "enablement…whereby members of the community are encouraged to use the media to identify, express and meet their needs rather than waiting for the social structure to do so for them" (Tinic 2006, 176). In my view, it is crucial to couple research that focuses on the potential agency immigrants employ in crafting alternative images with a discussion of the varied forms of resistance those same immigrants may face when attempting to get their stories told in mainstream media as well.

References

Abu-Laban, Y., and J. Garber. 2005. "The Construction of the Geography of Immigration as a Policy Problem: The United States and Canada Compared," *Urban Affairs Review* 40(4): 520–61.

Barber, M., and A. Rauhala. 2005. "Canadian News Directors' Study: Demographics and Political Leanings of Television Decision Makers," *Canadian Journal of Communication* 30(205): 281–92.

Belkhodja, C., and C. Richard. 2006. "The Events of September 11 in the French-Canadian Press," *Canadian Ethnic Studies* 38(3): 119–34

Cheng, H.L. 2005. "Constructing a Transnational, Multilocal Sense of Belonging: An Analysis of Ming Pao (West Canadian Edition)," *Journal of Communication Inquiry* 29(2): 141–59.

DiversiPro. 2007. "Research on Settlement Programming Through the Media." At www.diversipro.com.

Duck, J., R. Lalonde, and D. Weiss. (2003). "International Images and Mass Media: The Effects of Media Coverage on Canadians' Perceptions of Ethnic and Race Relations in Canada," *Australian Journal of Psychology* 55(1): 15–23.

Entman, R., and A. Rojecki. 2000. *The Black Image in the White Mind: Media and Race in America.* Chicago: University of Chicago Press.

Fisk, R. 2003. "Robert Fisk – September 11th: Ask who did it but for heaven's sakes don't ask why." A talk at "After September 11: TV News and Transnational Audiences" conference, September 9, Freedom Forum, London, U.K.

Fleras, A. 1994. "Walking Away from the Camera," in *Ethnicity and Culture in Canada: The Research Landscape,* ed. J.W. Berry and J.A. LaPonce. Toronto: University of Toronto Press, pp. 340–84.

——— 2007. "The Politics of Ethic and Aboriginal Media in Canada: Crossing Borders, Constructing Buffers, Creating Bonds, Building Bridges." Paper prepared for the Media and Minorities and Integration Conference at the University of Dortmund, June 21–22.

Fleras, A., and J. Kunz. 2001. *Media and Minorities: Representing Diversity in a Multicultural Canada*. Toronto: Thompson Educational Press.

Frideres, J. 2006. "Interview with Jim Frideres," *Canadian Diversity* 5(2): 47–48.

Gillespie, M. 2006. "Transnational Audiences after September 11," *Journal of Ethnic and Migration Studies* 32(6): 903–21.

Greenberg, J., and S. Hier. 2001. "Crisis, Mobilization and Collective Problematization: 'Illegal' Chinese Migrants and the Canadian News Media," *Journalism Studies* 2(4): 563–83.

Henry, F., and C. Tator. 2002. *Discourses of Domination: Racial Bias in the Canadian English-Language Press*. Toronto: University of Toronto Press.

Henry, F., C. Tator, W. Mattis, and T. Rees. 1995. *The Colour of Democracy: Racism in Canadian Society*. Toronto: Harcourt Brace.

Hier, S.P., and J.L. Greenberg. 2002. "Constructing a Discursive Crisis: Risk, Problematization and Illegal Chinese in Canada," *Ethnic and Racial Studies* 25(3): 490–513.

Ismael, T.Y., and J. Measor. 2003. "Racism and the North American Media Following 11 September: The Canadian Setting," *Arab Studies Quarterly* 25 (1/2): 101–36.

Jiwani, Y. 2006. *Discourses of Denial: Mediations of Race, Gender and Violence*. Vancouver: UBC Press.

Karim, K.H. 1993. "Constructions, Deconstructions and Reconstructions: Competing Canadian Discourse on Ethnocultural Terminology," *Canadian Journal of Communications* 18(2): 197–218.

―――― (ed.). 2003. *The Media of Diaspora*. London: Routledge.

Karim, K.H., M. Eid, and B. Ebanda de B'béri. 2007. *Settlement Programming Through the Media*. Toronto: Citizenship and Immigration Canada, Ontario Region.

Lee, W.-N., and D.K. Tse. 1994. "Becoming Canadian: Understanding How Hong Kong Immigrants Change Their Consumption," *Public Affairs* 67(1): 70–95.

Lehrman, S. 2005. *News in a New America*. Miami, FL: John S. and James L. Knight Foundation.

Li, P. 2003. "The Place of Immigrants: The Politics of Difference in Territorial and Social Space." *Canadian Ethnic Studies* 35(2): 1–13.

Lorimer, R., and M. Gasher. 2004. "Mass Communication and Modern Society," in *Mass Communication in Canada*, 5th ed. Don Mills: Oxford.

Macdonald, I. 2006. "Teaching Journalists to Save the Profession: A Critical Assessment of Recent Debates on the Future of US and Canadian Journalism Education," *Journalism Studies* 7(5): 745–64.

Mahtani, M. 2001. "Representing Minorities: Canadian Media and Minority Identities," *Canadian Ethnic Studies* 33(3): 93–133.

———— 2008. "Racializing the Audience: Immigrant Perceptions of Mainstream Canadian English-Language TV News," *Canadian Journal of Communication* 33(4): 639–60.

Mahtani, M., and A. Mountz. 2002. "Immigration to British Columbia: Media Representations and Public Opinion." Working Paper Series 02-15. Vancouver: Vancouver Centre of Excellence for Research on Immigration and Integration in the Metropolis.

Miljan, L.A., and B. Cooper. 2003. *Hidden Agendas: How Journalists Influence the News*. Vancouver: University of British Columbia Press.

Nesbitt-Larking, P. 2007. *Politics, Society and the Media*. Toronto: Broadview Press.

Poynter Institute. 2007. At www.poynter.org.

Thobani, S. 2003. "War and the Politics of Truth-Making in Canada," *International Journal of Qualitative Studies in Education* 16(3): 399–414.

Tinic, S. 2006. "Global Vistas and Local Reflections: Negotiating Place and Identity in Vancouver Television," *Television and New Media* 7(2): 154–83.

Vukov, T. 2003. "Imagining Communities through Immigration Policies: Government Regulation, Media Spectacles and the Affective Politics of National Borders," *International Journal of Cultural Studies* 6(3): 335–53.

Zhou, M., W. Chen, and G. Cai. 2006. "Chinese Language Media and Immigrant Life in the United States and Canada," in *Media and Chinese Diaspora: Community, Communications and Commerce*, ed. W. Sun. London: Routledge, pp. 42–72.

Chapter 9

The Discourse of New Individual Responsibility: The Controversy over Reasonable Accommodation in Some French-Language Newspapers in Quebec and Canada

CHEDLY BELKHODJA

This research examines the intrusion of the language of individual responsibility into advanced democratic societies and particularly into the debate in Quebec over reasonable accommodation. Some observers believe that, in recent years, democratic societies have become more difficult to read and describe than in times gone by. With the upsurge in what are considered new tensions and threats, such as terrorism and Islamic fundamentalism, as well as repeated requests for accommodation by ethnocultural groups, the sense of living together in a common culture—the basis of membership in the nation-state—is, according to some commentators, increasingly under attack. Identities are less clear-cut and more diffuse, and identity differences are widening. Media coverage of certain stories has intensified and dramatized the respective situations: consider the violence in French suburbs; confrontation between Whites and young Lebanese in the Cronulla district of Sydney; the situation in the Netherlands in the wake of the murder of filmmaker Theo van Gogh; and reactions to the Danish cartoons of the prophet Mohammed. In such a context, a more openly critical discourse maintains that multiculturalism policy has gone too far and has been too quick to embrace the values and customs of newcomers without protecting the foundations of a common identity (Banting, Courchene and Seidle 2007; Gregg 2007). Some suggest that "pluralistic sensibility"

Immigration and Integration in Canada in the Twenty-first Century, eds. J. Biles, M. Burstein, and J. Frideres.
Montreal and Kingston: McGill-Queen's University Press, Queen's Policy Studies Series.

has lost ground in our democratic societies, as evidenced by, for example, the breakdown in the management of ethnocultural diversity, and the difficulties surrounding the possibility of accommodating the many expressions of difference in the public sphere (Salée 2007).

This chapter addresses the questions raised in this introduction. It begins with a short description of the theme of individual responsibility, which is increasingly a focus of political and media discourse. Second, it analyzes the situation in Quebec, presenting the preliminary findings of a research project under way on the coverage of reasonable accommodation in five French-language newspapers: *L'Acadie-Nouvelle*, *Le Droit*, *Le Soleil*, *La Presse*, and *Le Devoir*. Finally, it concludes with a few broader considerations on the emergence of a "conservative sensibility" in Quebec.

The Discourse of New Individual Responsibility

The theme of individual responsibility reflects an ideological sea change that has been taking place in Canadian political culture over the last twenty years or so. There are two important considerations here. First, responsibility is a key feature of the neo-conservative, populist discourse of the Right, with its insistence on the values of the marketplace, morality, and individual rights at the expense of a more collectivist vision of society. Second, responsibility also reflects the concept of the growth and vitality of contemporary individualism. In this new framework of responsible citizenship, individuals not only have rights—they also have responsibilities. This discourse of responsibility grew out of the premise that individuals must be encouraged to take charge of their lives—and that they in fact want to do so—in order to develop and thrive. This more active concept of citizenship centres on the individual, who is willing to take on responsibilities in an advanced liberal society (Doheny 2007; Dean 2004; Ilcan and Basok 2004).

The theme of individual responsibility has become a feature of the Canadian press over the last few years, especially since September 11, 2001. In this new political context, a need clearly emerged to reframe rights and responsibilities as a result of a change in public opinion (Stein 2007). Writing in the *Globe and Mail*, Jeffrey Simpson summarizes the new way of viewing citizenship as follows: "It's just assumed that people have responsibilities and understand them, whereas rights have to be stipulated, asserted and explained.[...] This way of looking at the world assumes and encourages responsibility by citizens for each other usually, but not exclusively through the agency of government" (Simpson

2005). In the *Globe and Mail* and *National Post*, journalists like Christie Blatchford, Margaret Wente, Jonathan Kay, and Andrew Coyne call into question Canadian accommodation that implies a definition of Canada as a nation that welcomes diversity and grants rights to ethnocultural minorities. In their opinion, it is time to take responsibility and make people aware of what is going on around them, particularly in the religious activities and institutions of Muslim immigrants: "What are the Islamic private schools and mosques in our country teaching and preaching? Most non-Muslim Canadians don't have a clue. They didn't in Britain, either. The lesson is that it's time for all of us to pay attention. If we don't do it for our own sakes, let's do it for the Muslim parents" (Blatchford, *Globe and Mail*, 16 July 2005). In addition, the journalists say, Muslims must be encouraged to be more responsible, watch over their neighbourhoods, think about the education of their children, and expose extremists. The articles by Sheema Khan in the *Globe and Mail* often broach these issues. Moderate Muslims must become involved and denounce the use of violence in the name of religion. This is apparently one of the main challenges facing the Muslim community.

A new critical view of integration is emerging around an economic, individualistic discourse. Martin Collacott, a former diplomat now working with the Fraser Institute, expresses this view in several major dailies. As far as he is concerned, immigrants come to Canada with responsibilities, including that of accepting Canadian values in order to gain and maintain their citizenship: In a March 1, 2006 article in the *National Post*, he noted that immigrants should be required to take an oath that they are committed to Canadian values and will give their complete allegiance and loyalty to Canada. Moreover, their future behaviour would have to reflect this commitment. A week later he added:

> Greater emphasis has been given in recent years to the rights of newcomers than to their obligations to Canada. This likely has been a contributing factor in encouraging some of them to treat this country as a base from which to engage in, or mount support for, their favourite conflicts abroad. (Collacott 2006)

The Situation in Quebec

In Quebec, the argument that the goal of Canadian multiculturalism policy is to reduce Quebec's relative weight in the country is well established: [translation] "Canada has imposed a multicultural vision of the country to deny the existence of the Quebec people and has tried (unsuccessfully) to impose institutional bilingualism so as to avoid having to recognize the biculturalism of its founding peoples" (Seymour 1997, 128).

This criticism of Canadian multiculturalism emerged in a very specific context, that of the Quiet Revolution and the affirmation of a distinct Quebec identity under Jean Lesage. After many years of absence from national affairs, post-Duplessis Quebec resumed its role in the Canadian federation and demanded its share of constitutional powers. The principle of institutional and linguistic duality, based on the constitutional pacts of 1774 (*Quebec Act*) and 1791 (*Constitutional Act*), guided the Quebec government's actions. During the 1980s, Quebec was faced with the more visible presence of immigrant communities, so it came up with its own policy on pluralism—interculturalism (Gagnon 2000). The purpose of the policy was twofold: to promote respect for ethnic diversity and to create opportunities to share a common identity.

The criticism that multiculturalism undermines the interests of the Quebec people and its national self-affirmation is well documented. The argument first took shape in the 1970s and still enjoys currency in Quebec society. Stéphane Kelly (2001) presents the multiculturalism policy as a means of neutralizing advocates of a federalism based on the duality of the two founding peoples. At the time, according to Kelly, Trudeau wanted to [translation] "undermine Laurendeau's bicultural ideal" (Kelly 2001, 207) and recognize the role and place of ethnic communities, particularly in the West, which was home to Ukrainians and a number of other ethnic communities. In Kelly's opinion, the multiculturalism policy provided an opportunity for ethnocultural pressure groups to express their position more openly during the constitutional debate of the 1980s.

Over the past few years, criticism of Canadian multiculturalism has extended beyond the political arena and the tensions between Quebec and the federal government. The arguments for national and linguistic duality and against any recognition of a mosaic of identities have shifted to an argument centred on Quebec identity. Catherine Bouchard points out that since the early 1990s, efforts to define the Quebec nation have incorporated reflections on ethnicity and cultural and religious divisions (Bouchard 2002, 71–77). Critics recognize Quebec's multiethnic character as a factor that enriches and enhances the blueprint for Quebec society; but at the same time they condemn Canadian multiculturalism for fragmenting identities. Another consideration is the recent political trend in Quebec, which reflects major changes since the breakthrough of Stephen Harper's Conservatives in the last federal election and the success of the Action démocratique du Québec (ADQ) in the provincial election of March 2007 (Labelle and Icart 2007). According to Labelle and Icart, after a considerable lag, Quebec is following the lead of Ontario and Alberta by being influenced by a new populist, conservative discourse that dovetails well with the argument against the recognition of ethnocultural minorities. According to Victor Armony (2007b), like other populist leaders, Dumont calls on his fellow citizens to defend and promote the values of Quebec society and take actions that will strengthen Quebec's national identity, while at the same time condemning the political elite's subservient attitude to demands by community representatives (2007b, 7).

In 2006, the accommodation controversy made an explosive entry onto the Quebec political and media scene (Armony 2007a; Labelle and Icart 2007). The legal value of reasonable accommodation that was recognized in legislation introduced in the 1980s was overshadowed by a number of facts reported by the media—almost like a soap opera of events threatening the very foundations of Quebec liberal society. In March 2006, the Supreme Court of Canada handed down a major decision on the right to wear the kirpan as a sign of religious freedom. In early November 2006, the media reported several requests by the Hasidic Jewish community of Outremont, including one to ensure that young male students in a religious school could not see inside the YMCA gym located next door, the refusal of some Hasidic men to co-operate with women police officers, and an issue of denying men access to prenatal classes (Armony 2007a, 162). In December, the debate shifted to the issue of celebrating Christmas and reactions of frustration on the part of a majority of Quebecers with what they considered unreasonable demands by a minority that did not want to offend the sensibilities of non-Christians. In an article published in *La Presse* (December 22, 2006) and entitled "Joyeux Noël, quand même!" [Merry Christmas anyway!], Mathieu Bock-Côté set the tone:

> Ça y est! Un autre interdit. Et pas un petit : plus de fêtes de Noël! Trop traditionnelles. Trop chrétiennes. Surtout trop occidentales, et pas assez inclusives. (p. A31)

In January 2007, the Quebec town of Hérouxville created its own code of conduct, which caused a great deal of unease and embarrassment in Quebec. With all the international and national coverage, the small village of 1,338 inhabitants in the St-Maurice valley became a very strange case in the context of Canadian pluralism and Quebec interculturalism. In Quebec, the "Hérouxville affair" widened the divide between the metropolis of Montreal and its surrounding regions, which were portrayed and even ridiculed by the media as places inhabited by old-stock Quebecers with little acceptance of multicultural diversity. André Drouin, a member of the Hérouxville municipal council, was invited to appear on the popular TV talk show *Tout le monde en parle*, and he outlined the code of conduct that newcomers had to follow if they wanted to settle in the village. His arguments illustrated some features of the populist discourse, such as plain speaking, the condemnation of elites, a mistrust of difference, a paranoid feeling that there is an urgent need to act before "the immigrants take over," and an appeal to the down-to-earth goodness of "his" people. As Victor Armony points out, it was no accident that the identity backlash was concentrated in ethnically homogeneous areas (2007a, 166). The "Other" became a caricature of someone who was considered hostile and a threat to a well-established, reassuring order.

On 8 February 2007, Premier Jean Charest responded to all the media frenzy and tried to calm things down by announcing the creation of a public commission. The Consultation Commission on Accommodation Practices Related to Cultural Differences would be chaired by two well-known figures: historian, sociologist and novelist Gérard Bouchard and philosopher Charles Taylor. The Bouchard-Taylor Commission was given the following mandate:

- take stock of accommodation practices in Quebec;
- analyze the attendant issues bearing in mind the experience of other societies;
- conduct an extensive consultation on this topic; and
- formulate recommendations to the government to ensure that accommodation practices conform to the values of Quebec society as a pluralistic, democratic, egalitarian society. (https://www.accommodements.qc.ca/commission/mandat-en.html)

More than 300 briefs were filed by organizations and individuals. An extensive consultation process was launched in Gatineau on 10 September 2007, and ended in Montreal on 13 December 2007. The commissioners are to submit their final report in late March 2008. The media closely followed the hearings, which were designed to offer a forum for dialogue between the commissioners and the general public.

French-Language Newspapers

Our sample comprises over 1,500 texts from five newspapers representing the main French-speaking regions of Canada: *Le Devoir, La Presse*

(Montréal), *Le Soleil* (Quebec City), *Le Droit* (Ottawa), and *L'Acadie-Nouvelle* (New Brunswick). The texts were identified by the EUREKA.CC database through a search for the term "accommodements raisonnables" [reasonable accommodation] in all articles (news stories, editorials, letters to the editor, opinion pieces). The time range is one year (from 1 November 2006 to 30 October 2007). This first part of the research work gives the results of a quantitative overview of the newspapers. The second part gives a qualitative interpretation of reactions to the reasonable accommodation issue. Analysis focuses on editorials, opinion pieces, and letters to the editor.

Table 1: Articles by Newspaper and Type

	L'Acadie-Nouvelle	Le Droit	Le Soleil	Le Devoir	La Presse
News*	38 (75%)	185 (74%)	242 (73%)	269 (62%)	450 (73%)
Editorial/Opinion: analysis and letters to the editor	12 (25%)	66 (26%)	92 (27%)	162 (38%)	166 (27%)
Total	50 (100%)	251 (100%)	334 (100%)	431 (100%)	616 (100%)

*"News" includes current affairs, economy and finance, arts and entertainment, sports and leisure.

Source: Eureka.cc

Over the 12 months, the reasonable accommodation issue received a tremendous amount of coverage in the Quebec media. During the 12-month period preceding the start of the controversy (from 1 November 2005 to 31 October 2006), overall use of the term in the target publications was limited: *La Presse* (n=19), *Le Devoir* (n=9), *Le Droit* (n=1), *Le Soleil* (n=1), *L'Acadie-Nouvelle* (=0). The Montreal newspapers were the loci of the real debate. *Le Devoir* published more opinion pieces and analyses by intellectuals and academics than did the other newspapers, while *La Presse* included more letters to the editor on the subject.

New Brunswick's *L'Acadie-Nouvelle* gave the issue little coverage, although columnist Rino Morin Rossignol commented on what was going on in Quebec. Some journalists alluded to events in Quebec and made conjectures about the consequences of immigration to New

Brunswick's Acadian communities. For example, editor-in-chief Jean Saint-Cyr wrote:

> Relativement à l'abri du phénomène de l'immigration, comme Acadiens nous avons beau jeu. On peut se défendre d'être raciste ou xénophobe, personne ne peut nous contredire tant que nous ne vivons qu'entre nous. Mais comment accueillerions-nous une vague importante d'immigrants dans nos communautés? (*L'Acadie-Nouvelle*, 15 November 2007, p. 12)

Because Ottawa is so close to Quebec, *Le Droit* followed the issue closely, giving a slightly different perspective—that of Franco-Ontarians. It expresses both concern about francophone immigration and deep concern over the focus on relations between the majority and minorities in Quebec. One reader recalls Ontario's recent anti-francophone past and francophones' fear of having to live under the law of the English-speaking majority. He makes the following rather striking remarks:

> La tentation est grande de transposer cette déclaration aux francophones minoritaires au Canada. Est-ce à dire que la protection constitutionnelle dont jouissent les francophones brimerait « le droit fondamental » de la majorité anglophone au pays ? Il y a dans de tels propos un risque élevé de dérive qui mène d'abord à tous les excès de langage. Or, aux dernières nouvelles, les mots sont encore porteurs de sens. Et de la parole aux gestes, il n'y a souvent qu'un pas. (Pierre Bergeron, *Le Droit*, 5 February 2007, p. 4)

Figure 1 shows the breakdown of articles by month over a 12-month period. Note that the number of news articles went up, particularly after the Hérouxville affair and the Charest government's decision to set up a public commission. The increase also coincided with the provincial election of March 2007 and the popularity of the ADQ and its leader, Mario Dumont.

By focusing on reactions published in the newspapers, we could draw some interesting conclusions about the concept of individual responsibility; certainly, the newspapers provided space for many expressions of opinion on such subjects as the place of religion in public life, the adverse consequences of the Canadian multiculturalism policy's recognition of diversity, and the widening divide between Montreal and the regions. However, the analysis in this chapter deals only with the theme of individual responsibility.

The first major theme of these newspapers was reflective of the majority's feeling of being threatened by the demands being made by

Figure 1: Number of Articles by Month (2006–07)

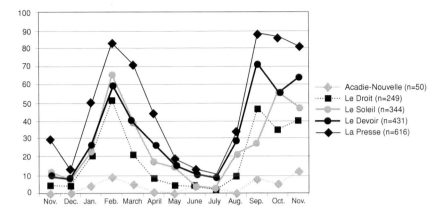

Source: Eureka.cc

ethnocultural minorities. Represented in a variety of forms, this major-ity was saying it no longer had to accede to all the unreasonable and dangerous requests and demands by minorities. Several letters to the editor expressed this view:

> Le port du kirpan, les exigences des juifs hassidiques ou les demandes au sujet des jours d'examens pour les étudiants et bien d'autres faits du même genre nous portent à nous demander si nous sommes devenus des étrangers dans notre propre pays. (Rosaire Desjardins, *Le Soleil*, 21 No-vember 2006, p. 20)

> Le débat public sur les accommodements raisonnables s'est littéralement embrasé lors de l'allocution de Jacques Godbout, qui a soutenu que la société québécoise, si elle continue sur ce chemin, sera portée à disparaître, car « ces tribus qui immigrent avec leurs costumes, leurs coutumes, leur religion et leur télévision » nous imposeront leurs vues. Par conséquent, nous devrions nous lever contre cette « immigration massive » avant qu'elle ne nous assimile. (Laurie Duguay, *Le Devoir*, 14 June 2007, p. A6)

> S'il y a un comportement à éviter, c'est bien celui où une majorité en ar-rive à se soumettre à certains diktats d'une minorité. (Pierre Bissonette, *La Presse*, 18 August 2007, p. A25)

> La classe moyenne a exprimé son ras-le-bol. […]Elle ne se reconnaît pas dans les accommodements raisonnables non-raisonnables, comme le

kirpan à l'école, les fenêtres bouchées au YMCA et, ce qui allait devenir la cerise sur le sundae, le vote des femmes voilées. (Pierre Bouret, *Le Droit*, 28 March 2007, p. 20)

These advocates maintain that immigrants must be made aware of the fact that integrating means adapting to the manners, conventions, and customs of the host society. Old-stock Quebecers convey this discourse in a variety of ways and pass it on to the immigrants themselves—for example, by arguing that Muslims must take responsibility and speak out, especially against religious fundamentalists:

« Si l'immigrant ne va pas patiner, le Québécois ne viendra pas faire de la danse latino ! » Du haut de ses 16 ans, Isaac Imanishimwe est convaincu : l'intégration des immigrants, c'est une partie qui se joue à deux. (Valérie Gaudreau, *Le Soleil*, 24 March 2007, p. 19)

Le débat sur les accommodements raisonnables aidera peut-être des gens à réaliser qu'il y a des limites à ne pas franchir et que la moindre des choses pour les immigrants est de s'adapter à notre culture et non le contraire. (Rolland Vallée, *La Presse*, 12 October 2007, p. A23)

In some writers' opinion, governments must take a more responsible approach to selecting countries as sources of immigration and make it clear that "good" immigrants are the ones that can integrate easily into the host society:

Nous pouvons être plus prévoyants dans nos politiques d'immigration en favorisant la venue de cultures qui sont compatibles entre elles, compatibles avec et complémentaires à notre propre culture. Est-ce trop demander que nos gouvernements, démocratiquement élus, soient là pour protéger et défendre notre mode de vie? (Jacques Bastien, *Le Droit*, 3 March 2007, p. 24)

Thus, for these writers, responsibility meant more than a position taken by the responsible individual; the term also had a collective connotation. Some articles in the newspapers conveyed a more nationalistic dimension—that of the Quebec nation—which must take charge of its own destiny too. Another argument states that it is time to take responsibility as citizens and counter the intolerant, racist attitudes being expressed in some quarters. Commenting in *La Presse* on the brief submitted to the Bouchard-Taylor Commission by Councillor Drouin of Hérouxville, Alain Dubuc wrote:

Ce mémoire est un torchon, une présentation pseudo-scientifique étayée par un document d'appoint immonde, intitulé Mode de vie du Québec, qui est un prototype de littérature raciste. Il faut dire les choses comme elles sont, parce qu'à force de marcher sur des oeufs, et de vouloir respecter tout ce que disent les gens, nous sommes en train, par notre silence, de cautionner l'inacceptable. (2 November 2007, p. A19)

Conclusion

One's first impression is that the media have given "reasonable accommodation" a largely sensationalist spin, particularly by reporting the wild, demagogic remarks of individuals testifying at the Bouchard-Taylor Commission hearings. However, the entirety of the statements in the French-language press of Quebec, Ontario, and New Brunswick suggests that people's reactions did differ. Many statements referred to values such as tolerance, openness to diversity, and respect for other people, as illustrated by a letter against intolerance signed by about 200 Quebecers (*La Presse*, 1 November 2007, p. A21).

Examination of the newspaper articles shows that the reference points of identity and citizenship have changed in recent years. In a sense, the reasonable accommodation issue in Quebec reflects the current tendency in some quarters to call into question social-democratic pluralism.

Responsibility is generally portrayed primarily as a characteristic of the individual; but analysis of the Quebec newspapers brought out its collective dimension as part and parcel of the development of the Quebec nation. Thus, the meaning of integration has changed. Immigrants are now being asked to be responsible, productive workers; to adopt the shared values of the host society; to learn the language; and, above all, to avoid becoming dependent on government assistance.

In short, the type of debate going on in Quebec is different from that going on in English-speaking Canada. Focusing particularly on the importance and the role of the past and history of the Quebec nation, the debate that has engaged Quebec society has been more in-depth and has in many instances not been understood in the rest of Canada. The media have referred to a "Quebec identity malaise," characterized by confrontation between two camps, *Us* and *The Other*—between the advocates of diversity and plurality of identities and the defenders of the traditions of a Quebec and French-Canadian majority. One is left with the impression that there was no longer any communication between the past and the present, between a cosmopolitan Montreal metropolis that is open to the world and the land of the first settlers.

This new dynamic of Quebec identity was conveyed primarily in the Montreal newspapers by intellectuals in opinion pieces and by columnists. In short, pluralist sensibility seems to have lost ground in Quebec public life because it has been competing with another discourse that has found clearer expression in recent years—a new conservative sensibility that is presented as a paradigm of change (Beaudry and Chevrier 2007; Bock-Côté 2007).

This new sensibility, as conveyed by certain Quebec thinkers and intellectuals, is based on several specific claims. The first is that granting accommodation to all minorities leads to fragmentation (division, dispersal) of society, through the recognition of private interests acting as full-fledged lobby groups. In the opinion of the proponents of the new sensibility, multiculturalism defends the cultures of groups reflecting the shift from the traditional or Old Left to a pluralist or New Left in the early 1990s. Some writers establish connections between the New Left and the emergence of new ideologies, such as feminism, multiculturalism and even Islamism (Rousseau 2006). The majority culture feels that it is under attack from demands by every ethnic and religious minority.

Their second claim is that pluralist openness has resulted in a "loss" and that there is therefore a need to reconnect with the goal of building or rebuilding a Quebec national society. This is a major concern for some members of the Quebec francophone elite: on what foundation can the shared national project be built? Should there be a return to the heritage of French Canada or to the ideal of the Quiet Revolution, to the "policy of national greatness" defended by Jean Lesage and to the ideas of the inspirational sociologist, poet and author Fernand Dumont in his oft-quoted 1993 book *Genèse de la société québécoise* [Genesis of Quebec Society]? The new conservative thinkers all express the fundamental principle of historical continuity and rejection of the concept of *rupture* (a recurring word) between pre-1960 and post-1960 Quebec.

The third claim is that requests or demands for reasonable accommodation reflect the dominance of postmodern theories of "deep diversity." The proponents of the new conservative sensibility are constantly criticizing postmodern society and the multiplicity of identities in an increasingly egalitarian democracy. The dispersal of identities leads to the growth and celebration of unfettered, total individualism. Gilles Labelle contends that the multiplicity of identities has become nothing more than a choice presented to the fully developed individual: "Essentially, a society of individuals is a society of individuals without ties who can choose any identity whatsoever, depending on their affinities" (Labelle 2007, 296, translation). Thus, in the opinion of a number of these writers, conservatism is the only alternative offering something different from the discourses of the neo-liberal Right and the identity politics of the New Left, whose arguments "share a common foundation, that of radical individualism" (interview with Marc Chevrier, in Cloutier 2007, 33, translation). A key feature of the conservative sensibility is a recognition of the "practical" importance of a political tradition that needs to be defended, as opposed to an ideological position. As Mathieu Bock-Côté (2007a) points out, all that is required is to rehabilitate conservatism as the only contemporary radical option for promoting change.

Finally, the criticism of diversity and demands for accommodation clearly illustrates the new importance of certain attitudes and values that were formerly peripheral to public debate. Stating that multiculturalism is no longer the ideal integration model no longer sends shockwaves through society. Several writers condemn Canada's multicultural drift to multiple identities in shrill, emotional tones. Columnists flout the requirement of political correctness and rake the *doxa* of identity pluralism over the coals. Ordinary citizens ("real people") feel more concerned and feel the need to speak out and express their opinion on all kinds of subjects. It is important to explore the issue further by analyzing the rise of populism in democratic societies. Populism is no longer just an extremist ideology defended by political parties; it is now a commonly used rhetoric and style for establishing a new relationship among individuals. Populism claims to be an alternative that can provide a constructive response to the frequently expressed feeling of disaffection from politics, and it proposes to remedy the problem in its own way by re-establishing the connection between the elites and ordinary people. In today's climate of individual responsibility, populism invites individuals to take charge of their own political lives. However, this does not overshadow the fact that the populist recipe contains some ingredients that are less than democratic—demagoguery and manipulation.

References

Armony, V. 2007a. "Identité, minorité, équité," in *La cité identitaire*, eds. J. Beauchemin and M. Bock-Côté. Montreal: Athéna, pp. 153–70.

——— 2007b. *Brief to Consultation on Accommodation Practices Related to Cultural Differences*. At http://www.accommodements.qc.ca/documentation/memoires.html.

Banting, K., T.J. Courchene, and F.L. Seidle (eds). 2007. *Belonging? Diversity, Recognition and Shared Citizenship in Canada*. Montreal: Institute for Research on Public Policy.

Beaudry, L., and M. Chevrier. 2007. *Une pensée libérale, critique ou conservatrice? Actualité de Hannah Arendt, d'Emmanuel Mounier et de George Grant pour le Québec d'aujourd'hui*. Lévis: Presses de l'Université Laval.

Bock-Côté, M. 2007a. *La dénationalisation tranquille*. Montreal: Boréal.

——— 2007b. "Le multiculturalisme comme idéologie," in La cité identitaire, eds. J. Beauchemin and M. Bock-Côté. Montreal: Athéna, pp. 61–81.

Bouchard, C. 2002. *Les nations québécoises dans l'Action nationale. De la décolonisation à la mondialisation*. Saint-Nicolas, QC: Presses de l'Université Laval.

Cloutier, J-F. 2007. "Entrevue avec Marc Chevrier," *L'Action nationale* 98(3), March: 29–40.

Collacott, M. 2006. "Newcomers Must Put Canada First." *National Post*, 7 March.

Dean, H. 2004. "Popular Discourse and the Ethical Deficiency of 'Third Way' Conceptions of Citizenship," *Citizenship Studies* 8(1), March: 65–82.

Doheny, S. 2007. "Responsibility and the Deliberative Citizen: Theorizing the Acceptance of Individual and Citizenship Responsibilities," *Citizenship Studies* 11(4): 405–20.

Gagnon, A.G. 2000. "Plaidoyer pour l'interculturalisme," *Possibles* 24(4), Fall: 11–25.

Gregg, A. 2007. "Identity Crisis Multiculturalism: A Twentieth-Century Dream Becomes a Twenty-First-Century Conundrum," *The Walrus*, 1 February. At http://www.walrusmagazine.com/.

Ilcan, S., and T. Basok. 2004. "Community Government: Voluntary Agencies, Social Justice, and the Responsibilization of Citizens," *Citizenship Studies* 8(2), June: 129–44.

Kelly, S. 2001. *Les fins du Canada selon Macdonald, Laurier, Mackenzie King et Trudeau*. Montreal: Boréal.

Labelle, G. 2007. "Repenser la domination: « société des identités » ou « société des individus déliés »?" in *La cité identitaire*, eds. J. Beauchemin and M. Bock-Côté. Montreal: Athéna, pp. 291–301.

Labelle, M., and J-C. Icart. 2007. "Une lecture du débat en cours sur l'accommodement raisonnable et le racisme au Québec," *Globe* 10(1): 121-36.

Rousseau, G. 2006. *La nation à l'épreuve de l'immigration?* Boisbriand: Les Éditions du Québécois.

Salée, D. 2007. "The Quebec State and the Management of Ethnocultural Diversity: Perspectives on an Ambiguous Record," in *Belonging? Diversity, Recognition and Shared Citizenship in Canada*, ed. K. Banting, T.J. Courchene, and F.L. Seidle. Montreal: Institute for Research on Public Policy, pp. 105–42.

Seymour, M. 1997. "La souveraineté du Québec : Un objectif légitime," *L'Action nationale* 87(6): 109–39.

Simpson, J. 2005. "Ask Not What Your Country Can Do For You." *Globe and Mail*, 19 June, p. A17.

Stein, J.G. 2007. "Searching for Equality," in *Uneasy Partners: Multiculturalism and Rights in Canada*, ed. J.G. Stein et al. Waterloo: Wilfrid Laurier University Press, 2007, pp. 1–22.

Conclusion: Canadian Society: Building Inclusive Communities

JOHN BILES, MEYER BURSTEIN, AND JAMES FRIDERES

Introduction

Canada has long been a world leader in welcoming and accepting immigrants, which in turn has contributed to Canada's growth and prosperity, as well as helping to shape our current society. Immigration is
helping Canada to attenuate the disruptions associated with its decreasing birth rate and to respond to shifting economic realities. Immigrants
help to boost Canadian competitiveness in several fields, such as the
sciences and engineering, as well as contributing to Canadian entrepreneurship. The impact of immigration is evident in our daily lives—
in the food we eat, the entertainment we watch, and the religions we
profess. And yet, for all the good it creates, we find that immigration
also generates widespread changes that can be unsettling for communities across the country and challenges associated with the integration
of these diverse new populations.

In many ways, the political reaction to immigration is nearly as old
as Canada itself. But there are important differences today compared to
a century ago. For example, in the 1960s, the majority of the immigrants
living in Canada were from the United Kingdom, the United States,
and other Western European countries. However, by the twenty-first
century, immigrants from Asian, Latin American, and African countries now make up well over two-thirds of the flow, with over 80 percent of recent arrivals coming from developing countries. In fact, over
half of the immigrants who have arrived since the 1970s and three-
quarters of those who came in the 1990s are members of a visible minority group. About seven out of ten individuals identified as visible
minorities are immigrants. It is estimated that by 2017, visible minorities

Immigration and Integration in Canada in the Twenty-first Century, eds. J. Biles, M. Burstein, and J. Frideres.
Montreal and Kingston: McGill-Queen's University Press, Queen's Policy Studies Series.

will make up 20 percent of the total Canadian population. We also find that population projections of specific religions demonstrate major shifts over the next decade. For example, Muslims now make up less than 2 percent of the population; but by 2017, it is estimated they will comprise just over 4 percent of the population, reflecting a 145 percent increase. Likewise, Sikhs and Hindus are expected to show major increases of 72 percent and 92 percent respectively by the end of the next decade (Bélanger and Malenfant 2005). These new demographic facts have changed the dynamics of immigrant integration and the responses by native-born Canadians to immigrants (Rifaat 2004).

Throughout history, migration has represented a courageous expression of an individual's will to achieve a better life. Today, this opportunity is open to millions more individuals than ever before. Globalization allows an increasing number of people to look for opportunities in countries far removed from their own. Their reception is, however, uncertain and depends on local realities, institutions, attitudes, and perceptions (Weidenfeld and Sussmuth 2005). Moreover, where settlement services are provided, there is insufficient analysis to determine their contribution to immigrant integration along the dimensions identified by the authors of this volume. Migration can create burdens and benefits for both sending and receiving countries, as well as for migrants themselves, a result that is highly dependent on how immigrants are integrated by their host societies (Fix 2006). When successful, immigrants remit earnings back to their home countries and provide a substantial economic force to their homeland (Ratha 2003; Nonnenmacher 2007). Similarly, immigrants returning home bring with them expertise and capital that buttresses local economies, as well as innovations and new ideas that enhance the social and economic structure (Spencer 2003).

Similar patterns occur within the host countries themselves: immigrants either can be a burden or an asset, depending upon the quality of their integration. For example, in a globalized environment, openness to immigrants can be an important foreign policy asset, useful in trade, cultural exchanges, and peacemaking. In contrast, if barriers prevent immigrants from participating socially, culturally, politically and economically in their new country, they will inevitably become a burden.

In summary, positive integration creates a "virtuous cycle" just as exclusion creates a "vicious" one. Measurements of outcomes allow us to determine which cycle we are moving along.

The success of immigrant integration depends on the mutual adaptation of immigrants and the host society (Bouchard 2007). To achieve this mutual adaption, both immigrants and the host society must undertake interventions as soon as possible after entry (Papademetriou 2003). This two-way street approach to integration is embedded legislatively in both the *Canadian Multiculturalism Act* (1988) and the *Immigration and Refugee Protection Act* (2001). Despite this legislation, Canada still lacks empirical evidence pointing to the success or lack of success of our two-way approach to immigrant integration. There are three problems with the assessment data: it is one-dimensional, it does not recognize intra-group diversity, and it is not dynamic and lacks comparability. As such, comparisons over time and among regions using this data are virtually impossible.

Integrating Immigrants

Today, Canada confronts a migration context that is different from that which the country experienced in earlier periods. Specifically, the increase in international mobility and the reduced cost and greater ease of entry has meant that many migrants can maintain social, political, cultural, and economic ties in two or more societies simultaneously. This has delayed the completion of integration—a process that we now understand may take generations. This new fluidity of context means that we must also develop new ways of understanding "integration." Contemporary approaches to the concept of integration recognize that culture is an amalgam of different influences and that it has evolved and will continue to evolve. For example, the cultural dimensions of integration are subject to re-invention, especially as later generations re-discover and re-interpret their ancestral heritage (Ray 2002).

As mentioned in the Introduction, one of the shortcomings of this volume is that it considers each sphere of integration in isolation. This is a necessary approach to ensure that each is carefully considered and identified. However, the chapters in Part I show that Canada is working with a fixed model of integration. Hopefully, in the future, researchers will be able to generate a multilevel method of analysis which integrates the various dimensions of integration.

The model employed in this volume is depicted below (see Figure 1). It reveals that "motivating conditions" shape public discourse. This discourse explores the growing immigrant and refugee population across the country, the concentration of immigrants in low wage jobs, and the need to build better social services for these growing populations (Hulchanski 2007). It also describes an increasing diversity and expanding cultural and linguistic competence within Canada, as well as the need to develop a strong and viable support system to promote the well-being of all community members. Finally, it reveals the fact that the host society has come to realize that it needs to make Canada more inclusive and accepting if society is to become cohesive, effective, and efficient. As such, there is a basis for Canadians to want to address the issue of immigrant integration.

Figure 1: A Two-Way Process: Working Framework for Identifying Immigrant Integration

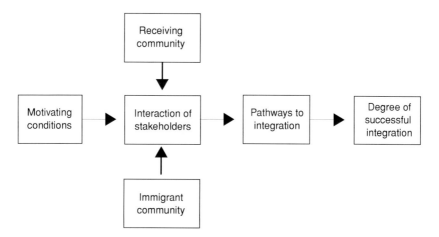

Immigrants find themselves with a declining return to their human capital investments. They find that their returns on their investments have gained less than previous cohorts who had lower levels of human capital. On the other hand, the host society is spending ever more on integration programs and arguably, getting less in return. Why? Is there a decline in successful integration of immigrants? Are barriers being created by the host society that prevent integration or at least lengthen the process? These "motivating conditions" have encouraged various stakeholders to address the issue of immigrant integration.

The model in Figure 1 also represents the fact that there are two communities involved in the process of immigrant integration—the receiving (host) community and the immigrant community—and both are integral parts of the solution. The two communities and other stakeholders (e.g., government agencies and immigrant-based organizations) come together, and all are part of the integration process. This duality highlights the two-way nature of the integration process. Both communities are integral stakeholders in the process, and both must contribute to the process of integration. The result is a complex pattern of two-way interactions that produce important pathways for immigrant integration, such as English/French language acquisition, equal treatment under the law, community support and engagement, and opportunities for the two communities to work together toward a common goal. The outcomes and milestones that we observe along these pathways reflect the degree of successful immigrant integration. But how would we know if the outcome was successful? The subject of this volume is to identify and operationalize indicators of successful integration.

We find that some newcomers are very successful in the labour market and enjoy positive relations with other Canadians (Hiebert 2006). Nevertheless, substantial evidence shows that major constituent groups within the overall immigration movement face barriers on every major integration front, such as in education, employment, law, health, and civic participation (Green 2006). Moreover, while significant numbers of immigrants and second-generation immigrants are well integrated along dimensions such as language acquisition, some areas, such as employment, continue to be problematic (Ray 2002).

For Canada's immigration model to succeed, immigrants must be encouraged and assisted to weave themselves into the host society's economic, social, political and cultural spheres as soon as possible after arrival. This is not to advocate assimilation, but rather to ensure that integration barriers are dissembled, that receptivity is enhanced, and that immigrants receive a fair return on their human capital assets and thereby contribute as early and fully as possible to their communities. In short, successful integration ensures a positive-sum game for both immigrants and Canadians of longer tenure. In the end, integration will enrich and strengthen the social and cultural fabric of Canadian society and promote economic and social success.

Today, formidable challenges stand in the way of integration: the sheer number of immigrants; the compositional changes that have sharply increased religious, racial, and ethnic diversity; economic restructuring; and increased geographical dispersion of where immigrants choose to settle. Communities are faced with demands by immigrants for assistance and transformative institutional changes that are costly and sometimes engender resentment. Sometimes these demands for change come from very large demographic groups, and failure to adapt to them is an affront to democracy. Alternatively, sometimes these changes are necessary in smaller, less diverse communities to attract and retain highly skilled immigrants. In either case, refusal to change is not an option.

Measuring Integration Outcomes

This volume seeks to improve the foundation of a new discourse and set of policies that can meet the challenges and opportunities posed by new forms and sources of immigration in the twenty-first century. Its intended audience includes policy analysts and policy-makers at all levels of government, as well as other public and private stakeholders. The aim is to broaden and clarify the scope of the national dialogue on immigrant integration. In this dialogue, robust, transparent, and comprehensive measures are needed to demonstrate that the investment of scarce social resources is producing valuable returns. The measures presented by the authors of this volume constitute a step in this direction.

Specifically, the goal of this volume has been to identify a set of empirical indicators that could be used to measure integration and to do so in a manner that is both clear and rigorous. Uniquely, it has tackled all four spheres of Canadian life—social, cultural, political and economic—and has paid attention to both sides of the two-way approach to integration. Too often, public discourse, research, and policy discussions focus on simply one area (usually economic outcomes) and on only one side of the two-way street. We contend that Canada will be able to move forward only when we understand the complexity of the Canadian context and the roles and responsibilities of both immigrants themselves and Canadian society as a whole.

With this goal in mind, the chapters in Part I provided the reader with both theoretical and operational definitions of integration and, most importantly, with measures to explore how we are faring (see Table 1 below). The authors began with a broad review of the literature to identify how the concept of integration has been defined and employed in both the academic and policy context. These surveys reveal the multidimensionality of the integration concept and allow the reader to more fully understand the different meanings the concept has taken on over the years. Nevertheless, while exposition of the concept reveals that its meaning has some "openness," it also reveals that the term is subject to empirical verification.

Thus, operationalization was the next task of these authors. Throughout Part I, they have identified a range of indicators that could be used to assess the nature and level of immigrant integration. The actual choice of indicators has depended upon the sphere under discussion (e.g., cultural, political, etc.) and the context in which the indicators are being evaluated (e.g., urban, rural, religion, generation, etc.). For example, agencies focusing on economic issues will want to ensure that these indicators are measured to assess the level of economic integration taking place and to situate immigrant economic activity in the overall economic performance of the region or the country at the time. What is important is that all spheres be measured using consistent, long-term indicators that will allow "umbrella" agencies, such as Citizenship and Immigration Canada, to acquire a holistic picture on the integrative successes of immigrants. As well, policy-makers need indicators that depict both sides of the two-way integrative process.

Table 1: Empirical Indicators Currently Available for Measuring Immigrant Integration in Four Dimensions

Economic	Social	Cultural	Political
Annual income	Associational involvement	Intercultural competency	Citizenship
Occupation			Voting
	Feeling of security and belonging	Cultural participation	
Labour force participation			Political engagement
	Intermarriage rate	Intercultural dialogue	
Unemployment			Civic engagement
	Immigrant/host contacts		
Education achievement		Language proficiency	
	Perceived discrimination		Political representation
Expertise/job match		Immigrant content in mainstream media	Knowledge of rights and responsibilities
	Residential segregation		
Use of Social services			
	Assimilation resistance	Cultural labour force participation	Knowledge of Canadian politics
Poverty rate			
		Level of volunteerism	
Duration of job	Understanding of Canadian institutions		
		Literacy rate	
	Outreach services for immigrants	Intercultural events	

Part I has revealed there are several such indicators available for use by the various actors in the immigration field. Perhaps Citizenship and Immigration Canada could play an important co-ordinating role, as well as serving as a repository for data sets collected by different agencies, academics, and others. Other organizations, such as the Metropolis project, might also contribute to this effort. These data sets could then be made available to different agencies and departments, as well as to scholars who are developing theories and conducting basic research in the area of immigrant integration.

Table 1 identifies a set of indicators for each of the dimensions reviewed in Part I. New indicators also were identified in the various chapters and these will need to be considered as we evaluate the measurement process over time. While Table 1 identifies specific indicators within each of the four dimensions, it is recognized that there is some overlap among them.

Many of the authors noted that data sets measuring integration already exist within a variety of sources. Whether from the General Social Survey, the Ethnic Diversity Survey, Census, Longitudinal Immigration Database, Longitudinal Survey of Immigrants to Canada, or from several academic and polling sources, there is data that can be used to empirically test the many dimensions of integration. The authors have drawn from this wealth of indicators and identified what they see as the most useful and theoretically important indicators.

Part II provided extensive contextual information to allow policy analysts and academics to better understand the suggested empirical indicators. This contextual information also demonstrates that there are no easy fixes. It shows that the nature and range of actors in the field of immigrant integration has increased dramatically over the past few years, and that the level of resources allocated to the challenges of integration has exponentially increased. It also demonstrates that no single organization has a monopoly on power, ideas, or resources. The conclusion is that the stakeholders need to learn how to plan and work together if they want to succeed. This contextual information also becomes important where integration indicators must be interpreted and evaluated. It is only through this contextual lens that we can fully interpret the various indicators that are proposed by the researchers in this volume. In addition, the contextual data needs to be configured in a way that would allow analysts and policy-makers to identify the success of second-generation immigrants. Finally, it may suggest that the target of our measuring efforts may need to be expanded in the future.

There is an urgent need to identify the sources and indicators that track integration changes over time. Moreover, "benchmarks" need to be established to assess the changes that are taking place. Benchmarks will allow agencies to develop meaningful strategic plans and goals for the future. In the best of all possible worlds, this could be completed through longitudinal panel data sets (e.g., New Canadian Children and Youth Study). However, in the absence of such data, we need to find cross-sectional indicators of integration that have been collected by various social agencies.

The past decade has shown that only through sustained immigration will Canada be able to grow, attenuate the labour force demands, and moderate problems associated with a homogeneous population in a global environment. As a result, immigration has come to the fore of public discourse. Media stories about immigration are common, and the emergence of new service agencies has confirmed the importance of this transformation. At the same time, the changing dynamics of immigration and integration as well as the multiplicity of actors involved in immigration and integration reflect the complexity of the process.

If Canada is to compete for the "brightest and the best," immigrants must be confident they will not face barriers and exclusion. Thus, Canada cannot afford to neglect the talents of either newcomers or established residents. The country has chosen a high immigration pathway from which it will be very difficult to deviate. Given this track, scale, and composition of Canada's intake, the immigration system cannot be permitted to fail. Yet to successfully manage integration, we must be able to measure and calibrate our interventions along many dimensions. Economic success will not guarantee social cohesion. Nevertheless, this volume is a start toward improved planning, and it is intended to launch further discourse among the stakeholders.

References

Bélanger, A., and E. Malenfant. 2005. *Population Projections of Visible Minority Groups, Canada, Provinces and Regions 2001–2017*. Ottawa: Statistics Canada / Canadian Heritage, Minister of Industry, Cat. No. 91-541-XIE.

Bouchard, G. 2007. "Shaping Canada's Future: Immigration and Refugee Policy," *Institute for Research on Public Policy Choices* 13(3): 2–21

Fix, M. 2006. *Immigrants' Cost and Contributions: The Effects of Reform*. New York: Migration Policy Institute.

Green, S. 2006. *Rethinking Immigrant Integration in Germany*. Washington, DC: Johns Hopkins University, American Institute for Contemporary German Studies.

Hiebert, D. 2006. *Beyond the Polemics: The Economic Outcomes of Canadian Immigration*, RIIM Working Paper. (Available at www.riim.metropolis.net.)

Hulchanski, D. 2007. "The Three Cities within Toronto," *Research Bulletin* 41. University of Toronto, Centre for Urban and Community Studies: pp. 4–6.

Nonnenmacher, S. 2007. "Recognition of the Qualifications of Migrant Workers: Reconciling the Interests of Individuals, Countries of Origin and Countries of Destination," *International Journal on Multicultural Societies* 9(1): 91–122.

Papademetriou, D. 2003. *Policy Considerations for Immigrant Integration.* Washington, DC: Migration Policy Institute.

Ratha, D. 2003. *Workers' Remittances: An Important and Stable Source of External Development Finance.* Zurich: Global Development Finance 2003, World Bank.

Ray, B. 2002. *Immigrant Integration: Building Opportunity.* Washington, DC: Migration Policy Institute.

Rifaat, C. 2004. *Immigrants Adapt, Countries Adopt...Or Not: Fitting Into the Cultural Mosaic.* Montreal: New Canadians Press.

Spencer, S. 2003. *The Challenges of Integration for the EU.* Washington, DC: Migration Policy Institute.

Weidenfeld, W., and R. Sussmuth. 2005. *Managing Integration: The European Union's Responsibilities Towards Immigrants.* Washington, DC: Migration Policy Institute and the Beartelsmann Foundation.

Index

Contributors

CHRISTOPHER G. ANDERSON, Wilfrid Laurier University

CHEDLY BELKHODJA, Université de Moncton

JOHN BILES, Metropolis Project

JEROME H. BLACK, McGill University

MEYER BURSTEIN, International Consultant

HÉLÈNE DESTREMPES, Université de Moncton

JOHN FOOTE, Policy Research Group, Department of Canadian Heritage

JAMES FRIDERES, University of Calgary

M. SHARON JEANNOTTE, Centre on Governance, University of Ottawa

JACK JEDWAB, Association for Canadian Studies

MINELLE MAHTANI, University of Toronto

PATRICIA RIMOK, Conseil des relations interculturelles, Gouvernement du Québec

RALPH ROUZIER, Conseil des relations interculturelles, Gouvernement du Québec

MARJORIE STONE, Dalhousie University

ARTHUR SWEETMAN, Queen's University

CASEY WARMAN, Queen's University

Queen's Policy Studies
Recent Publications

The Queen's Policy Studies Series is dedicated to the exploration of major public policy issues that confront governments and society in Canada and other nations.

Our books are available from good bookstores everywhere, including the Queen's University bookstore (http://www.campusbookstore.com/). McGill-Queen's University Press is the exclusive world representative and distributor of books in the series. A full catalogue and ordering information may be found on their web site (http://mqup.mcgill.ca/).

School of Policy Studies

Robert Stanfield's Canada, Richard Clippingdale, 2008   ISBN 978-1-55339-218-7

Exploring Social Insurance: Can a Dose of Europe Cure Canadian Health Care Finance?
Colleen Flood, Mark Stabile, and Carolyn Tuohy (eds.), 2008
Paper ISBN 978-1-55339-136-4 Cloth ISBN 978-1-55339-213-2

Canada in NORAD, 1957–2007: A History, Joseph T. Jockel, 2007
Paper ISBN 978-1-55339-134-0 Cloth ISBN 978-1-55339-135-7

Canadian Public-Sector Financial Management, Andrew Graham, 2007
Paper ISBN 978-1-55339-120-3 Cloth ISBN 978-1-55339-121-0

Emerging Approaches to Chronic Disease Management in Primary Health Care,
John Dorland and Mary Ann McColl (eds.), 2007
Paper ISBN 978-1-55339-130-2 Cloth ISBN 978-1-55339-131-9

Fulfilling Potential, Creating Success: Perspectives on Human Capital Development,
Garnett Picot, Ron Saunders and Arthur Sweetman (eds.), 2007
Paper ISBN 978-1-55339-127-2 Cloth ISBN 978-1-55339-128-9

Reinventing Canadian Defence Procurement: A View from the Inside, Alan S. Williams, 2006
Paper ISBN 0-9781693-0-1 (Published in association with Breakout Educational Network)

SARS in Context: Memory, History, Policy, Jacalyn Duffin and Arthur Sweetman (eds.), 2006
Paper ISBN 978-0-7735-3194-9 Cloth ISBN 978-0-7735-3193-2
(Published in association with McGill-Queen's University Press)

Dreamland: How Canada's Pretend Foreign Policy has Undermined Sovereignty, Roy Rempel, 2006
Paper ISBN 1-55339-118-7 Cloth ISBN 1-55339-119-5
(Published in association with Breakout Educational Network)

Canadian and Mexican Security in the New North America: Challenges and Prospects,
Jordi Díez (ed.), 2006   Paper ISBN 978-1-55339-123-4 Cloth ISBN 978-1-55339-122-7

Global Networks and Local Linkages: The Paradox of Cluster Development in an Open Economy, David A. Wolfe and Matthew Lucas (eds.), 2005
Paper ISBN 1-55339-047-4 Cloth ISBN 1-55339-048-2

Choice of Force: Special Operations for Canada, David Last and Bernd Horn (eds.), 2005
Paper ISBN 1-55339-044-X Cloth ISBN 1-55339-045-8

Force of Choice: Perspectives on Special Operations, Bernd Horn, J. Paul de B. Taillon, and David Last (eds.), 2004   Paper ISBN 1-55339-042-3 Cloth 1-55339-043-1

New Missions, Old Problems, Douglas L. Bland, David Last, Franklin Pinch, and Alan Okros (eds.), 2004   Paper ISBN 1-55339-034-2 Cloth 1-55339-035-0

The North American Democratic Peace: Absence of War and Security Institution-Building in Canada-US Relations, 1867-1958, Stéphane Roussel, 2004
Paper ISBN 0-88911-937-6 Cloth 0-88911-932-2

Implementing Primary Care Reform: Barriers and Facilitators, Ruth Wilson, S.E.D. Shortt and John Dorland (eds.), 2004   Paper ISBN 1-55339-040-7 Cloth 1-55339-041-5

Social and Cultural Change, David Last, Franklin Pinch, Douglas L. Bland, and Alan Okros (eds.), 2004   Paper ISBN 1-55339-032-6 Cloth 1-55339-033-4

Clusters in a Cold Climate: Innovation Dynamics in a Diverse Economy, David A. Wolfe and Matthew Lucas (eds.), 2004   Paper ISBN 1-55339-038-5 Cloth 1-55339-039-3

Canada Without Armed Forces? Douglas L. Bland (ed.), 2004
Paper ISBN 1-55339-036-9 Cloth 1-55339-037-7

Campaigns for International Security: Canada's Defence Policy at the Turn of the Century, Douglas L. Bland and Sean M. Maloney, 2004
Paper ISBN 0-88911-962-7 Cloth 0-88911-964-3

Understanding Innovation in Canadian Industry, Fred Gault (ed.), 2003
Paper ISBN 1-55339-030-X Cloth 1-55339-031-8

Delicate Dances: Public Policy and the Nonprofit Sector, Kathy L. Brock (ed.), 2003
Paper ISBN 0-88911-953-8 Cloth 0-88911-955-4

Beyond the National Divide: Regional Dimensions of Industrial Relations, Mark Thompson, Joseph B. Rose and Anthony E. Smith (eds.), 2003
Paper ISBN 0-88911-963-5 Cloth 0-88911-965-1

The Nonprofit Sector in Interesting Times: Case Studies in a Changing Sector, Kathy L. Brock and Keith G. Banting (eds.), 2003
Paper ISBN 0-88911-941-4 Cloth 0-88911-943-0

Clusters Old and New: The Transition to a Knowledge Economy in Canada's Regions, David A. Wolfe (ed.), 2003   Paper ISBN 0-88911-959-7 Cloth 0-88911-961-9

The e-Connected World: Risks and Opportunities, Stephen Coleman (ed.), 2003
Paper ISBN 0-88911-945-7 Cloth 0-88911-947-3

Knowledge Clusters and Regional Innovation: Economic Development in Canada, J. Adam Holbrook and David A. Wolfe (eds.), 2002
Paper ISBN 0-88911-919-8 Cloth 0-88911-917-1

Lessons of Everyday Law/Le droit du quotidien, Roderick Alexander Macdonald, 2002
Paper ISBN 0-88911-915-5 Cloth 0-88911-913-9

Improving Connections Between Governments and Nonprofit and Voluntary Organizations: Public Policy and the Third Sector, Kathy L. Brock (ed.), 2002
Paper ISBN 0-88911-899-X Cloth 0-88911-907-4

Governing Food: Science, Safety and Trade, Peter W.B. Phillips and Robert Wolfe (eds.), 2001
Paper ISBN 0-88911-897-3 Cloth 0-88911-903-1

The Nonprofit Sector and Government in a New Century, Kathy L. Brock and Keith G. Banting (eds.), 2001   Paper ISBN 0-88911-901-5 Cloth 0-88911-905-8

The Dynamics of Decentralization: Canadian Federalism and British Devolution, Trevor C. Salmon and Michael Keating (eds.), 2001   ISBN 0-88911-895-7

Institute of Intergovernmental Relations

Comparing Federal Systems, Third Edition, Ronald L. Watts, 2008 ISBN 978-1-55339-188-3

Canada: The State of the Federation 2005: Quebec and Canada in the New Century – New Dynamics, New Opportunities, vol. 19, Michael Murphy (ed.), 2007
Paper ISBN 978-1-55339-018-3 Cloth ISBN 978-1-55339-017-6

Spheres of Governance: Comparative Studies of Cities in Multilevel Governance Systems, Harvey Lazar and Christian Leuprecht (eds.), 2007
Paper ISBN 978-1-55339-019-0 Cloth ISBN 978-1-55339-129-6

Canada: The State of the Federation 2004, vol. 18, *Municipal-Federal-Provincial Relations in Canada,* Robert Young and Christian Leuprecht (eds.), 2006
Paper ISBN 1-55339-015-6 Cloth ISBN 1-55339-016-4

Canadian Fiscal Arrangements: What Works, What Might Work Better, Harvey Lazar (ed.), 2005
Paper ISBN 1-55339-012-1 Cloth ISBN 1-55339-013-X

Canada: The State of the Federation 2003, vol. 17, *Reconfiguring Aboriginal-State Relations,* Michael Murphy (ed.), 2005   Paper ISBN 1-55339-010-5 Cloth ISBN 1-55339-011-3

Canada: The State of the Federation 2002, vol. 16, *Reconsidering the Institutions of Canadian Federalism,* J. Peter Meekison, Hamish Telford and Harvey Lazar (eds.), 2004
Paper ISBN 1-55339-009-1 Cloth ISBN 1-55339-008-3

Federalism and Labour Market Policy: Comparing Different Governance and Employment Strategies, Alain Noël (ed.), 2004   Paper ISBN 1-55339-006-7 Cloth ISBN 1-55339-007-5

The Impact of Global and Regional Integration on Federal Systems: A Comparative Analysis, Harvey Lazar, Hamish Telford and Ronald L. Watts (eds.), 2003
Paper ISBN 1-55339-002-4 Cloth ISBN 1-55339-003-2

Canada: The State of the Federation 2001, vol. 15, *Canadian Political Culture(s) in Transition,* Hamish Telford and Harvey Lazar (eds.), 2002
Paper ISBN 0-88911-863-9 Cloth ISBN 0-88911-851-5

Federalism, Democracy and Disability Policy in Canada, Alan Puttee (ed.), 2002
Paper ISBN 0-88911-855-8 Cloth ISBN 1-55339-001-6, ISBN 0-88911-845-0 (set)

Comparaison des régimes fédéraux, 2ᶜ éd., Ronald L. Watts, 2002   ISBN 1-55339-005-9

Health Policy and Federalism: A Comparative Perspective on Multi-Level Governance, Keith G. Banting and Stan Corbett (eds.), 2001
Paper ISBN 0-88911-859-0 Cloth ISBN 1-55339-000-8, ISBN 0-88911-845-0 (set)

Disability and Federalism: Comparing Different Approaches to Full Participation, David Cameron and Fraser Valentine (eds.), 2001
Paper ISBN 0-88911-857-4 Cloth ISBN 0-88911-867-1, ISBN 0-88911-845-0 (set)

Federalism, Democracy and Health Policy in Canada, Duane Adams (ed.), 2001
Paper ISBN 0-88911-853-1 Cloth ISBN 0-88911-865-5, ISBN 0-88911-845-0 (set)

John Deutsch Institute for the Study of Economic Policy

The 2006 Federal Budget: Rethinking Fiscal Priorities, Charles M. Beach, Michael Smart and Thomas A. Wilson (eds.), 2007
Paper ISBN 978-1-55339-125-8 Cloth ISBN 978-1-55339-126-6

Health Services Restructuring in Canada: New Evidence and New Directions,
Charles M. Beach, Richard P. Chaykowksi, Sam Shortt, France St-Hilaire and Arthur
Sweetman (eds.), 2006   Paper ISBN 978-1-55339-076-3 Cloth ISBN 978-1-55339-075-6

A Challenge for Higher Education in Ontario, Charles M. Beach (ed.), 2005
Paper ISBN 1-55339-074-1 Cloth ISBN 1-55339-073-3

Current Directions in Financial Regulation, Frank Milne and Edwin H. Neave (eds.),
Policy Forum Series no. 40, 2005   Paper ISBN 1-55339-072-5 Cloth ISBN 1-55339-071-7

Higher Education in Canada, Charles M. Beach, Robin W. Boadway and R. Marvin McInnis
(eds.), 2005   Paper ISBN 1-55339-070-9 Cloth ISBN 1-55339-069-5

Financial Services and Public Policy, Christopher Waddell (ed.), 2004
Paper ISBN 1-55339-068-7 Cloth ISBN 1-55339-067-9

The 2003 Federal Budget: Conflicting Tensions, Charles M. Beach and Thomas A. Wilson
(eds.), Policy Forum Series no. 39, 2004
Paper ISBN 0-88911-958-9 Cloth ISBN 0-88911-956-2

Canadian Immigration Policy for the 21st Century, Charles M. Beach, Alan G. Green and
Jeffrey G. Reitz (eds.), 2003   Paper ISBN 0-88911-954-6 Cloth ISBN 0-88911-952-X

Framing Financial Structure in an Information Environment, Thomas J. Courchene and
Edwin H. Neave (eds.), Policy Forum Series no. 38, 2003
Paper ISBN 0-88911-950-3 Cloth ISBN 0-88911-948-1

*Towards Evidence-Based Policy for Canadian Education/Vers des politiques canadiennes
d'éducation fondées sur la recherche,* Patrice de Broucker and/et Arthur Sweetman (eds./
dirs.), 2002   Paper ISBN 0-88911-946-5 Cloth ISBN 0-88911-944-9

*Money, Markets and Mobility: Celebrating the Ideas of Robert A. Mundell, Nobel Laureate
in Economic Sciences,* Thomas J. Courchene (ed.), 2002
Paper ISBN 0-88911-820-5 Cloth ISBN 0-88911-818-3

The State of Economics in Canada: Festschrift in Honour of David Slater, Patrick Grady and
Andrew Sharpe (eds.), 2001   Paper ISBN 0-88911-942-2 Cloth ISBN 0-88911-940-6

The 2000 Federal Budget: Retrospect and Prospect, Paul A.R. Hobson and
Thomas A. Wilson (eds.), 2001 Policy Forum Series no. 37, 2001
Paper ISBN 0-88911-816-7 Cloth ISBN 0-88911-814-0

Our publications may be purchased at leading bookstores, including the Queen's
University Bookstore
(http://www.campusbookstore.com/), or can be ordered online from: McGill-
Queen's University Press, at
http://mqup.mcgill.ca/ordering.php

For more information about new and backlist titles from Queen's Policy Studies,
visit the McGill-Queen's
University Press web site at:
http://mqup.mcgill.ca/